PEOPLE I

Malcomb Bailey III	Operating officer hired to satisfy the regulators
Ralph Bailor	Jones Bylor broker and Broker Jim's competitor
Blackhard & Funkelstein	Legal firm for Broker Jim's brokerage company
Chrispina	Filipina, Broker Jim's bookkeeper
Daniel Brewster	Manager at Montcalm who first hires Broker Jim
Frank Brocknor	New broker-actor promoter
Elmer T. Campbell	"Jiggs," wealthy broker at Jones Bylor
Saul Carlson	Ominous character and local acquaintance from Montcalm
Dave Connors	Stockbroker and friend of Brocknor
Cotton Head Kid	Ted Baxter, inspector from NASD
Rex Donovan	Partner with Homes Module Corporation
Benjamin Ergstein	Young client who launches Broker Jim's career
Winona Flowerbell	Wealthy Native American whose charms tempt Broker Jim
Jim Gordon	Broker Jim's uncle
Major Gray	John Taylor, Broker Jim's executive vice-president
Mr. Hackett	Sales manager at Jones Bylor
Herman Hershel	"Big Belly," State Securities official
Wayne Howard	Partner with Home Modules Corporation
Jones Bylor	Broker Jim's first stockbrokerage connection
Daniel Lews	Broker Jim's friend and partner
Lois	Broker Jim's first wife
LSW	Local Securities of Washington, Broker Jim's firm
John L. Lucas	Wealthy, irascible ex-rancher and broker at Jones Bylor
Mae Belle	Early client and supporter of Broker Jim
Sonada McLean	Broker Jim's second wife
David McLean	Sonada's son
Sven Nordoff	Broker Jim's client and close friend
Michael O'Keefe	Real estate salesman at Ocean Shores
Gordon Palimeer	Executive vice-president of Tiger Hackett
Raja Singh	Broker from India
Miss Shirley	Secretary at Renndag Securities and later at Jones Bylor
Rosco Tallon	Broker Jim's mentor at insurance inspection agency
Bill Tedmore	Retired Navy captain and broker at Jones Bylor
Silas Tidler	Oversexed, religious fanatic and owner of lumber yard
Tiger Hackett & Co.	Hackett's company
Warrior	Samuel Jackson, big producer who joins Broker Jim's firm

Broker Jim

by

J. Glenn Evans

First Paperback Edition, 2002

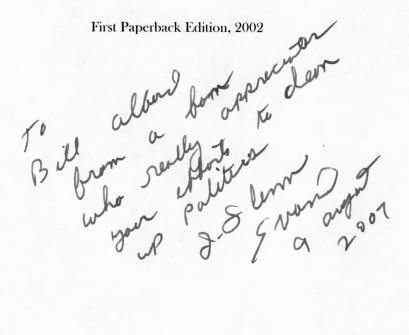

To Bill Alberd from a book who really appreciate your efforts to clean up politics

J. S. Glenn Evans

9 August 2007

ISBN: 0-7596-8208-9 (e-book)
ISBN: 0-7596-8209-7 (Paperback)

Library of Congress Number 2002093060

This book is printed on acid free paper.

Printed in the United States of America
Bloomington, IN

Cover concept by *Michael Magee.* Cover design by *Kelsey Fernkopf.*

1stBooks – rev. 07/26/02

TO BARBARA

and a very special thanks to Michael Magee, William Murdoch, Bill Riddling, Leonard Tews, Ursula Zilinsky, Thomas Hubbard, and Verne Carlson who read sections of the manuscript and offered their support and comments, and finally to Robert Ray, who taught me so much about scene-building in his writing classes at the University of Washington.

ONE

I got to the office at four in the morning, two hours earlier than usual. On my desk was a framed snapshot of me with my mother out in a cotton field, a picture taken forty-eight years ago. I had always tried to follow her advice, be honest. Maybe that was what caused my agitation now. I paced the floor around my big teakwood desk, a desk that overpowered my office, somewhat like LSW dominated the region's local securities business. We dealt in the securities of small companies and helped to make them big. Resting on one corner of my desk was a hand-tooled leather plaque, placed there by my fourteen-year-old stepson, David, on Father's Day, when he was ten years old. It read James Bradley, Big Cheese. It sometimes embarrassed me, but I was too proud of him to remove it. It was the file on the other corner that made me uncomfortable.

I sat down and glanced up from the stack of paperwork on my desk. I met the eyes of Sonada, my wife, looking down at me from her portrait on the wall. How could I have brought her to this? She didn't even know about my problem. I hadn't told her.

On top of my paperwork was the latest copy of *Northwest Financial News*. Chrispina must have put it there after I left yesterday. A glance, and I saw that the paper had published an article on me. There was a big photograph of me sitting at this desk, captioned "Local Securities Czar." There were laudatory quotes from Blackhard of Blackhard & Funkelstein, the firm that handled most of our legal and prospectus work. I knew the article was coming out but had not expected it so soon. They commented on our modest headquarters, located in a well-kept older, eight-story building. We were on the sixth floor. My brokers had been telling me over and over again, "Let's move to the new Financial Building. We need a more prestigious office. We've outgrown this dump; let's move." Local Securities of Washington had started right here. My first office rent had been only $400 a month.

When Nixon bombed Cambodia and our markets had all but dried up, these people trusted us. When our building manager saw me struggling to make rent payments, he said, "Don't worry, Jim, we trust you." He let the rent slide a couple of times until we could catch up. Now we rented most of the floor and paid

J. Glenn Evans

$10,000 a month. He was our friend when we needed him. These brokers could protest all they wanted, but I wasn't about to move. You stick with the people who don't let you down.

At six-thirty I heard my traders across the hall open up for the day's business. Later the stockbrokers came in, just beating the New York Exchange opening, seven o'clock our time, but ten for the New Yorkers. Not that beating the opening really mattered; we didn't do much in Big Board stocks. Each day had the excitement of a kid's baseball game, but the players had grown taller and older.

"Thank God you're here," Marlo, my head trader, said as he cracked the door and stuck in his bald watermelon head. "Raja is giving me hell again."

"What else is new? He gives everybody hell." Raja was our most productive salesman, originally from India, where I sometimes wish he had stayed.

"He wants to unload 50,000 shares of Roundup Plastics on me. I've got too much in inventory already."

"Tell him I'll take 3,000 at five, two at four and the rest at three dollars a share. If he wants more, he can give us time to work it off. He didn't buy it all at once."

"Okay, but he'll wail like a banshee. Our Roundup quote is five dollars a share."

"Yes, but most people don't dump 50,000 shares of a thinly traded stock all at once."

"Okay. You're the boss. You can listen to him scream."

"Tell him, take it or leave it."

"Will do."

Just as Marlo left, John Taylor stood in the doorway. I always thought of him as Major Gray, his military rank, crop of gray hair and well-trimmed mustache that made him look like Walter Cronkite, the famous newscaster.

"Got time for a coffee?"

"Sure." It was seven o'clock. Our markets never really got going until eight or eight-thirty. We walked over to our favorite coffee spot in the basement of the Rainier Tower. On the tunnel walls, along the way were pictures of old Seattle, the Smith Tower, Dexter Horton Building, and Pioneer Square. At eye level, in an alcove at the east end of the concourse, stood a terra-cotta Indian head, salvaged from the White-Henry-Stewart Building that had once stood on this spot. The high ceiling of the coffee shop gave a man room to breathe, and the service was quick. You got your own.

We sat down with coffees and lit our first cigars of the day. We each smoked six to ten a day. Major Gray nodded at the newspaper he had laid on the table. "I see you made the headlines. I'm highly honored to be having coffee with such a celebrity."

I said, "Don't you know, there's always glory before the fall? The big news splashes on tycoons. Just wait, the bad news starts to come out."

"Don't kid me, Jim. We've just begun to grow."

2

"Things aren't what they seem. We read the good news about the tycoon, and then he fails, goes bankrupt, or goes to jail."

"I'll make your bail."

"Thanks. It's nice to know that I have friends like you around. Say, John, do you realistically think we can quickly move a big chunk of our inventory?"

"Month's early."

"I know, but I'm in a hell of a bind."

"Maybe I can rev up Raja. He's always good for an extra hundred grand or so, especially, if we can throw in an extra quarter into his commission pot."

"Raja's a pain in the ass," I said.

"I know. He drives a sales manager to distraction. If I give him a quarter, he wants half. If it's a half, he wants a dollar. There's just no satisfying that man. He does deliver the goods, though."

I looked at my watch. "Seven forty-five. Listen, John, I've got to get back to the office. Some things to clean up before my eleven-thirty meeting with the banker."

"You go on," he said. "I'll stay here, finish my coffee and read about a local celebrity I know." He grinned. "Good luck with the banker."

Back at the office, I asked the receptionist, "Any messages?"

She chuckled and handed me a fresh stack of phone calls, a good quarter-inch thick. I quickly thumbed through them and pulled out a couple for immediate response. The rest I democratically put at the bottom on the inch-high stack already on my desk. I'd call them when I got to them. Most messages come from people who want something, or they want you to do something for them. Not many offer to do something for you, unless it costs me money. Let them ferment a while. With age they might get better or go away.

Into five minutes, and Raja was there. He stood at my door, white turban bouncing like an angry beehive.

"Your markets are no good! You quote five dollars. Now you offer me only half that."

"I thought I was being generous. You bought most of that stock at half the price I'm offering you."

"It's a rigged market. Wait 'til the SEC hears about this."

"Fine, you just go tell 'em what a bad guy I am. Then, we both can find new jobs."

"You're not fair."

"Look, Raja, we've made you a good offer for that size of block. You don't take it now, you'll risk market changes."

"The trader said you would pay five for the first 3,000 and four for the next two and three for the rest."

"That's right, if you act now. Two hours from now it might be different."

"You're being prejudiced."

"No, I'm just tired of your raising hell all the time about everything."

3

"You quoted five dollars and now you offer me much less than that," he said, pounding his fist on my desk.

"What do you expect? You hit me with 50,000 shares all at once. You know a quote is good for only 100 shares, 1,000 at most."

"Your markets are not honest!"

I smiled at him, and said, "Take it or leave it."

"I'll check with my clients."

Just as Raja left, I heard a tap at my open door. Chrispina, my Filipina bookkeeper, came in. Quiet and efficient, she was my best and oldest employee. She had been with me since the earliest days, right after my first partner, Daniel Lews, left. She had started out working only on Saturday, but now she worked full-time.

"Mr. Bradley, there are three gentlemen here to see you."

"Do they have an appointment?"

"They said they didn't need an appointment."

"Oh? Who are they?"

Before she got a word out, three men stalked into my office. Like three robots in unison, they pulled out their IDs and shoved them in my face. They reminded me of soldiers at attention.

The short one with thick dark hair and heavy brown-rimmed glasses said, "We're from the Securities & Exchange Commission."

"Nice to meet you," I said, "but we're a state broker-dealer and not regulated by the SEC."

"Doesn't make any difference," the same man said.

"I'm from State Securities Commission," the second one said. He had a GI haircut, white shirt, tie, coat draped over his arm. "We're here to audit your firm."

"We're a state broker-dealer. Why is the SEC here?" I asked.

The man from the state said, "Mr. Hershel called them in to give us a hand. We don't have the trained personnel for this kind of investigative work."

"Big..." but I cut myself short. Herman Hershel, a senior state securities regulator, was Big Belly to me, ever since my first visit to Olympia ten years ago when I set up Local Securities of Washington, or LSW, as everyone called us. Hershel was corpulent, and not too bright. I had seen his authority at State Securities grow over the past ten years. The more his belly hung over his belt, the more powerful and arrogant he became.

The third man stood before me, saying nothing. His identification card showed that he too was from the SEC. This silent one looked at the file on the corner of my desk. It was marked "Personal Financial." Without a word, he picked it up, glanced through a few pages, and then put the file in his briefcase.

"That's my personal file," I said.

"We'll be interested in that too," the silent one said, not returning the file.

4

Raja, again, stood outside my doorway. He impatiently danced up and down like a man who needed to relieve himself. When he realized the room was full of official-looking people, his turban disappeared.

The dark-haired SEC guy in the brown-rimmed glasses said, "We need a desk and an office." His tone told me this was not a request. "We may be here for a while."

"That's fine," I said. "You can use my office. I'm going to be out of town for a few days."

"Where?" the state man asked.

I started to say "None of your damn business," but choked it off and said, "I'm due in Dallas tomorrow afternoon for three or four days."

"What for?" asked the state man.

"Need to meet with my partners on a little private oil venture down there."

"You will give me the address and phone number where you can be reached," Big Belly's state man said.

"I am staying at the Dallas Towers the first night, and then I might be out in the oil fields."

"You will call us each day and keep us informed as to your whereabouts."

"Seems hardly necessary. I'll be back in three or four days."

"We want to know where you are," Big Belly's man said.

"If you say so. Chrispina can direct you to all of the files. She has been with me since we started."

"We may have some questions that need immediate answers," the state man said.

"John Taylor, he's our executive vice-president. He can answer your questions."

I pressed the intercom button. "Chrispina, these gentlemen are securities regulators. Show them every courtesy and give them whatever they ask. They will be here for a few days, and will use my office while I'm out of town."

"Yes, sir."

I cleaned off my desk, put everything on the floor in the corner, pointed to my chair, and said, "Be my guest."

I then gave them a "go fuck yourself" nod, and walked down the hall. I went to Major Gray's office to call my banker. He wasn't back yet from his coffee. I then dialed the bank president and when he came on the line, I said, "Sorry, Dick, I can't make it to lunch today. Can you reschedule me sometime next week?"

"That's fine, Jim. I'm free Thursday."

"Good! I'll see you when I get back from Dallas."

What else could I say? I couldn't ask my banker to loan me money until I knew what these Regulatory Heavies had in mind. They had a sack over my head and a gun at my brain, and until they left, I was helpless. I silently started to pray,

"Oh God, please keep the cash flow coming in faster than the checks that I've got to cover."

What a hell of a time to have securities regulators come in on me! Just as I was bringing it together. I looked at Major Gray's desk calendar. I'd remember this day, August 6, 1984, a day that would live in infamy, as F.D.R. had said. Yesterday, I had a foreboding that something bad was going to happen, and it did.

August was warm and the sun was shining all around Puget Sound. With these guys hovering, how could I do any hard thinking at my office? They wanted to see records, not me. They wouldn't believe anything I'd say, anyway.

I reached for the office intercom. "Chrispina, I've got a few things to do. I'll be gone the rest of the day. Just show them whatever they want. Give them whatever they ask."

I scribbled a note to Major Gray to cooperate with them, and answer any questions they had. "They're just doing a routine audit," I wrote.

I went to my car and drove out toward Magnolia and parked. Its high bluff overlooked Puget Sound. I got out and looked around. It was a steep drop-off. I remembered the disturbed girl who had once worked for me. She was manic-depressive and had jumped off the Aurora Bridge. I got back in the car and looked at the horizon. Seeing, but not seeing, I stared out at the water and the ships coming into the harbor. I thought of those stockbrokers back in '29, and how they handled their problems. After a while, I got back in the car and headed for the Arboretum. Its tall trees, cool shade and green grass calmed my spirit. I drove slow and easy through the park, then parked in one of the lots, and just stared ahead of me. Then, after a while, I drove back to the bluff. That's the way the day went. There were no solutions. I solved no problems. The time just passed. By now it was late afternoon and I headed home.

As I came in the backdoor, I saw Sonada in the dining room. She looked down at me from a high stepladder. She had just started to place a strip of striped wallpaper down from the ceiling of the room that was both a dining room and library.

"You sick?" she echoed from her perch. There was a smudge of white paste on her right cheek.

"Nope, just thought I'd come home early and enjoy a cigar out in the back yard. Have some thinking to do."

"I never see you 'til after dark. You must be sick."

"No, no. Just thought it would be nice to come home and enjoy the flowers out back. You spend so much time planting, watering, caring for them, and I never even take the time to notice how beautiful they are."

She secured the top of the strip, wiped the smudge from her cheek with her arm, and came down to finish smoothing the bottom part of the wallpaper. "My flowers won't be any competition for your cigar."

"They look pretty."

Upstairs, I changed from my Brooks Brothers blue pin stripe suit into a pair of olive-drab trousers and a short-sleeved red sports shirt. I went outside, and sat down on a green lounge chair in the backyard. Even as late as August, there were lots of beautiful flowers still in bloom. Sonada knew all their names. She had made the backyard a park. She had practically rebuilt the inside of the old house, high ceilings and all. That morning she had said she wanted some new cupboards in the kitchen.

I told her, "If I had known you wanted a new house, I would've built you one."

She stuck her tongue out at me and went on fixing breakfast. She knew she'd get whatever she wanted.

Sitting in the warm sunlight, a little cloud of cigar smoke wafted skyward. A robin darted in to grab a worm before the rotating sprinkler caught him on its return. Two squirrels playfully chased each other across the top of the brown wooden fence. Apples hung from the fifty-year-old tree that had come with the place. They had a blush of red, not quite ripe yet. I had made some apple cider our first year here. It was great. The second year was not so good. I got busy and didn't do things just like it should have been done. As I sat there, I wondered why I hadn't spent more time like this. Getting rich wasn't all it was cracked up to be. More problems than fun.

Here I was with a beautiful wife and David, a fine fourteen-year-old son. I hardly ever saw them in the daytime, and rarely even on weekends. There was always another business trip or another deal to do. David was the best part of the bargain, a ready-made family. He was only four years old then. Now it was Boy Scouts and baseball. He had even earned his Eagle rank in the minimum time. Did I now put my family in jeopardy because of my too aggressive expansion? These regulators could wipe me out.

I heard David's bicycle come up the driveway and then go in the garage. Then in a few moments, he pushed his way through the back gate. He was loaded down with manuals and a telegraphic key.

"Hello, Son."

"Hi, Dad. You okay?"

"Just home a little early to relax."

"Is everything okay, Dad? I never see you before sundown." He came up and sat down on the wooden deck in front of me.

"No, Dave. It's okay. Where've you been with all that stuff?"

"Bob and I are working on our communications merit badge, learning the Morse Code."

"Are you learning anything?"

"Dit da-dit dit dit-dit dit dit."

"Ass!"

"How'd you know that?"

7

"I was once a Boy Scout myself," I said. "We learned a few things we didn't always share with girls. Anyway, is that the way a general should be talking?"

"I'm not a general."

"Thought you earned yourself a general's badge."

"Dad! That's not a general's badge. It's an Eagle's. I'm not in the army."

"Just joshing."

"It takes more merit badges to earn the right to wear additional palms on the Eagle badge."

"I see. Maybe I'll join you on one of those hikes this fall before winter sets in. Guess I can't wait too much longer. That last snow hike almost did me in."

"That was more'n two years ago and you haven't gone out with us since. The guys still talk about those tales you told around the campfire about robber barons. Golly, what they got away with then! No wonder they were rich."

"That was before the SEC."

"Dad, my patrol is still wondering what happened to you, Old-Hide-in-the Sleeping-Bag. That's what they call you."

"Colder than hell out there last time I went out with you guys. Snow all over the place," I said.

"Don't wait too long or there'll be more snow. Gotta go, Dad. Promised Mom I'd repair the chair down in the basement," and he was gone.

Sonada stuck her head out the upstairs bedroom window. "By coming home early, you're in for a special treat."

"What's that?" I asked, wondering if we were on the same beam.

"Wait and see," then she disappeared.

I shut my eyes, sucked in the warm summer air, and recalled a more pleasant time when I was carefree. A time when I didn't have my own firm. I was just a stockbroker for somebody else. Then I had real money to spend, cash in hand, and no hungry firm to gobble it up.

I must have fallen asleep because when Sonada called again, an hour had passed, and it was dusk. The sun was almost down.

The dining room table was all set, and there was candlelight. Pork chops, fried okra and dried black-eyed peas, my favorite meal. My favorite since I had helped mother pick fresh okra from the garden back in those Oklahoma Depression days. Fried okra and pork chops was a feast in those brown bean and corn bread days. Mother fried the okra in bacon grease after dicing it up and dipping it in cornmeal. Sonada used olive oil.

"Is this my surprise?"

"One of them." A knowing glance passed, not seen by David who was trying to read a book by candlelight.

After we had finished eating, Sonada said, "Jim, you're awfully quiet tonight. Is anything wrong?"

"No, my thoughts are on the Dallas trip tomorrow."

8

"Oh, is that all? You're not happy unless you're gadding about somewhere on some kind of deal."

"Guess so. Sometimes it's nice to get away from the downtown Ulcer Gulch, but it's kind of wonderful to be home too."

"You love it down at that office, or you'd be home early more often," she said as she started to pick up the dishes. David jumped up to help her. "Are you sure you're all right?" she insisted again. "You haven't been raving about them damn regulators, them damn Democrats and them damn government forms you have to fill out. Not one word about any of them. It's just not natural. It's been too quiet this evening."

"No, Hon, everything's fine. Just got a few things to work out."

"Let me know if there's anything I can do to help you," she said.

"Ha, you help me! You work all day down at that damn office. Come home, fix dinner and run this place. I should help you."

She smiled and said nothing, the way martyrs often do.

Quit her job, I thought. How in the hell would she have any money for the house? Most everything I made went right back into the business; yet everybody thought I was rich. Ha! On paper, and that was only money when you could sell it. I had a steak reputation and a baloney pocketbook. No! I was not going to worry her about my quagmire. I'd handled crises before, lots of them. So why disturb her now, besides she worried too much anyway. Risk was my business, not hers. Like President Truman once said, "If you can't stand the heat, get out of the kitchen." Sonada would be awfully upset if she knew the gambles I had to take in this business. Yet, if I didn't take the gambles, there'd be no progress. No, no, I must not start alarming her now.

I got off the plane in Dallas. My three oil partners were at the gate to greet me. The native Texan among them was the only one who didn't have on a cowboy hat. He was our waterflood specialist who looked like Hoss Cartwright of Bonanza TV fame, big and friendly. My second partner was a bespectacled, short-statured college professor type, who looked odd in a cowboy hat and boots. He didn't look like a top-notch jungle-exploring geologist. This past year he had retired from a large international oil company, as head of their South American exploration division. Like me, he was the only one who carried a briefcase. My third partner, also in cowboy hat and boots, was a friend from South Africa. I had met him through his brother. Their family had large mining interests there. South Africa enjoyed playing the oil game. He was a thin man with a sharp eye, and didn't miss a scent that smelled like a buck. He made money mixing people with deals, ones that didn't require him to risk his own money. South Africa had introduced me to the others, and had assembled our project.

"Gentlemen, this is a surprise. How did you know which flight I was on?"

"Called your office," South Africa said. "We've got problems with Conan."

"What this time?"

"We'll drive you over to the Towers. We can talk on the way."

We walked out to Waterflood's car. It was a Cadillac of older vintage that showed signs of keeping company with a lot of oil field roads.

Settled in the car, we headed towards town. Nobody said anything; seemed we all had our own thoughts. I looked out the window at the passing land. God must have slapped this country in anger, it was so flat.

Finally Geologist said, "Conan wants more cash up front."

"That's tough," I said. "The deal is signed."

"I know, the son of a bitch," Waterflood said. "He already has your fifty grand down. Now, he can get contrary."

"I thought you Texans were men of your word."

"Hell! Jim, that son of a bitch ain't no Texan. The man's a California transplant," Waterflood said.

"Besides having a swelled head, I think his bank is pressing him," South Africa added.

"Too bad I didn't have him down in South America," Geologist said. "Those jungle natives knew how to handle his type."

The Dallas Towers loomed up in front of us like a Texas phallus with a hard-on for oil.

"Let's have a drink and plan strategy," South Africa said as we got out of the car. "You can check in after that."

"Okay."

We sat down in cane-bottom chairs around a table made for playing poker and dominoes in the barroom. The decor was a replica of an old western saloon. It only lacked men, armed with six shooters, at the bar.

"What's with these South American natives?" I asked Geologist. "How would they solve our problem with Conan?"

"I was just being frivolous, but they do know how to handle turgid heads."

"How's that?"

"Shrink them."

"They still do that?" I asked him incredulously.

"Did when I was down there."

"You got back okay."

"I don't have a big head," Geologist chuckled. "Sad tale, though. One of my local guide friends disappeared. It wasn't until years later that I found out what happened to him."

"What happened?" Waterflood asked.

"On one of my trips into the interior, I was offered a shrunken head. Traded a frying pan for it and brought it home as a souvenir."

"You bought it?" asked South Africa.

"Scarce artifact. Sure, I bought it. Took it home, but when I looked at it closer, there was something strange about the damn thing that bugged me. The thing looked familiar and haunted me a bit. Then I realized that it was my lost friend, the guide."

"That sounds like a Texas tall tale," South Africa said.

"Texas bullshit," was Waterflood's reaction as he yawned.

"No. Honestly. I'll show it to you sometime."

There was a sad, serious look on his face. I believed him, and said, "No. I'll take your word for it."

South Africa got back to business. "Tomorrow, we have an appointment with Conan at his banker's office at 3:30."

"How serious do you think our problem is?" I asked.

"Conan tells me that he has someone else who will pay all cash up front," said Geologist. "Bankers like cash."

"Depends on his banker, whether he will support our side," Waterflood said.

"I doubt seriously if I can come up with any more money than I have already personally committed. That fifty came from my own funds," I said. "The rest of the funding has to come from an outside underwriting. I can't raise the money through my firm because the project is out of state."

"What are the prospects that these funds can be raised?" South Africa asked.

"Excellent," I said. "Daniel Lews, my former partner, has been kind enough to arrange an underwriting for me through a friend of his."

Actually, I thought to myself, "Those regulators in Seattle could louse up my finance on this project. If it got out that I had problems with the SEC, that underwriting firm would quickly drop my project. Now, with my files infested by the SEC, any delays they created could spell fatality to all of my operations."

"We'll get something worked out with Conan," South Africa said.

"By the way," I said. "I haven't seen where my fifty grand has gone yet. I haven't even seen the property yet."

"That's easily solved, Jim," Waterflood said. "I'll pick you up early in the morning and we'll drive out to the field. It's only seventy-five miles out."

"Great! But I better get checked in."

"Pick you up at six in the morning. That'll give us plenty of time to get back for the three-thirty meeting."

"Anyone want to have breakfast?" I asked.

"You guys won't see me at five in the morning," South Africa said.

"Okay, we'll see you guys at the banker's office tomorrow afternoon," I said. I didn't really expect them to accept my early invitation.

As I stood up, Geologist opened his briefcase and pulled out a thin wooden box of cigars. "Here's a little something to keep you company while you're here in Dallas."

11

I glanced at the box, and then at Geologist. He had a sly grin on his face. It looked like he still had his South American connections. This was a box of pure Cuban cigars. "Thanks," I said. He sure knew how to ease a man's lonesomeness.

As I checked in at the hotel, the desk clerk gave me a questioning eye as they often did in these Bible Belt places. A man alone, no luggage, just a briefcase. In their little minds, they think you're there to debase some of their Texas women. This is the way I always traveled—light, with just a few overnight things stuffed in the bottom of my briefcase. To these Texans I might look like a carpetbagger out for sex, but I found that I could move a lot faster when not bothered with luggage.

"There's a message for you, Mr. Bradley," the clerk said in a tone more respectful, when he realized I was one of his customers with a reservation. Once in my room, I looked at the message. Sure enough, it was from Big Belly's man, demanding to be called back immediately upon my arrival. I dialed my office and Chrispina put me on the line with Big Belly's man.

"What can I do for you?" I asked.

"Where is your file of active personnel?"

"That's confidential information that I keep locked in my office. Chrispina's got the key."

"Okay, thanks. Did you have a nice trip?"

"Just fine. Thank you."

Not more than ten minutes later, Big Belly's man called again. "How many brokers do you have?"

"Forty. There's a file for each one."

"Okay, thank you."

These guys could be awfully generous with their phone calls, especially when someone else picked up the tab. Chrispina could have easily answered all those questions. Then, I got it. These jokers think I'm down here in Texas to flee over the border. They think I might leave the country with cash embezzled from my firm. That's the only reason for these silly calls. They want to make sure I'm still here. The trouble runs deeper than I thought. This is not a routine audit. These guys suspect fraud, and I'm the one being stalked. I needed to get back to Seattle pronto.

That evening I looked out the hotel window just as the city lights were coming on. It was a first-class room, high up. There was the regulation table, a couple of chairs and a Gideon Bible—same as the fleabag hotels I used to stay in. I lit one of Geologist's Cuban cigars and took a sip of brandy from my silver flask. Cigars always tasted better with brandy. I had come prepared. Some places down here, you couldn't even buy liquor. I felt sorry for people who couldn't control their drinking. The stuff never bothered me. It eased the pain of being away from home. How many nights had I stayed away from home chasing deals? Probably as many as there are skirts on Broadway.

The Dallas lights were different from those back home. No lights in the world twinkle like the lights of Seattle on a misty night. Oh, how I missed them. Sonada, David, home. Just how much always hit me when sitting alone in a faraway hotel room. Even if I lost everything else, I'd still be a wealthy man if I could keep them. It doesn't always work that way, though. Women need security. Being poor certainly hadn't helped marriage with Lois, my first wife. I knew what loss of money did to others. Love and poverty make a poor marriage salad. I had a friend whose wife had taken the suicide road over just such a loss. No, that must not happen to me. Yet, being poor wasn't all bad. I remembered a poor time. Sometimes, I wished I were back there.

TWO

Dust and grasshoppers spread across the dry land. Sweat oozed from bodies like a squeezed dishrag. The stock market didn't really matter. That was a far-off place where rich men jumped off buildings because they didn't want to be poor. In rural Oklahoma where I lived, being poor was no shame. Everybody was poor, I thought.

I'd heard my mother talk with her friends about how things were when she was young, before she got married. Times were good then. She said you found your fun. Young folks, if they had a car and no money, could always tap a little gas. Drip-gas, they called it; the big oil companies wouldn't miss it. Boys took their best gal for a ride, went to the Saturday night dance, and church the next day, even if they were bleary-eyed. Everyone knew what service station they patronized by the backfires their cars barked. Sometimes on the way home from the dance, after a little rotgut whisky, which was cheap, they parked and played house. If they goofed, there might be a shotgun wedding, but they'd think about that later. At other times when things were slow, to get the adrenaline going, they could always snitch a watermelon. Hell, it was going to waste out in the field, anyway. Just don't get shot.

It was the Fourth of July, 1937. I would be seven in December. They called me Jimmy then. We were poor folks. That's all grown-ups talked about, how good poor people were, and how Roosevelt was trying to help them, and how awful those Hoover Republicans had been. They said you judged a person by how honest he was, not by how much he had. That's what they told me.

I looked forward to that evening. It would be fun to sit in the front yard and watch the fireworks go off in town, just a mile south of us. Big red skyrockets would zoom across the sky. After that we would pop the firecrackers and light some sparklers that Mother had bought with our egg money.

Mother and Daddy had already had breakfast. He was outside harnessing the mules for the day's work in the field. My sister, Connie, and I were having breakfast in the kitchen where we always ate. It was warm there, close to the cookstove. The radio was on. We were listening to Homer and Jethro and

14

everything else that was going on in the world, except when the sponsor came on and advertised some cow feed.

"Mother, I'm tired of biscuits and gravy," I said. "Can't we have some eggs for breakfast?" I looked towards the icebox where I had seen a big box of eggs.

"We don't have any eggs, Son."

"I seen some in the icebox."

"Son, you know those are Mr. Adams's eggs. We sold our half to buy you some clothes, when you start school in the fall."

"There's lots of them in there. He won't miss a teensy-weenie two or three eggs."

"No, Son, that wouldn't be honest. Now, hurry up and finish your breakfast. I'm canning green beans today. You can be Momma's little man and help wash the fruit jars. Your hands are small. You can clean them so much better than I can."

"Some of them eggs shur would taste good right now, Mother. I'm tired of biscuits and gravy."

"No, Son, maybe next week. Now you hurry up, we've got lots of work to do." When I saw the sadness in her eyes, I shut up. I knew they were Mr. Adams's eggs, but I tried. It wasn't fair, him getting all those eggs. We did all the work.

The morning like to have never went. I crawled under the house to look for fruit jars. I rummaged in old boxes there and in the storage shack out back. Next, I washed them in a tub filled with hot sudsy lye-soap water that stung my hands. About lunchtime, I was tired. I sat on the floor, bent over that old washtub, and that wasn't any fun. I would much rather have played Tarzan in the barn.

At last, Mother came over and gave me a hug. "Son, you've been a godsend as Mother's little helper. I think you can go play now. But first, I want you to take a lunch down to your daddy. He's down in the south field with Mr. Winters. They've been baling hay all morning out there in the hot sun."

"Can I stay down and help them?"

"I don't mind, if it's all right with your dad. Just don't get in their way." She handed me a paper sack and said, "There's enough in there for you and Mr. Winters, as well as your daddy."

"Thanks, Mother."

She also handed me a gunnysack with a couple of fruit jars filled with cold well-water and chipped ice from the icebox. I put the food sack on top of the jars in the gunnysack, and threw it over my shoulder like I had seen Daddy do.

"I'll see you at sundown when the cows come home," I said, just like I heard Daddy say many times.

As I looked back, Mother smiled and said, "You won't last that long. You'll be back up here and playing Tarzan in the barn in an hour or two."

"No, I won't."

"We'll see."

"Mommy, can I go?" Connie yelled out.

"No, field work's for men," I said, not losing a step to get away.

"You wouldn't like it," I heard mother say, trying to calm her down.

I just kept going fast as I could. Who wants a four-year-old sister tagging along? I could still hear her wailing as I reached the barn. Where I was going was for men, not women.

I was barefooted, had on my straw hat and my blue and white striped overalls. I was ready for a man's work. On the backside of the barn, where they could no longer see me, I stopped and felt the up and down boards, unpainted like our house. The boards were gray like the sky on a rainy day, which I hadn't seen for quite a while. The touch of the boards felt like Mother's Sunday-go-to-meetin' coat. The soft gray wood grains tickled the palm of my hand. Boards on the house felt the same way. Connie's wailing had stopped, so I had made my getaway. As I entered the woods behind the barn, the shade of the trees felt cool. The crickets were singing.

It was different when I reached the west pasture. There, the sand on the path in the open field was so hot, I walked fast, even ran to keep from burning my feet. I had to keep a sure eye out for sandburs. It hurt to stand in the hot sand on one foot, while you picked them out of your other foot. I could taste the salt from the sweat running down my face as I crossed the open field. The cool water jars felt good against my back. I saved my shoes for school. Going barefooted was fun, especially when it rained, and the mud squished between your toes. I wished that it would rain. There'd been almost none since spring.

The grass on each side of the path was taller as I got nearer the bottom field. There were crows in the sky and some were caw-cawing from the fence row. I ran along the path through the tall grass to feel the breeze on my face. With my free hand, I clipped the grass tops like an airplane wing clipping the treetops. The grasshoppers flew out of my way as I came up on them. They were like horses pulling my chariot, like I had seen in a picture show about Rome. I was a king out here. I didn't hold my hat and say, "Yes, sir," and "No, sir," to the likes of Mister Adams. I'd had seen Daddy do that when Mr. Adams came out in his big car to collect his share of what we growed.

Out in the middle of the field was a cabin that belonged to Ol' Drake. His cabin was surrounded by a garden patch, which he kept green by carrying buckets of water from the creek. Ol' Drake was sittin' in the shade and whittlin'. He was tall and thin, and looked like a scarecrow without his Sunday-go-to-meetin' suit on. He stood up as I got near and raised his hat and yelled a greeting, "How's Mistah Jimmy?"

"Jus' fine, taking my daddy his dinner."

"Sho nuff. I seen 'em dis mornin' and him and da haying man, worked up a storm of dust." Ol' Drake shouted like he was hard of hearing. "Never seen so much hay and dust fly. Lordy, Lordy. They's goin' like a spring tornado."

I waved and hurried on. I'd rather stop and talk, but Daddy's drinking water would get hot. Ol' Drake was a man who liked to talk. Once he got started, I wouldn't be able to get away. I liked him a lot. We were friends. He taught me how to fish. He showed me how to swim in the creek by dog paddling. All the grown-ups called him Nigger Drake. My teacher from up north said you were supposed to call him Negro, not "Nigger." Negro sounded funny to me. I didn't care what they called him. He was my friend.

As I reached the edge of the hayfield, there were blue and yellow and speckled butterflies fluttering around. They flitted away as I got near. I couldn't catch them like fireflies at night. Fireflies were fun to catch. I'd put them in a jar and pretend I was carrying a lantern.

I could see Daddy on the other side of the field pulling the rake with Captain Jack and Lieutenant Jim. They were two mules Daddy named after the bosses in his National Guard outfit. The rake was a big spider with all of its legs in a row. Daddy was the spider's body. As I got closer, I could hear Daddy bark out commands to his officers like he was their general. He yelled, "Gee" and "Haw," which meant for them to turn left or right. Daddy said I'd been named after Lieutenant Jim because I was about as stubborn as his old mule. Mother said that wasn't so, that I'd been named after Uncle Jim, her brother. Uncle Jim was the only one in the family that had any money, and he had lots of it. Mother said he squeezed a penny until it squawked, and he knew how to keep money. That was why he never gave us any of it. That's what she said, but I'd seen him slipping her money 'most every time he came for a visit.

When Daddy saw me, he pulled a lever that lifted up the spider's legs, like I'd seen the preacher's wife lift up her dress when she walked across our front yard. He drove the mules towards the big pecan tree on the edge of the far side of the field where Mr. Winters was operating his hay-baler. It was powered by a mule pulling a pole around it. Daddy had told me that there were fancier balers that ran on gasoline, but they weren't for poor folks. Gasoline cost money; hay and corn you could grow.

The mules brayed as they headed towards the shade of the pecan tree. By the time I got across the field and caught up with them, Daddy was watering them from the two buckets of water he had brought down that morning. Mr. Winters had already unhitched his mule, and was sitting on his haunches like I had seen pictures of kangaroos. He sat in the shade of the pecan tree, waiting for his vittles.

"You're a sight for sore eyes," Mr. Winters said as he brushed the sweat and dust from his face with his wet shirtsleeve. He smelled like a man who had worked in the hot sun all week, and missed his Saturday night bath.

"Well, Son, what's for dinner today?" Daddy asked me, knowing full well what it was, bacon and biscuit sandwiches, cool water and a raw tater or two with a little salt.

17

After we finished eating, Mr. Winters said in a studied tone, "Be done 'bout this time tomorrow." Then he got up and walked over to a clump of bushes on the other side of his baler. I heard him pee, almost as loud as a mule pees.

While we were alone, I whispered, "Daddy, how much does Mr. Winters charge us for baling this hay?"

"He gets one bale for every eight that he puts up."

"Daddy! You mean we get to keep only three bales out of every eight we grow?"

"Guess that's right, Son. Mr. Adams gets four. Mr. Winters gets one so that leaves three for us. You get that smart in school already?"

"I don't think that's fair. Why should Mr. Adams get more hay than we do? He don't do no work."

"He does a different kind of work, Son. He's a lawyer, an educated man. He don't have to work out here in the field like we do. He owns the land. That's his capital so he gets half."

"Why do we have to pay to have his hay baled?"

"We're partners with Mr. Adams. We do the work and baling is part of the work. He buys the seed and he owns the land, so we split fifty-fifty. Mr. Adams gets half of the baled hay. That's our agreement."

"That's still not fair."

"That's what we agreed to do, and a man is only as good as his word."

"I wouldn't of made a deal like that!"

"Son, we didn't have much choice. We had to have a place to live, and that was the only deal he would make. He has the capital. We don't, so that's the best deal I could make."

"What's capital?"

"That's money that's used to make more money. He spent money to buy this farm. With money he buys seed for us to plant. Mr. Adams sometimes loans me money to tide us over between harvests, which I pay him back when we sell the crops."

"When I grow up, I'm going to have capital, because I ain't gonna be poor. I bet I make more money than both Adams and Winters put together."

"Mr. Adams and Mr. Winters," he corrected me.

When Mr. Winters came back over towards us, he stretched and scratched his back against the tree trunk like a bear I had seen in a movie. He almost looked like a bear with his black beard. Mother once told me she couldn't stand a man with beard. It was like "kissin' a goat's butt."

When I asked her if she had ever kissed a goat's butt, she didn't answer me.

"Son, I hope you do get rich," Daddy said with an air of hopelessness.

I didn't realize then just how much the Depression had battered him down. When he and Mother first married, he had just gotten out of a first hitch in the U.S. Marines. Mother told me just how strong Daddy was then.

She said, "He could whip a bear. He was so full of piss and vinegar."

That's what the Marines did to men. At least that was the idea I got from the picture shows. Daddy bought a little farm with the money he had saved in the Marines. We lost it all when the local cotton gin would only pay five cents a pound for cotton.

I noticed that people paid attention to Daddy. He looked like Abe Lincoln, without a beard, and I know he was about as honest as Mr. Lincoln. Daddy was a tall man and a slow talker. He walked even slower—swung his big feet out in front of him that looked like shoe boxes, and slung his arms back and forth like my swing over Wewoka Creek. His hair was black and mine was red. Mother said that he was my stepfather, but that didn't matter none. To me he was the only real daddy I ever had. I didn't know my first father. Mother said she caught him trifling on her with her best friend. She said she even caught them doing it in the back seat of the car. She looked like she was mad when she talked about it. She wouldn't tell me what they were doing and what trifling meant, but I figured it was something bad.

Mother told me that my first daddy kidnapped me one time, when I was two years old. He took me to the Gulf of Mexico. I didn't remember it, but Mother said it happened. Uncle Jim went out to the farm of my first daddy's mother. He told Grandma Allen to make her son return that baby to his mother pronto, or he would sic the police on him. He'd put them after him like wolfhounds. She got the picture. Her old man, Grandpa Allen, raised wolfhounds. I never met those grandparents. I only knew them from what I heard my mother say. Mother also told me that another time my first daddy tried to visit me when I was asleep, so I did not get to see him. She said that my real daddy chased him off, and said, "Don't come back." I guess my first daddy was smart. He didn't come back. My real daddy was big and strong. I bet he could even bulldog Captain Jack and Lieutenant Jim if he wanted to.

"Daddy," I asked, "Why do we farmers have to work and Mr. Adams doesn't? He don't do any work, but he still gets half of what we grow?"

Dad looked towards Mr. Winters and chuckled his funny, hee-hee laugh. He said, "Farming is about the only kind a work a man with a strong back and weak mind can get. Mr. Adams has an education. You study hard, and maybe you can become a lawyer like him and make lots of money."

"I don't wanna be no lawyer and steal eggs from poor farmers."

Daddy didn't say anything to that. He just seemed to be trying to think of something to say.

I guess I let him off the hook by saying, "Daddy, can I stay down here and ride on the rake with you?"

"Guess so. Maybe I'll even teach you how to drive the team."

"Let's go to work," I said, eager to get started. The mules had long since finished their grain, and the two men were just whiling away the time. Finally,

Daddy got up and hitched Captain Jack and Lieutenant Jim to the rake again. Mr. Winters, reluctantly, got up from his haunches and hitched his mule to the pulling-pole that circled and powered the hay-baler.

Off we went, chugging and clanging, across the field. I rode on Daddy's lap. He held me so I wouldn't fall off and be raked up with the hay by the steel claws of the spider's legs behind us. He let me hold the reins. "Gee, haw," I yelled, imitating the way he barked at the mules. Those stubborn mules just ignored me, but they jumped to attention when my daddy spoke. It was fun for a while to ride the rake and yell, "Gee, haw." I bounced up and down on Daddy's lap. His leg bones cut into my bottom. Playing Tarzan in the barn would be more fun.

"Daddy, I think I'll go help Mother some more."

"Whoa." The team stopped. He laughed and said, "I didn't think it'd take long for you to get tired of this. Good job. You stayed longer than I thought you would."

I hurried back up the trail towards home. I'd swing on the grapevine, that big rope that hung from the roof of the barn. That would be a lot more fun and a whole lot cooler than working out in the hot sun. About halfway up the path I found a stick that was just right. I mounted it like the cowboys I'd seen in Westerns, jumping on from behind. I trotted the rest of the way home with the stick between my legs and singing, "Yippee yi yee. Yippee yi yay. Get along little doggies. We're headin' for Cheyenne and I'm gonna play Tarzan when I get to the barn. Yippee yi yee, yippee yi yay."

Just as I rounded the barn, I saw Mr. Adams's new Packard sittin' in the front yard. He had come to get our eggs. I decided to trot on up closer and have a look-see. Just as my horse reached the front porch, I imagined a train comin' down the steps, loaded with a carload of eggs and ridin' high. If I hurried, I could cross the tracks and beat the train. I'd seen cowboys do that all the time. I made it just in time! I looked back over my horse's tail, and there sittin' on the ground was Mr. Adams in his fine white summer suit, covered with dust and broken egg yellows. He didn't have his usual city smile that meant, "I'm better than you." His legs were hunched up and his belly resting on his knees. He looked up from under his fancy cream-colored, store-bought Panama hat, amidst broken eggs all around.

"You damn brat! Why don't you watch where you're going?"

"You didn't blow your whistle, Mr. Adams? Didn't you see me comin'? Weren't you lookin' down the tracks? You shoulda blown your whistle. You mighta run over me."

Mother appeared on the porch, and looked down at the yellow mess.

"Oh! Mr. Adams, I'm so sorry. I'll give you our share of the eggs next week."

He stood up in the middle of a pond of broken eggs, looked up at Mother, all the while dustin' and wipin' slimy eggs off his self. Chickens pecked at the yellow goodies on the ground.

"I would certainly hope so." Without another word, he went to his car. He mumbled something I couldn't understand. I think it might have been cuss words. There wasn't any grass in the front yard. The chickens had taken care of that, and now they were cleaning the dust-peppered eggs up off their yard plate.

I could swear I heard my mother chuckling to herself. She turned her head, so I couldn't see her face. She went back in the house. She didn't bawl me out like I thought she would. I guess she thought the sight of Mr. Adams sitting there among all those broken eggs was worth the price of a week's eggs.

In September I started my first day of school. I walked a mile and a half to the highway to catch the school bus. I was almost to the highway when I saw a billy goat in the front yard of a house near the sandstone county barn. He looked mean. Those big horns were dangerous. I wanted to run back home. I slowly backed off. That billy goat looked at me. I couldn't go home. I had to get to school. Mother would whip me if I went back home. She had taken me to school yesterday to meet the teacher, and see how things were set up, and it was all arranged. I had to be there. I jumped down in the ditch on the opposite side of the road from him. I slowly crawled on my hands and knees until I got well past that house. For a whole week I crawled in the ditch. That billy goat was always in the yard. I wouldn't tell Mother the real reason why the knees of my pants were so dirty. I didn't want her to think I was a coward.

That Friday, as I crawled up from the ditch on the other side of the house, a boy stood on the road.

"What's you doin' down there in that ditch?"

"I'm afraid of that billy goat," I said, and I really was.

"She won't hurt you. Come on up. I'll show you."

I didn't want to, but I followed him into his yard. That goat ran up to us like a dog that wanted to be petted.

He said, "Go ahead and pet her. She's a nanny goat, not a billy. She won't butt you. Just don't run from her."

I touched her, but I was ready to run if I had to. The goat's fur was soft and warm and I continued to pet her.

Then I said, "I'm Jimmy. What's your name?"

"I'm Johnny Loadstar. How long you been crawlin' in that ditch?"

"All week."

"I saw you out there yesterday and told my mother. She said I was to watch for you. She bet you were afraid of Nanny."

"That's right, I was."

"My favorite cowboy is Gene Autrey," Johnny said like he owned him. "Whose yours?"

I liked Gene Autry too, but I could think of only one other name that moment. "Tom Mix," I said. I was stuck with Tom Mix from then on.

"Well, I got to get on, or I'll miss my bus," I said.

"My mother drives me to the bus stop. Ride with us."

His mother was a beautiful, refined lady, like my teacher. I liked her. Johnny also had a horse named Pet. We became best friends, and I got to ride behind him on Pet all over the countryside. I didn't know then that he was a friend that would last a lifetime.

The next three years went fast. More school, more corn and cotton to chop. I learned how to plow and pull the rake and shout with my ten-year-old authority. Captain Jack and Lieutenant Jim learned to obey me. I often swam with two brothers, Bob and Rick Jolson. Rick was the same age as me, and Bob was a year older. They lived on a farm just below us that got flooded out almost every other year in the spring. Their land was richer than ours, being bottom land, so they made out better than we did, even if they were flooded out every other year. Dog paddle is what they called my way of swimming, dog paddle. That's the way they said they learned to swim, kick their feet and paddle like a dog pitched in the pond. We certainly didn't have to worry about stepping on any sharp fish fins in Wewoka Creek. The creek was full of salt water from the nearby oil wells, which killed all the fish years ago. Old Indians who sat on the streets downtown would sometimes talk about how big the fish were before the oil boom had ruined everything.

About this time a funny-looking man showed up in the newsreels at the Saturday cowboy pictures shows. He looked a lot like Charlie Chaplin. When he'd get excited, he barked like a dog. I couldn't understand what he said. Mother said he was the leader of Germany, that place that always made trouble in Europe. She said my Uncle John on my daddy's side had been gassed in World War I, when he went to fight the Germans, and that's why he was simple-minded. The grown-ups made Hitler sound pretty bad. Times got better, though. Farm prices went up. My older cousin and I made some show money by selling scrap iron we found on the farm.

That fall, just before I turned ten, Mother said, "Let's take a walk in the woods, Son."

She was quiet as we walked along and gathered poke-salad greens, like Grandma and I used to do when I stayed all night with them.

"Son," she said, "You're going to have to be the man of the house. Your dad's National Guard unit has been called up. He's got to go to the army. We're gonna have to leave this farm and move to town."

I didn't say anything. I just felt sad. I could see Mother fight to keep from crying. Almost as if talking to herself, she said, "If you're gonna enjoy this life, you gotta learn to enjoy your miseries too, or you miss out on a lot of living."

"Will Daddy be safe?"

"I don't know, Son."

At the auction, I knew my dad was crying in his heart, as he watched them sell Lieutenant Jim and Captain Jack. Strangers led them off. I watched too, and saw them disappear down the lane behind the blackberry bushes. I thought I saw tears in Daddy's eyes, but he was a man who did not cry. He'd told me before that real men don't cry. Our things went cheap. I think our neighbors felt ashamed at what they paid, but they took our stuff anyway. It had been a hot day, but then some clouds came over and made it cool. The clouds threatened rain, but it didn't rain like everybody wished. Most of the people were festive. They drank our free coffee and punch, ate our donuts, and talked about how things were getting better. The gray of the day made me sad. I wondered how it would be to live in town. What would there be to do?

THREE

Monday, Daddy was gone. He was a buck sergeant in the 45th Division of the Oklahoma National Guard. The pay he earned helped us on the farm. The Federal Government nationalized the Guards, and he went to Fort Sill in Lawton for a year's training. Uncle Jim came out in his car with a trailer behind. He helped us move our things to a garage apartment in town. Rent was six dollars a week. We wouldn't go hungry. There was an army allotment from Daddy. Mother got a job in the laundry. She fed flat pieces like sheets and tablecloths into a mangle that dried and pressed them.

I baby-sat Connie. She was seven years old and stubborn. She acted like a little sister. I delivered the Wewoka paper which made me twenty-five dollars a month. The paper came out six days a week and on Sundays there were funnies. I liked the funnies, especially the Katzenjammer Kids. I collected twenty cents a week from each subscriber, and got to keep six cents of it. Sometimes I went back two or three times before my customers would pay me, because they had no money. When I got a second route, and hired another boy to work for me, I made another fifteen dollars a month. With both routes, I made about half as much as Mother earned. The laundry paid her twenty dollars a week. Vacations were not in the owner's vocabulary. Connie would bug me for a dime or quarter. Sometimes I would give it to her, sometimes not. When I didn't, she called me stingy.

I told her, "I'm being frugal, not stingy. I don't have money to waste."

I gave a lot of my money to Mother to help pay the rent. She ordered a typewriter for me on her Montgomery Ward's account. I paid for it at ten dollars a month. I also took a correspondence course in writing. The stories I read by Jack London and Mark Twain, and the poems by Robert Frost, James Whitcomb Riley and Edgar Allen Poe seemed magical. That's what I wanted to be when I grew up, a writer.

After a while Mother left the job at the laundry and got a job slinging hash at a restaurant-beer joint. When Daddy came home on leave, they argued. He didn't like her working there. She said the laundry work was too hard. If she had to work, she would work wherever she wanted to. That's the way it was. He went back to camp.

I was ten years old when they bombed Pearl Harbor, but by the end of the month I would be eleven. It was a clear day, but cold so I wore the black sweater my dad gave me when he came home on leave. The headline was spread all across the top of the page. "PEARL HARBOR BOMBED!" I asked our circulation manager where Pearl Harbor was. He didn't know, so we asked the front office, and they said somewhere in the Hawaiian Islands.

They sent Daddy overseas. We'd get letters, but we didn't know where he was. They blacked out some of his words. Mother said they censored his letter. I didn't know what that meant so I looked it up in the dictionary. It said, "An official in time of war who read mail and removed information that might be useful to the enemy." I didn't like the idea of some stranger reading Daddy's mail. He wouldn't squeal to the enemy.

When I was twelve, I joined the Boy Scouts. Johnny Loadstar, my friend who still lived out in the county, near the county barn, joined the Scouts with me. I talked him into it, but we joined a neutral troop together. He was Presbyterian and I was Baptist, so we joined a troop that was sponsored by the Methodist. Every month, after we became First Class Scouts, we made the limit of three merit badges that we were permitted to receive at one Court of Honor. It made me proud to pin a duplicate badge on my mom, who always came to these award ceremonies. She sat there in her print dress among the businessmen, doctors, lawyers, judges and their wives, all the local people who had money. I knew she felt out of place, but she always came. Johnny and I set out to make Eagle Scout, and we did.

The Boy Scouts was a whole new world for me. We camped out and learned Indian ways. We were patriotic and helped on Scout paper drives. From studies to get the Scout merit badges, I learned that there were many ways to make a living. You could be an architect, a bookbinder, a geologist, a civil servant, an explorer, but I still wanted to be a writer.

It was a cloudy Sunday afternoon, and we were all at home. Connie and I helped Mother make chocolate fudge. The wonderful smell of it cooking made us fuss over who got the spoon and who got to scrape the pan. We didn't make it often since sugar was rationed.

A strange man knocked on the door. He handed Mother an envelope. She opened it. From where I was, I could see short printed lines. She began to cry. When she got hold of herself, she read it to us. It was a telegram from the War Department. Daddy wouldn't come home. He was killed in action.

Later, a letter came from his commanding officer. It told how bravely he had died, somewhere in North Africa, while trying to rescue a wounded comrade.

After the war in 1946, a blind veteran from Daddy's old National Guard outfit gave me an inkling of the kind of soldier Daddy was. He said, "Sergeant Bradley got busted, lost his stripes, even spent some time in the brig. There was this private whose wife came to visit him, just before we shipped out. He couldn't get a pass because he was on guard duty. Your dad gave him his pass and took his place. First Lieutenant Jim Rolland caught your dad standing guard in the private's uniform, and busted him. It took your dad more than a year to earn his stripes back, and that was after he got transferred to another unit that went to North Africa. Loaning that pass probably cost him his life, because most of my Guard buddies made it back home."

"Did Dad really do that?" I asked.

"Yep. Rules didn't mean a thing to Sergeant Bradley if they got in the way of helping one of his men," the old blind soldier said as his voice withered away.

At seventeen and almost through high school, I still wasn't absolutely sure what I wanted to do. Boy Scout merit badges exposed me to all kinds of successful people in different trades and professions. Still, I didn't know. I certainly didn't want to be a poor farmer. To become a writer still had appeal. Robert Frost's poetry touched me. Shakespeare wasn't much fun, but my high school English teacher crammed him down my throat. Jack London and Mark Twain, they wrote the real stuff. I'd never been too fancy with words. At school spelling bees, I never got tired standing up. What I knew best was that I didn't want to be poor. I had been that too long.

Sunday, late August 1947, Uncle Jim stopped by for a visit at Grandpa's farm. We sat on the front porch while Grandma fixed dinner, which city folks called lunch. It was one of those summer days you sizzled like bacon out in the sun. Way out in the open field, across the road, we could see the heat waves do their distant dance. It was not a day to work. Most folks in the South or Southwest had sense enough to stay in on days like these, unless they were somebody's hired man and had no choice. Uncle Jim was rich. He'd made it big out West in the lumber business. He and I, lazily, sat there on the front porch and watched chickens scratch the gravel and peck at watermelon rinds. Grandpa's front yard had no grass. Like our old farm place, the chickens took care of that. At least the lawn didn't have to be mowed. I leaned back against the wall in my cane-bottom chair. The old farmhouse was a two-story affair, an unpainted gray. It was built fifty years ago when Grandpa and Grandma first came up from Tennessee. The land was bought with Grandma's boarding house money. Their farm was two miles north of Mr. Adams's old place, where we once had sharecropped. Mr. Adams, now gone, never did like me much. I think he never forgave me for wasting all those eggs when he tripped over my stick-horse.

Grandpa, fully dressed, lay on his bed in the front room. He read Western shoot-'em-ups, and recovered from his Saturday toot. He always brought enough bootleg whisky home to last him through Sunday. Grandma had already given him his Sunday morning comeuppance, but Grandpa, long ago, had figured out how to

handle that. He'd just take another slug to show her who was boss, and went back
to bed and laid down with his westerns, where men were men.

I could hear the cowbells in the distance as we talked. Uncle Jim's sawmill was
out in Oregon, and he was on his way back home from New York. He'd been
back there to talk with some of those moneyed Jews, as he called them, about
finance. He always stopped by for a visit with the old folks when he had the
chance.

"Jews are not bad folks," he said, "once you get to know them, especially if
they like you. They sure come in handy when you need some money. Tell me,
Jimmy, what do you want to do with your life? Have you thought about what you
want to be?"

"Well, Uncle Jim, I want to go to college, and I think I want to be a writer."

"That don't pay so well. How about business?"

"Maybe," I said. "I did pretty well with my paper route, sold magazines and
traded a few things. Guess I kind of like buying and selling, especially when I don't
get skinned."

"Have you ever thought about being a stockbroker?"

"Aren't they the guys that jumped off of buildings?" I said it to be funny, but
from the look on his face, he didn't appreciate my sense of humor.

"Not anymore. They make a lot of money."

"That sounds great," I said, "Just what do they do, besides jump out of
windows?" I liked to jive him a little bit, all the airs he put on.

He leaned his chair back up against the wall, like me. I could tell he wasn't
comfortable. He came right back down on all fours. Since Uncle Jim had gotten
rich, he'd become quite a dandy, all dressed up in suit and tie, even in this
weather. He was miserable, but he wasn't going to be caught around his hometown
dressed like some hick farmer.

His brow furrowed like a field of terraces, and he said without a smile, "If you
are a stockbroker, you work with moneyed people. You learn how to make money
for yourself, and best of all you learn how to make money on other people's
money."

"Is that legal?"

"Sure it is. Bankers and insurance companies do it all the time."

"Is that why some folks call them crooks?"

"I hardly think so. But, you'll never make any real money if you work for
wages. You have to learn how to make your money work for you."

"You don't think I should be a writer?"

"Not if you want to make any real money. I think you should consider
becoming a stockbroker. That's the fastest way I know for a poor boy to get rich.
Beats sawing up trees. I do that, but I've made my real money speculating in
timber. Buying and selling, that's the way you make big money."

I thought about Mr. Adams and Mr. Winters, with their capital, how they had taken advantage of poor farmers. "I don't know whether I'd want to do that or not."

"Jimmy, take my advice, the securities business would be good for you. If I was starting over again, I'd be a stockbroker. You learn how to make money. You meet all kinds of rich people. You deal in the stock of big companies like General Motors, U.S. Steel, General Electric. If you want my advice, you'll study finance."

"How much does it pay?"

"Plenty." My uncle chuckled. "That's the right question to ask if you want to make money. Become a stockbroker, then you're a real capitalist." He emphasized *capitalist.* "There are a lot of wealthy stockbrokers." He jabbed his finger up and down at me. "If you want to make money, get where the money is."

"I don't know anyone who owns any stocks."

"Sure you do. I'd venture to say that a lot of those people you once delivered papers to owned stocks."

"You really think so?"

"Certainly. They have money. They don't broadcast it. They're just being smart. People with money know how to keep their mouth shut."

"Is that why I used to have go back two or three times to collect twenty cents for the paper?"

"No, I think in those days people just didn't have it."

"Well, I'd sure like to make some money."

Uncle Jim came alive. He was like a preacher who had just made a new convert. "Tell you what I'll do," he said. "Merrill Lynch has a little booklet that introduces investors to the market. I'll send you a copy as soon as I get back to my office."

"Thanks, Uncle Jim. I'd appreciate it."

"Jimmy, as soon as I get home, it's on its way. I also have some books on investments that I'll send."

"Gee, thanks."

Three days later, I received a whole pack of airmail stuff from Uncle Jim, postmarked from Portland, Oregon. I read all this stuff, and then went to the library for more. The more I read, the more fascinated I became. What a bunch of characters I met. A few were good, but most of them should have spent more time in Sunday school. J.P. Morgan would skin you alive if you crossed him. Daniel Drew could charm a snake. These were pretty rough guys to do business with. Daniel Drew, Jessie Livermore, Jay Gould, and Jim Fisk didn't seem much different than Jessie James. They used a pen and a bucket instead of a gun and a sack. They used their wits instead of doing honest work. I didn't find a single saint among them. If you wanted to do business with these guys, you'd be wise to plug up your ears and hide your pocketbook. There had to be some good honest hardworking stockbrokers. How else could they have raised all that money that put American industry in the forefront of the world? American businessmen even had more clout than those uppity royal asses of the British Empire. Bet that thought made old King George III roll over. I decided that maybe the business needed some good honest blood like me. That's what I'd do, become a stockbroker. Writing could wait. I wanted to get rich first.

FOUR

At high school graduation Mother came and saw them hand me the certificate as I crossed the stage, dressed in rented academic garb. I'd rather have saved the money than dress up like a clown. Connie had gotten married to a sailor, who had taken her out west to Bakersfield, got her pregnant a couple of times, and left her to make her own way. I was too bashful to ask a girl out, so I didn't go to the prom.

I had $500 saved from paper route money and later printer's devil work at the same paper. It was college, no matter what it took. I enrolled at Oklahoma A&M College. It was my first time away from home. All those big buildings, all the long halls, it was like being lost in a forest without a compass. That campus was my battleground. I hated to play soldier. Oklahoma A&M was a land-grant college. All male students were required to join the ROTC. They say bitching makes a good soldier, so I must have been a damn good soldier. I think Napoleon would have given up on me if he had been my corporal. He certainly wouldn't have pinched my ear like he did with those who pleased him. He could never sell his idea of glory to me. That's what politicians always spouted off about. He would have had me shot for barking, "I want out! I want out!"

I earned fifty cents an hour working in the college print shop. I saved on grub by helping in the cafeteria. I worried about where next year's money was coming from. My savings went fast.

I didn't have a girlfriend. There weren't many girls at A&M, and the fraternity boys had first pick. Work, study and class left me no time for frills and girls. Besides, girls made me shy. To overcome this, I took a dance class. Once my dorm-mates found this out, they insisted I take a broom and waltz around the room to show them the steps.

Summer came. I thought I might go up to the Kansas wheat harvests. Some fellows said it paid good money. I didn't relish more farm sweat in the heat and the dust. I didn't have a choice. My biggest problem was that I didn't even have money to get up to the wheat fields. I could hitchhike, but still I needed something to live on until payday. Mother certainly couldn't help me. I gave her money when I could.

School cleaned me out. I was as flat as a tortoise that hadn't made it across the road.

I called my uncle in Oregon for help. "Uncle Jim, I want to go to the Kansas wheat harvest to earn money for next year's college. Can you loan me $100 for a few weeks to cover my expenses up there? I promise I'll pay you right back."

"I'll do better than that, Jimmy. I'll send you some money to come to Oregon. I could use some help this summer."

"Now, Uncle Jim, I wasn't asking for a handout. You don't have to hire me."

"Jimmy, if I didn't need you, I wouldn't send for you. I can use the help. Pay will be better than you can make in wheat harvest. Believe me! I've been there."

"I'd love to come to Oregon for the summer."

"Good. It's done. Check's in the mail. I'm sticking in an extra hundred. See that your mother gets it. Don't let her know it comes from me."

"Thanks. I won't."

Midweek I headed west on the Greyhound bus to central Oregon. Monday morning, clad in blue jeans and a plaid lumberjack shirt, I became a chain slave that pulled lead-weight boards off a green chain. The town, Prineville, was infested with lumber mills as thick as woodpeckers in a dead forest. They feasted on private lands and the Ochoco National Forest. It didn't take me long to shed that lumberjack shirt. I thought farm work was hard. But, kid, if you haven't pulled green lumber, fresh cut off the log, from a moving chain, you haven't worked. You've heard tales of how hard the Ford assembly work is. That's for kids, when you compare it to steel-weight boards that come at you like mosquitoes on a summer night. That's what green lumber feels like, when you have to tip it up and slide it into a pile at the side of the chain, one after another all day long. Pancakes for breakfast was the only thing that would keep me standing up until lunchtime.

Being a nephew didn't cut any favors here. I didn't see much of Uncle Jim, except when he came out of his fan-water-cooled office and strutted around the yard like he was Napoleon out to view his troops. I was just a grunt and a private. I did appreciate the work though. That was the only way I could stay in college. After a month of green chain, I got a promotion. They moved me to the sort chain, and that was a snap. It was dry lumber and easy to handle. There you sorted lumber into piles according to grade as the boards came down the conveyor chain. Up on the chain, a registered lumber grader stepped from board to board and made grade marks on the lumber with a crayon on the end of a long stick. His other hand held another stick with a hook on the end. With that, he flipped the board over for a look at the other side. The grader had prestige, and we, the chain men, had none.

There was no cover for the sort chain. The sun just floated out there in the sea of space, laughed, and spit rays at us. We'd get so thirsty that a drip of water from the hydrant fifty foot away looked like Niagara Falls. Finally we got smart. We dry chain men would give the feeder, the guy who loaded the boards on the chain, the high sign. He'd pour it on. That lumber came so fast, we worked our asses off for a whole five minutes.

Then came the cherished cry, "Stop the chain! Stop the chain!"

The grader was so far behind he stepped on the boards that we were supposed to pull and stack. The chain stopped. I'd brush the sweat from my eyes with a swipe of my shirt sleeve and make for the water hydrant. It took at least three minutes for the grader to catch up. That water tasted so good and the rest felt so wonderful, it was like heaven to lie on my back and laugh back at that lazy sun resting up there.

Then back to lift, pull, and the push of boards to the stacks again. It was dumb-dumb work. So dumb-dumb that I started to play games. I'd see how little effort I could use to move a board and make it slide right into place, neatly stacked. I made fifteen bucks a day. That was big money to me, but small change to gyppos who loaded cars on a percentage basis. They made fifty bucks and sometimes a hundred or more. Their jobs were cherished positions, and not available to a poor relative.

When college started in the fall, I decided no more ROTC for me. I didn't want to be a soldier in the army. I knew I'd never make general so why waste the time. I switched to East Central State Teachers College at Ada, Oklahoma to study finance. Ada was thirty miles from my hometown, so I could get home for a visit to Grandpa's farm occasionally. An aunt took care of him. Grandma had died. Mother had moved west to be near Connie. About midterm my finances were no more. I was broke. I did everything that made a buck. I washed dishes, mowed lawns, served as a printer's devil on a small weekly newspaper. I peddled all kinds of junk, magazines and even an attachable gizmo that defrosted your refrigerator. All the time I didn't work, I studied for class, read books and magazines on the stock market, anything that would help to make me a rich stockbroker. I never wanted to be poor again.

Girls were like flowers, to be looked at. I couldn't afford them. Besides, I was shy around females. It wasn't that I didn't yearn for them, but I didn't quite know how to handle them. I'd heard all the locker room brags of conquest, but I didn't think much of those fellows. A man who kissed, went further and boasted about it to others, wasn't much of a man. I would certainly know how to keep my mouth shut if one of them ever did it with me. I'd be grateful and I certainly wouldn't welcome more competition by brags about what I'd done. I could just imagine how it would be to hold one of them up close and kiss her, and press her up against me. But, God, I was so shy. They were untouchables to me. I guess being scared of them was okay. I couldn't really afford them. I studied, worked and fought to survive. Girls would just have to wait.

But one Saturday afternoon when I was downtown, I ran into Betty. She was in my English class. She was well made. She smiled at me in recognition.

I said, "Hi." I couldn't remember her last name.

On impulse I blurted out, "Hey, there's a good movie on down the street. Would you like to go see it?"

"Sure. Why not."

We walked down the street, talked about minor incidents that happened in class. We laughed about Miss Smith, one of the old maid teachers, who some of the boys wrapped around their little fingers by bringing her a fresh rose every day. That's about all we had in common, other than she was a girl and I was a boy. A block from the theatre, I suddenly realized I only had fifty cents in my pocket. At the excitement of nailing a girl, I forgot I didn't have any money on me.

"You haven't seen this movie, have you?" I asked, hoping she would say yes.

"No. I think it'll be great. Nice of you to ask me."

Just as we reached the ticket window, I stopped, turned and looked at her. She was kind of pretty. I shrugged my shoulders, and I know my face turned red. "I'm sorry. I feel terrible. I just realized I only have fifty cents on me. Didn't get to the bank." I lied. I didn't even have a bank account.

"Oh! Is that all? Don't worry about it. I've got some money on me."

"I'll pay you back Monday."

"Really, that isn't necessary."

Next time I saw her in class, I paid her back, but I was so shamefaced, our relationship didn't go any further. I never got the nerve to ask her out again.

Later, I managed to scratch up enough money to buy an old Ford convertible. It was then I learned that girls were not untouchables. Hell, they were as hungry for me as I was for them. I didn't do any deep drills, just felt and smooched. With a car, dates were no trouble. All I had to do, was ask.

I managed to get in two years of college, and then the words began to come down from on high that we must save the world from Communism. I was registered for the draft and I could feel the wind blowing, so I joined the Air Force. I had my taste of the Army through the ROTC at Oklahoma State that first semester, and I wanted no more of that. My friend, Johnny Loadstar, joined the Navy. We had kept in touch, but he had stayed with Oklahoma State when I moved to East Central. In the Navy he got to fly, being attached to a Naval Air Station. I joined the Air Force to fly. After basic training, they stuck me in front of a typewriter and said, "You are a personnel clerk." After bouncing me around a couple of stateside bases, one of my personnel officers and I did not get along so well, so I ended up on Kwajalein, a small island in the Pacific Ocean. There, we wore Frank Buck hats and khaki shorts, sweated, and did without women.

When that hell was over, I got my discharge. The only good thing I could say about the Air Force was that having served in it, I could go back to college on the

GI Bill. It was pretty slim living on $110 a month, so I worked on the side and studied hard to become a stockbroker. I went back to East Central, there in Ada, Oklahoma. After my Air Force experience, I wasn't so shy of girls.

Back in college, Janie Wesmeyer became my main girl. She was a blond who loved to do the Mexican Hat Dance. I'd seen her perform at student dances. She excited my interest and I asked her out. She surprised me when she said yes. She was built, and how she could swing those hips, stomp those feet and bounce those boobs when she did the Mexican hat dance. If I had been a Catholic, I would have had something to tell the priest. She had a beauty fashion face that could make the movies, but she was fighting hard to keep from being plump. I met her at the Baptist Student Union, but I think she was more interested in meeting Baptist boys than in spiritual enlightenment.

We went out several times, usually to some school event, then before I took her home we would drive out to the lake, park in the moonlight and smooch. This helped me overcome my shyness with girls. Some people began to say we were going steady. Then one night I got a little carried away with my smooching. I got bold after a few kisses and played with her well-mades. She didn't stop me, and she got to breathing hard, and I messed the front on my pants. Something more powerful than me pushed hard and made me forget I was supposed to be married before I went all the way. I guess I should have just gone ahead and done it, but I thought I should ask.

As I started to remove her panties, I said, "Can I do it?"

She jerked up, pushed me away, stopped breathing hard, and said, "Take me home. I didn't think you were that kind. You're just like all the others!"

"I'm sorry," I said, and started to kiss her again.

She screamed, "Take me home this minute."

I didn't want her to tell everyone that I tried to rape her, so I took her home. She wouldn't go out with me anymore. I guess I broke the spell. I learned later, when I got into the sales business that I should have used the Assumptive Technique, just gone ahead and assumed that she wanted the goods. Asking her gave her time to think about it.

It was the last six months of college. Late Friday afternoon, most of the guys had gone home for the weekend, or were already committed.

"Hey, Jim," Charles Timmons shouted out to me as I walked across the campus on the way to the dorm after my last class. I knew him only slightly from sociology class. He didn't live in the dorm. "You want a date tonight? I tell you, she's a looker."

"Could be," I said as he caught up to me.

"This chick came down from Tulsa. Thought she'd surprise my girlfriend. We're stuck with her. She'll botch my weekend if I don't find her a date. Would you do me a favor?"

"Maybe I can help you out," I said.

"I'll pick you up, seven o'clock sharp. Be in front of the dorm. We'll go to a drive-in. Won't take you long to get acquainted there." He smiled, waved and took off in another direction. "See you at seven," he yelled back.

Charles was right on time. He drove up in his dad's old castoff Buick. He lived at home, off campus. She was in the back seat. She smiled sweetly. Charles was right. She was a looker, a petite redhead with it all up front. She was a lot more than I had expected for a blind date. She even outclassed his girlfriend.

"Jim, this is Lois," Charles said, as he looked at the girl in the back seat, "and Jeanne," who sat in front with him.

"Nice to meet you ladies," I said as I crawled into the back seat.

Lois smiled and scooted over closer to me as we drove off.

"You in college?" I asked.

"No, I work for the county as a typist."

"Tulsa County?"

"Yes. High school was enough for me."

I took her hand, and she did not pull it away.

At the drive-in theatre, we watched the old movie, *King Kong*, while we finished off our cokes and popcorn. Charles then said, "Time to get down to business." He gave Jeanne a long kiss, and then another one, and the movie went out for them.

I held Lois's hand and sat with my right arm over her shoulder. She snuggled up closer. Should I, or should I not? I hardly knew her. I finally got courage up enough to kiss her. Man! Could she smooch! If I had not seen that movie before, I would not have been able to tell you whether King Kong was a monkey or an ape.

Lois had to go home in the morning. There was a birthday party for her dad that evening, and she didn't want to miss it. We dropped the girls off at Jeanne's dorm. She'd made arrangements for Lois to stay with her. It was a long farewell in front of the dorm. I got her phone number and address, and had a date set up with her for the next Saturday night, there in Tulsa. I really couldn't afford to drive up there in my old jalopy, but I did it anyway.

After that, I drove up to Tulsa every two or three weeks, or as often as I could. Sometimes she came down to visit Jeanne, and we double-dated. There were a couple of times Charles and Jeanne drove up to Tulsa, and I went with them. I met Lois's folks and liked them. Her dad was a car dealer, and from the looks of their home, a successful one. Her younger brother and sister were nice to me.

Lois may have been a virgin, but she damn sure knew how to smooch. If my old time religion hadn't been such a leash, I felt sure I could have had her many times. Every weekend when she didn't come down, I drove up to Tulsa. I didn't push my luck, but minded my principles. I just might want to marry her someday. Everyone, from Grandma to the Baptist preacher who saved me, had said that you were supposed to be married before you did it. I guess I believed them because I behaved myself.

My sights were set on the West and the securities business. Poor boys still had a chance out west. That decision was made and I would not turn back. Maybe I was stubborn as my dad's mules had been, but that was the way my nose was turned and I knew how to plow a straight row.

I hated to leave. I loved Lois. At least I thought I did. We didn't get engaged. I wanted to keep my alternatives open. I almost weakened because she caused such an ache. I wanted her. We sat in the car, parked in a dark place under the trees that overlooked the Arkansas River and smooched. I almost put my hand up her dress, but caught myself and didn't.

"I'll write. I'll be back," I said.

"You won't come back." There were tears in her eyes.

I gave her one final hug, a long kiss and said, "Oh yes, I will." I drove her home.

She cried some more as I gave her that final goodnight kiss at her door.

My green 1940 Ford convertible was in fair shape. If I took it easy, it would probably make California. If it broke down, I'd just have to find a job and work a while. That ran through my head as I said my final, "Goodnight. I don't believe in goodbyes."

FIVE

We made it. I was proud of my old green gal. She didn't sputter once. We took those hills, and coasted down. She didn't even heat up in the desert. I stopped for a visit with my sister, Connie, in Bakersfield, California. I think she married early, mainly, to get away from home. She and Mother did not get along so well. Connie had two kids before she chucked her worthless, ex-sailor husband. Mother had given me the impression that they had been abandoned, but I guess Connie had kicked him out. She supported her kids. She worked as night auditor for a motel. She made enough to hire an old woman to baby-sit for her, and the kids loved her. Mother, when she first came to Bakersfield, baby-sat for Connie, but found that they did not get along any better out west, than they had at home. So, Mom found herself a good man, an auto mechanic, married him, and they moved to the desert. Mom's letters said they were happy. Once settled, I would go visit them.

Monday morning, just for fun, and to test my employability, I dropped in on the branch manager of one of those big New York Stock Exchange houses. No way would I settle in Bakersfield. It was all right, but I wanted a bigger pond. I impressed the branch manager with my ambition. He sent me to his regional office in San Francisco for interviews.

The next day, I caught the Greyhound bus. I feared my tired friend wouldn't make those San Francisco hills, so I left my green gal with Connie. With my BS in business and my old Woolworth leatherette-covered briefcase, I felt like I could conquer the world. As soon as I walked into this San Francisco office, I felt like I had a dishwashing apron on.

The cool wealth and dignity of that office exceeded all my expectations. I walked across the rugs and it felt like I was ankle-deep in salal in the valley of the giants. My best suit and tie, and I felt uncomfortable here. Desks were made of solid wood, rich and expensive. There was no veneer crap. I knew good lumber. The secretaries could have been movie stars. I shyly looked out over San Francisco Bay so I wouldn't have to look them in the eye.

The first two partners, already gray, looked minor league. They interviewed me.

"Your mother was a waitress and your father is dead?" asked the first one. He looked at the application the clerk had me fill out.

"Yes, sir."

He scratched his chin and looked at the other man and said, "We don't see many young men like this, who want to become a stockbroker." He looked at me and said, "Who do you know that has some money?"

"The banker back home is the only one I know who has any real money," I said. "And it doesn't all belong to him."

"How do you expect to make a living if you don't know anyone who has any money here in San Francisco, or for that matter, Bakersfield?" the second man asked.

"I get acquainted with people pretty easy," I said.

He smiled at the other one and said, "How long have you been in San Francisco?"

"About an hour."

He smiled at the other man.

"I like his optimism," his associate said. "Let's have him talk to Mr. Smith."

After Mr. Smith, I got passed on from one senior partner to another until I ended up with Mr. Balton, who headed the firm, or at least, was the West Coast manager.

"Why do you want to be a stockbroker?" was Mr. Balton's first question. "Why not real estate? Pays a bigger commission. How many people do you know in San Francisco?" Without waiting for an answer, "Will you work twelve to fifteen hours a day at low pay for two to three years while you build up a clientele?"

"Yes, sir."

He threw more questions at me. I answered him as best as I could. Mr. Balton's face was about as expressive as a poker player with three aces. I sensed that he liked me, though. He motioned for me to stand, and led me over to his office door. He pointed out a middle-aged, gray-haired man in a private office on the other side of the bullpen.

"See that man over there."

"Yes, sir."

"He built his clientele the hard way. He'd get up at four o'clock in the morning and go down to Fishermen's Wharf. Call on the fishermen one day, and then the next day, go over to the wholesale produce district and call on the commission merchants. He's a millionaire, and is now a partner. He paid a heavy price for success. He has ulcers."

"Sounds like his hard work paid off," I said. I didn't know what else to say.

He pointed a little farther down the row of offices on the other side to another man. "More ulcers! Two wives have left him. His kids hate him."

"He has ulcers too?" I asked. "Does he get up at four in the morning?"

Ulcers, I could take, but to get up at four in the morning? I remembered how much I hated to get up at that time, back when I was in Air Force boot camp at Amarillo, Texas.

"He did that for many years," was his reply. "You see that man over there with the heavy glasses on?"

"Yes, sir."

"He works twelve hours a day, and often more. His wife divorced him. Ran off with another man, a plumber, and later married him. The plumber left his work at the shop, didn't bring it home with him like our man did. She's now very happy. So you see, if you want to be a really successful stockbroker, there's a heavy price to pay."

I had noticed that all the brokers were older men, not more than two younger men in the whole outfit, and they both were a lot older than me. Mr. Balton motioned for me to take a seat again.

As we sat down, he offered me a cigar, which I courteously declined. It looked quite expensive.

As he lit his cigar, he said, "Commissions only run about 1 to 2 percent. You get only half of that. You have to sell almost $100,000 worth of securities to make yourself $500."

"One hundred thousand dollars!" I said, astounded at such a huge sum of money.

"Have you ever considered real estate?" he asked. "They make 5 percent and real estate is easier to sell than securities. There, you sell something that is real. We sell dreams. People can see, feel and touch real estate. With securities you're selling intangible ideas."

"General Motors makes cars, and they're real," I said.

"Stockbrokers don't sell cars. They sell pieces of paper. Cars, people need. Paper, they don't!"

My face must have leaked some hesitancy because next he said, "Look, I want you to go home and think about it. If you really want to be a stockbroker, you come back and see me in a couple of weeks. You think about it and we'll talk some more."

"Does that mean I have a chance?"

"Depends entirely on you. The industry needs new blood. Just look out there." With a sweep of his cigar hand, he pointed toward the bullpen. "A lot of these men have been here since the Depression days. Some of them even went through the Crash."

I thought to myself, "They look it."

"Thank you very much, Mr. Balton," I said. "I'll do just that. I'll see you in two weeks."

On the ride back to Bakersfield, I felt dejected, totally disillusioned. Ulcers! I didn't want ulcers and I didn't want to work with a bunch of old codgers. Especially I didn't want to get up at four o'clock in the morning. What was my uncle trying to do to me? Maybe I should just get a real job that paid me money, now. I could dream later. I wanted to make big bucks, but I didn't want to wait two or three years to make it. San Francisco was a wonderful place, but it sure made me feel like I was some place I shouldn't be. I decided that I wouldn't fit into that San Francisco office, so I told their Bakersfield branch manager the next day that I would pass. Still, I had to find a job quickly, before I ran out of money.

I next explored Los Angeles. This time I drove my car, and wished that I hadn't. It cost more money to park than to rent a motel back home. Besides, those people drove like they damn sure wished they were some place else, besides Los Angeles.

I found room and board for eighty bucks a month in an old converted Los Angeles mansion. There was a bathroom between my room and my neighbor's, which we had to share. That first evening we both got the urge and opened our respective bathroom doors at the same time. He was a fat man, maybe fifty-five. He introduced himself and invited me to come over for a glass of wine. I said no thanks, and let him go first. I didn't want to get mixed up with any winos.

Next morning at breakfast the fat man sat across the table from me. When he found that I needed a job, he said, "Why don't you go down to Hargo's Factoring? He might be interested in a bookkeeper." I knew bookkeeping, but that wasn't the way I wanted to spend my life. Still it might be a job.

I walked down right after breakfast. It wasn't far. The fat man gave me a note of recommendation to give Mr. Hargo. It was a flowery recommendation, and I don't know why. He hardly knew me. We just shook hands over a toilet stool and sat across the table from each other at breakfast.

Mr. Hargo looked over the application that I had filled out for him. Then he got up and closed the door that separated us from his clerk outside.

He said in a low voice, not to be overheard, "I see you're a college graduate with a minor in accounting."

"Yes, sir."

"I could use you as a bookkeeper. Pay would be $200 a month."

"Does that man out front need some help?" I had seen him working on the books as I came in.

He spoke even lower. "No, I would replace him."

"Is his work no good?"

"He's all right. I believe you might be better qualified."

I stood up to leave. "Mr. Hargo, I appreciate the offer but I don't think I want the job."

"What, what do you mean, young man?"

"If I took your job, I'd live in fear of every man that came in to talk with you. You'd best appreciate what you have." With that, I left.

It was a month before I found a spot. I got so desperate the fat man loaned me fifty bucks. I even had a glass of wine with him. He wasn't a wino. He was just being friendly. He was a good sort who seemed sincerely concerned about my need for a job. I called on stockbroker firms. One securities firm offered me $185 a month draw for at least six months, but a CPA said he would pay me $250 a month to start. As a junior accountant, I didn't have to pay any money back. I thought I would play it safe and take the job that paid me more money. I'd table my stockbrokerage ambitions for the moment. Maybe I could save money and then try again.

But that moment of optimism was brief. Hours and hours I fed numbers into the adding machine that spit out different totals each time. I was damn right disgusted. I was no bean counter. I wanted action. I didn't want to spend my life recording other people's doings. That seed my uncle planted was just bursting to bloom. I wanted to be a stockbroker. I made a terrible mistake when I didn't go back up to San Francisco. Just to think about it made me angry with myself. I let Mr. Balton bluff me. I let him con me out of a tremendous opportunity. He painted that sour picture of the securities business just to test me. Would I pay the necessary price to succeed? That's all he wanted to know. How stupid I was. The more I thought about it, the more disgusted I became with myself. He did say come back, and he would not have said that if he was not interested in me. I let him scare me away. In two years I could have sat on a stack of dollars, but with this job, I'd still be pounding on an adding machine's keys—something any dumb cluck could do.

Six months, I breathed that Los Angeles smog and I fought traffic battles. I was ready to hitchhike back to Oklahoma. I knew my old car wouldn't make it. I was trapped and tangled in adding machine tape. My $250 a month hardly paid room and board, and bought the gasoline. A junior accountant, big deal! I kept books for other people who did things. I was lonesome for Lois and things back home. Maybe I could dump the car and hitchhike back.

I thought seriously that I might go back up to San Francisco and try Mr. Balton again. I didn't like to backtrack. That was a sign of weakness. If I could hang on for one year and get my vacation, it would give me a chance to call on some Los Angeles brokerage firms. The CPA firm was a small, understaffed, independent outfit. Every day I was needed. I had to go here, go there, do this, do that. I felt like Old Black Joe, punch in those numbers, pick up that pen, grab the ruler, and draw that line.

Finally, six more months was enough of this torture chamber. It was Mr. Balton or nothing. I'd call him again. Maybe I'd still have a chance. That lunch hour, with a pocket full of quarters and dimes, I walked two blocks to an outside

41

telephone pay station. I dialed Mr. Balton's number. I wasn't sure what I would say but I'd convince him that I meant business this time. The operator said please deposit two dollars for three minutes.

After I fed the quarters in, I said, "This is Jim Bradley from Los Angeles. May I please speak to Mr. Balton?"

"Mr. Bradley, I am sorry but Mr. Balton died about three months ago. Can someone else help you?"

I stood there, held the phone, and said nothing.

"Mr. Bradley?"

"No, no, that will be fine. I'm terribly sorry to hear that. Thank you."

I hung up, walked back to the office with my hands in my pockets. I felt sorry about the mean thoughts that I had had towards Mr. Balton, who had outbluffed me. Now, I would have to start all over again and look for a brokerage connection.

With the Los Angeles smog and the daily traffic gauntlet, I'd be happier if I pushed a broom in Montana. At least there, I could breathe good air and rest my tired fingers from that machine dance. I was trapped. I didn't have enough money to go anywhere or try anything else. I was lonesome for Lois and things back home. We wrote to each other. I didn't tell her how miserable I was, only that I still loved her. I wondered who shared her kisses right now.

I found another room closer to work. My fat friend had started to leave roses in the restroom with little notes of endearment.

Three more months passed, and every chance that I could get a day off, I called on brokerage firms. I had to make a connection. I could not afford to go back up to San Francisco and try there. Some firms showed a slight interest, but I had no firm takers. I was too new to the area, they said.

A dark, smoggy, Friday morning, I sat at my metal clerk's desk and banged away at the adding machine. Over and over again, I tried to come up with the same damn figure for a total at the end of a long column of numbers. I was the only one there. No one else had yet come in. I had to work long extra hours to keep up. I was not the most efficient accountant. I sat there and added and re-added the same figures. The phone rang. I didn't answer it. This was my own catch-up time. Why should I have to solve somebody else's problem? I probably couldn't help them anyway. Besides this office didn't open this early. Didn't they know that? It kept ringing endlessly. Ring, ring, ring, it wouldn't let up.

Finally I jerked the phone up. "Hello." That's all I said. I was so mad at it.

"Jimmy," that's what Uncle Jim from Oregon still called me, "How would you like to go into business for yourself?"

"If it's anywhere but Los Angeles, I'd love to. What and where at?"

"Riverside."

"California?"

"Yes."

"Any smog there?" My eyes still watered on the way to work. They had not toughened up to the LA smog yet.

"There's some, but it's not so bad as in Los Angeles."

I don't know why I asked. Right then, I would have gone just about anywhere to get out of this accounting job and out of Los Angeles. "What's the business?"

"Lumber."

That excited me! Me, a lumber baron, just like my uncle. "Sounds great! What's the deal?"

"I've just purchased a 60 percent interest in a lumberyard operation that supplies housing tracts there in Riverside and the San Bernardino area."

"Oh, a lumberyard," I said and then caught myself. To disguise my disappointment, I said in a bright voice, "Sounds wonderful. How do I fit in?" My lumber baron vision had done a quick fade. What glamour was there in lumberyard work? They hadn't even made any movies of that.

"I'll loan you the money to buy a 20 percent interest. You'll be a partner."

"Uncle Jim, how did you get involved in the lumber business way down here in Southern California?"

"One of my best lumber customers needed some expansion money. He says he could make a lot of money serving all those new housing tracts going up all over the area."

"Count me in! How can I participate? I don't have any money."

"I said I'd loan you the money. I want somebody down there I can trust. I'll loan the $50,000 it takes. That sound good to you, Jimmy?"

"Wow! How can I ever pay back that much?"

"From the earnings."

"Partner, I'm in. Let's get started," I said just as the CPA head of the firm came in. He had his usual harassed, worried look of a man who had too many things to do. His eyes reflected a curiosity. Who could I be talking to this early in the morning? Who had a problem? I gave him no sign that I needed his help, so he went on to his office.

"I want you to run over to Riverside," continued my uncle. "Meet Mr. Tidler, Silas Tidler. He's the president. If you can convince him that you're a good man for the job, you're in."

"I'll go over tomorrow. Will he be there on Saturday?"

"Should be. He's open 'til noon. Maybe you can have lunch with him. I'll set it up."

"I'll be there."

"If it works out, I'll send him a check, and you a note for $50,000 to sign, 6 percent interest."

"Thanks, Uncle Jim. I won't let you down."

SIX

Saturday at daybreak, my old green gal and I plunged through and out of that LA smog. We burst into the sunny California desert near Palmdale. Once we reached Riverside, it wasn't the scene that I had visualized. I expected to find a beautiful river that flowed through town with lush green lawns and parks on each side. There was a river, but it was thirsty, and not far from being a dry riverbed. Above the banks, it was arid land. The only green, stolen from the desert, were the watered lawns. The grass sopped up scarce water like syrup on pancakes. Then I realized my mistake. Often, I had listened to Eve Arden's *Our Miss Brooks* radio show. It was Riverdale, not Riverside, where her rambunctious students, Archie and his friends, resided. They lived in a lovely dream world of yesterday, not Riverside at the edge of the California desert.

I met Mr. Silas Tidler and his wife, Mary, for breakfast at the Mission Inn. The place was a palatial hotel with tall cool rooms. Scattered throughout the hotel were medieval spirits dressed in knight's armor. You couldn't see the spirits, but their armor stood there, erect with sword, lance or mace in hand, ready to pounce on any invader who might disturb us.

Mr. Tidler was a handsome, tall, gray-haired man in his fifties. He didn't talk much, like he was above idle chatter. Mary was a bubbly, vivacious lady, not beautiful, not ugly. Her loose red hair, just turning gray, dangled on her shoulders. I could see her as an ally, right off.

We helped ourselves to breakfast. It was a buffet with all kinds of food, sausages, bacon, eggs, rolls, various melons, fresh fruit of all kinds, with tons of desserts. Fit for royalty, I expected to see the king come down the stairs any moment to join his knights for breakfast. Our table was out on a large patio encircled by the hotel. Above us was a high parapet with a large outdoor clock. On the hour came a loud clang, and two mounted knights approached from opposite sides of the clock, ready to do battle.

Mary talked and she talked. She'd ask questions and wouldn't wait for the answers. "How do you like beautiful California?"

She didn't give me a chance to say, but between breaths I managed to get in, "I haven't seen much of it before today. You know, I live in Smogville."

"Los Angeles?"

"Not sure, haven't been able to see any signs. My eyes are so watered up."

Mr. Tidler said, "Why all the Okies keep coming out to this hot dry desert is beyond me."

I winced at the term Okies, and said, "With all this lazy California sunshine, you need somebody out here who will work."

I could see Tidler grimace at this, but job or no job, I wouldn't put up with this Okie crap, especially when he was financed by an Oklahoman.

He said nothing, but just went back to his private thoughts.

"We didn't mean to be offensive," she said. "We thought that's what people from Oklahoma were called. Please forgive us."

"Sure." Her smile was so sincere, how could I not forgive the asshole?

"Your uncle speaks very highly of you," she said to move on to safer ground. "He said you worked your way through college, and that you are a hard worker and know lumber."

"I've handled enough of it to get pretty well acquainted."

"I think you'd be a real help to Si."

After we had eaten and settled back with coffee, Mr. Tidler finally said, "I wish I had your backer when I was your age. Your uncle put up $50,000 for your benefit. I hope you're worth it."

"He usually gets his money's worth," I said.

"We'll give you a try. Be here two weeks from today. You'll be my assistant. Your job is to do whatever I tell you to do. Two weeks should be enough notice to your present employer. I'd expect the same."

"That can be arranged," I said.

"Be here in two weeks then. Like I said, your job will be to do whatever I tell you to do. Pay is $500 a month."

Bells clanged in my head! Five hundred dollars a month! That's all I heard. That was double what I made at the accountant's. I might even be able to marry Lois.

"Thanks," I said, and looked straight into his gray eyes. "I'm sure we'll do okay. Uncle Jim says you're top-notch." I fibbed a bit. The real reason, I thought, was that Uncle Jim wanted me there to keep an eye on his investment.

No smile, but Tidler stood up and shook my hand like I was an untouchable.

"Monday week," he said. "It won't take long to see if you're worth your salt."

"You'll get your money's worth."

Mary, with respectful silence while the master spoke, smiled and said, "Have a good trip back."

He nodded a quick dismissal, and I left their august company.

That afternoon I arranged for a place to stay, room and board with breakfast and a packed lunch at $110 a month. Then I headed back to Los Angeles.

First thing Monday morning, I started the day with a lie. "Mr. Baird, I've enjoyed my work here, and I've really appreciated the opportunity."

He said, "I've seen you burn the midnight oil. I think you deserve a raise."

"Mr. Baird, I hope you will understand, and that my leaving will not inconvenience you, but I have to quit my job."

"Oh?"

"I've been offered an opportunity that I can't turn down."

"One of our clients decide to hire you?"

"No, sir. I've acquired an interest in a lumberyard over in Riverside."

"Riverside? That's a nice place."

"I told them I had to give you two weeks notice."

"A week should be enough. Roger says you'll finish that machine shop audit by then. No sense to start you on something new if you plan to leave. I wish you well." He nodded good morning.

Out in the lobby, my immediate boss, Roger, was talking to the secretary. "Wasn't that some accident on the freeway?"

"Yes," she said. "Such a shock."

"He asked for it. The way he drove up those freeways."

"What happened?" I asked.

"James Dean just killed himself on the freeway."

"That's a shame," I said. I didn't really want to ask who James Dean was. I'd never heard of him. Later, I discovered he was the famous movie star of *Giant* and *East of Eden.* Two movies that I enjoyed immensely.

"The way he barrel-assed up the freeways in his sports car," Roger said, "I'm surprised he didn't get it sooner."

"Roger," I said, "I'm leaving. I've acquired an interest in a lumber business over in Riverside."

"When're you going to piss off?"

"Mr. Baird suggested that I knock off after this week, when I'm finished with the machine shop audit."

"Okay." Then he turned back to his discussion with the secretary and the James Dean accident, like I didn't matter any more.

Saturday morning I made for Riverside. Everything I owned fit in two suitcases. That afternoon I settled in, and on Sunday I explored San Bernardino and Riverside. San Bernardino had places that made me think I was in old Mexico. I could see a slower pace than Los Angeles, but there was lots of activity. New housing tracts appeared everywhere.

Monday, I was up at five, and the rooming house lady fixed me a lumberjack's breakfast, pancakes, eggs and a heap of bacon. I had time so I walked over to Tidler's operation, Riverside Lumber and Development Company. It was located just at the edge of town near the railroad tracks.

Both of the Tidlers were already there, when I arrived at seven. Mrs. Tidler offered me a cup of coffee.

Mr. Tidler's comment was, "Did they fire you?"

"No. One week was a good breaking point."

"I'll bet."

The office was a small room, divided by a high counter. To move between the office part and the customer area, you lifted a hinged section of the counter. Along the wall, in the public area, there was a well-worn gray couch. At each end were bushel baskets of various size nails. Scrooge would have been comfortable here.

Outside there was no covered area, just rows of lumber all neatly stacked three piles high. The spread covered a city block or more, and I owned 20 percent of it. A yellow lift-truck and an orange one scurried about the yard like tumblebugs moving dung.

Mr. Tidler took his new partner on the grand tour. He introduced me to his four yardbirds, as he called them behind their backs. Fred was his head yardbird. He was a quiet, small-built, brown-haired man. He worked as well as bossed. Two of the yardbirds were husky young fellows named Pat and Mike, non-identical twins. They sorted and stacked lumber, and operated the lift-trucks. Matt was the other yardbird. He was an older Mexican man. He tallied lumber and filled orders.

Back in the office, Mr. Tidler described Matt as, "The best damn lumberman in town when he's sober."

Later that day I met Mr. Tidler's bookkeeper. God! She was beautiful. She had an endowed shape. Her face a vision, brown eyes and silky, dark hair that made you want to run your fingers through it. Just to look at her made my thoughts go bad. Wow! Just to smooch with her on that dirty old couch would be worth a month's pay.

"Irene, this is Jim Bradley," he said. "Jim, Mrs. Irene Maxwell. She will continue to keep my personal books, but you will take over the company books. Irene, see if you can break him in on them." She gave me a slight glance, smiled sweetly at Mr. Tidler, and said, "Yes, Si."

The first week was fun. Bookkeeping for a lumberyard was interesting. I figured outgoing board footage for inventory purposes, waited on drop-in customers, and tried hard to learn the retail lumber business. I had learned from my Oregon summer work that a board foot was a piece of lumber one inch thick, twelve inches wide and one foot long. A two-by-four one foot long, for example, being two inches thick would contain two-thirds of a board foot.

When freight cars came in loaded with lumber or hundred-pound bags of cement, we all became flunkies, even Mr. Tidler. At six, after the yard closed to customers, we poured on the sweat. We unloaded freight cars, sometimes worked past midnight and then back to our regular duties at seven in the morning. Matt always managed to avoid these sessions. He blamed his age, but I think he was just smart.

I made friends with the two young brutes, Pat and Mike. After I had unloaded a ton of cement, or twenty sacks, I felt like the ninety-pound weakling. You couldn't even hear Pat and Mike breathe, and I was panting worse than a dog in the summer. They joshed me, at first, about my "sissy" office job, but finally they accepted me as one of them.

After these midnight work sessions ended, Mr. Tidler set us up to a sirloin steak dinner and all the beer we wanted at a popular tavern-cafe, called Little Brown Mug. Mr. Tidler always skipped out after the steak dinner, but we stayed on and indulged further. Fred would stay, sleepy as he was, I think, to shoo us home early enough to get up for work the next morning.

At the third one of these midnight sessions, after Mr. Tidler had gone on home, I asked, "What do you guys really think of Mr. Tidler?"

Fred said, "I think he's a great man. I've been here five years, and he hasn't done anything to make me change my mind."

"Works your ass off," said Mike, "but he's a square shooter."

"Same here," says Pat. "We've been here three years and he hasn't screwed us yet."

"What pushes him?" I asked. "He's one of the hardest-driving men I've come across."

"His brother," said Fred. The waitress topped our coffee cups and looked at her watch.

"How's that?" I said. "I've never heard him mention a brother."

"Seems he had to play second fiddle to a successful older brother who he once worked for," said Fred. "He told me that to get away from him, he went up to the Yukon Territory and found enough gold that the old miners left to start this business. And now, by damn, he would outgrow his brother."

"Has he?"

"No!" said Fred. "His brother died before he caught up with him, and willed all his money to the church."

"Guess Mr. Tidler won. He's still here," Pat said.

"Nope. He don't think so," Fred continued. "He's resolved to build up a net worth double that of his brother, before he reaches the age his brother died. Then, he can leave more money to the church than his brother left."

"Talk about brotherly love. Sounds a little sick to me," I said.

"Nope. Don't think so," said Fred. "You should see how he treats us at Christmas time, how much he does for his church. The man's a saint. He's a deacon, you know."

"The Lord works in strange ways," said Mike.

"Damn sure does," Pat put in. "I think the Lord has a better racket than the IRS."

"How's that?" I asked.

"Makes Mr. Tidler kill himself and us too, just to out-donate his dead brother."

Mike said as an afterthought, "Nobody fights that hard to pay taxes."

"Let's go home," Fred said, to the delight of the waitress who stood off to the side with a wipe cloth in her hand. That ended my probe into the insights of Mr. Tidler that night.

After several more of these midnight work sessions with nothing going, but work, eat, sleep, and more work, my thoughts raced back to Oklahoma and Lois. She wrote that she was faithful to me, but I sometimes wondered, the way she had liked to smooch. Every time my eye caught pretty Irene, when she came in for Mr. Tidler's books, and I smelled her perfume, I knew I had to do something about my problem.

I went to a Saturday night public dance over in San Bernadino. As I approached, the music sounded Mexican. I went inside. I never saw so many beautiful women, all dolled up. It was a man's candy store. I looked around, all these beautiful young senoritas and some of them smiled at me. I was the only white face there, except for a bartender across the way. None of the men was smiling. I made my way over to the bar.

"Is this place only for Mexicans?" I asked.

"Don't ask me. This is where the Union sent me."

I didn't stay. I went home and looked at a picture of Lois.

It was May and I felt rich. I had stacked up $1,500. Monday after quitting time, Mr. Tidler and I were the only ones left. I figured up the day's tickets, and he fussed around with something in his office over in the corner.

Finally I got up enough nerve to ask, "Mr. Tidler, may I take a couple of weeks off and go back to Oklahoma to get married?"

"Go on back. Might do you some good. Put the fire out. Maybe then, your mind will be on the lumber business," said the man who always took a jab when he could.

When I called, Lois wanted more time to plan, but I only had two weeks. Two days later, I was in Tulsa. Made it back in two days. That old 1940 Ford made it without a single breakdown. Prewar cars, that's the way they made 'em—twenty years old and still going.

Lois's family insisted on a big splash. I think they bragged to their kin about the rising young executive their daughter was marrying. Uncle Jim came back and served as my best man. Lois's parents demanded that we take their second car, a '56 Plymouth, only three years old. I sadly parted with my old faithful green.

We headed west in grand style with our new used Plymouth, pulling a small trailer with Lois's things and all our loot. We made it out of Oklahoma and through the edge of Texas just fine. When we hit the heat of the Arizona desert, on the road to the Grand Canyon, the car began to heat up. Again and again, I had to stop and add more water to the radiator from the two canvas bags we had brought along on the good advice of a service station attendant.

"What's wrong with you? Don't you know how to drive a car?" Lois demanded.

"There's not anything we can do, but take our time and add water," I said.

"What have you done to my mother's car?"

"When we get to a service station, we'll have them flush out the radiator."

"It was okay when they gave it to us."

"I wish I had kept my old flivver. At least it don't bitch about the heat like you do."

She looked straight ahead, and wouldn't talk to me for an hour, and I liked that. If I knew I had enough gas to drive back to the last service station we'd passed, I'd take her back home, leave her and her mother's car too. Used goods or not, her family could have her back. I didn't know how far it was to the next gas station, but it couldn't be as far as the last one we'd passed. I drove on and hoped one would show before I ran out of gas. You think you know a woman. Just marry her, and then you find you've married a stranger. The cooing stopped at the first sign of trouble.

We were almost to the Grand Canyon before we came to a service station. While they flushed out the radiator, we sat in the shade at the side of the building and drank cold pop. Out of the heat, Lois's frustration subsided, and she tried to be sweet to me. I played along and forgave her for the moment, but I wished I'd left her in Oklahoma. Had she been a wise choice for a wife? That night at the lodge she tried to make up for her bitchiness. I took advantage of her remorse. The rest of the trip was uneventful.

We arrived at our new home Sunday afternoon. I carried Lois over the threshold of the small furnished cottage I had rented before I went back to get married. It was located at the back of the main house where my old landlady lived. We made love. She made no comment on my choice of a place to live. Later we got up and went to the store for some items and she fixed dinner.

Monday, as soon as I arrived at the lumberyard, Mr. Tidler called me into his private office, the cubbyhole in the corner. "You didn't file the state sales tax report before you left. They penalized us for late payment. Irene found the form under a stack of papers."

"She told me she'd file the tax reports for a while, until I caught on to the bookkeeping."

He grimaced "You're the bookkeeper. It's your responsibility."

"I'll pay the penalty. How much was it?"

He ignored my question.

"Irene's back on the books again. You will work out in the yard. Give you a better feel for lumber."

"I felt enough lumber up in Oregon when I pulled it off the green chain."

"Nevertheless, you're out in the yard, where you'll earn your pay. And another thing, your salary drops to $300 a month. That's more in line with what the other men make."

"What do you mean? I left my job in Los Angeles to come here. We have an agreement. My salary is $500 a month."

"I said we would start you at $500."

"My contract calls for $500 a month and that's what it should be."

"Show me your contract."

"You know it's verbal."

"Words don't cut ice with me. I've already discussed it with your uncle. It's okay with him. Your salary is reduced to $300 a month. That's fifty dollars more than you made in Los Angeles."

"How much do I owe you for the late payment penalty?"

"Ten dollars," he said.

I pitched a wadded-up ten-dollar bill in front of him and walked out. It bounced to the floor and I let it lay. One minute more I would have slugged the pious bastard. I was trapped. Most of my money had gone for the trip, and now I had a wife to support.

Out in the yard I came upon a stack of lumber that had fallen over, bumped by one of the lift trucks. I re-stacked it, viciously.

Fred came by. "When you finish with that, give Matt a hand. He's sorting lumber over there," and he pointed to the other side of the yard.

"Yes," I said, and didn't look up.

His tone told me that he already knew of my changed status. Tidler had already discussed his plans to put me out into the yard, and under his supervision. That move had been decided before my return. Now I was just another Tidler yardbird. When I finished with that pile, I went over to where Matt worked. He looked like he could use some help. He broke down larger piles of lumber that had been shipped in from places up north, with town names marked on the side of the piles. They sounded exotic to me, Seattle, Everett, Enumclaw, Yakima. There were also names of places in Oregon that I was familiar with—Prineville, Bend, Redmond.

We sorted lumber by size and grade. After we covered a stack with a layer of boards, we would stop a moment while Matt recorded the footage on his tally sheet. Occasionally I would throw on a couple of cross-sticks or stickers to stabilize the stack before we put on the next layer of boards. I noticed he used a crayon to change the grade marks, and always upwards.

"What are you doing?" I asked. "Why are you changing the grade marks?"

"Those dumb graders up north don't know lumber."

"Isn't it dishonest to change those grade marks?"

"No. It don't make no difference. Lumber just goes in tract houses in places that don't get seen. That's what Mr. Tidler told me."

"Oh, I see," I said, but I thought, no wonder Tidler made such good profits. A little like the stock market: buy low, grade high. Sounded more like watered stock to me. Wall Street didn't have a monopoly on crooks. I wondered what Tidler told his Lord on Sunday.

All day, Matt and I tore down loads. We sorted, we stacked and re-stacked by size and grade. The sun was a furnace in the sky. The hotter it got, the slower we moved. I didn't know which was the worst, the boredom or the heat.

Right after lunch, with the sun at its hottest, Tidler sprang from behind a stack of lumber. He'd watched us from the shade there.

"Let me show you guys how to stack lumber!"

He got on one end of the pile with me on the other. Lumber moved like a full-steamed paddle wheel. I never saw lumber move so fast and sweat dripped off my face like a flood. Matt tallied and skipped the grade changes. Tidler, cocky, moved like a bucking stallion, but I kept up with the son of a bitch. He worked at this pace for thirty minutes, then suddenly stopped.

"There! See how easy it is." Then, he went back into his cool office.

Matt and I kept up the pace for about ten minutes, then back to our slow plod. When quittin' time came, I went back in the office to clean out my personal things from the bookkeeper's desk. Irene wasn't there, and Tidler was busy with a customer out front. I noticed my ten-dollar bill, still on the floor. I left it there. I didn't give a damn if the rats ate it. I wouldn't pick it up.

Next day Matt and I worked way out in the yard amidst lumber stacked three piles high. I heard a strange rumble. I looked at Matt. There was terror in his eyes. He shouted, "Get at the end of a pile! It's an earthquake."

I had never been in an earthquake before. I wondered if the earth would break open and we'd fall in, like I'd seen in movies. There was no place to run. The whole lumberyard bounced. It was like I was standing up and riding on a wagon. Safe at the end of a pile, I looked at the lumber. I became more fascinated than frightened. For a few moments I stood there and watched acres of lumber piles do a boogie-woogie. After it stopped, I looked around. Matt was gone. I didn't see him anywhere.

I called out, "Matt, where are you? Are you all right?"

After a few moments he came out from behind a stack of lumber. There was a sack in his hand.

"Let's celebrate." He tipped his bottle, took a big swig. "We survived another earthquake. Want a little nip?"

"No, thanks."

He took another swig, and then returned the bottle to its hiding place.

Only two stacks fell over, so no serious damage was done. We restacked them and headed back towards the office to look for something else to do.

We saw Tidler's preacher drive up and go in the office for his weekly conference. Mr. Tidler was well regarded by his church group. Deacon of his church, he was a generous and pious man. Every week this preacher came out. They spent considerable time on church matters. We knew his conference would last an hour or so. We had finished the job that we had been working on. We didn't see much else to do, so Matt went off and hid somewhere with his bottle. I tidied up the yard, picked up loose paper that seemed to grow everywhere in Southern California.

The preacher left after a couple of hours of spiritual business. I'd even seen the two of them down on their knees in prayer one time. The godly Mr. Tidler, back to his own affairs, came out to the yard. He saw me at this make-work job.

"Mighty damn expensive garbage help. Can't you find something better to do than that?"

"Yard's pretty messy. Thought I'd clean it up."

"I've got something for you to do. Go clean up that mess against the fence. Pull out the nails." He pointed to a pile of scrap lumber with rusty nails still in the boards and some old lumber pilings used to stack lumber on. These are short pieces of timber with thick boards nailed to the outer edges that create legs so the lift trucks can get their prongs under the stacks of lumber.

"You mean pull..."

"God dammit, I said clean it up," and he left.

"You want all those nails pulled?" I yelled after him.

He ignored me and went on back to the office.

He surely didn't want me to pull the nails out of those pilings. They were expensive to make. That seemed dumb. Maybe he had some other use for them. I wasn't going to chase after him. I had begun to plain out dislike the man. I wasn't his flunky. I was a partner. I owned 20 percent of the business. But who was I to argue with the great god Tidler? If he wanted the nails pulled out of those pilings, he'd get the nails pulled out of those pilings.

I worked hard and pulled plenty of nails. This kept me busy the rest of that day and into the middle of the next morning. It was hot dirty work and the sun burned on. With a swish of my shirtsleeve I wiped the sweat from my forehead. Just as I finished up, Tidler came out of his nice cool office. He looked my way, and then came over on the double time. He gasped for breath as he pointed to my new stack of timbers made from the pilings. They stood almost shoulder-high. They were neatly stacked without a single nail in them.

With his hands on his hips, he stood there and looked at that big pile of timbers from the broken-down pilings, and said, "Kiss my bloody fuckin' ass. Kiss my bloody fuckin' ass." He didn't look at me. He just turned around and sauntered back into the office like he had been skunked.

I decided right then that I had better give some serious thought to our future. It didn't look too great here. I had heard truck-driver tales of how beautiful Seattle was and what a wonderful place that Northwest country was to live in. I remembered the beauty of the Oregon country. On the way home I stopped at the newsstand that sold out-of-state papers. I picked up a copy of *The Seattle Times* and the *Seattle Post-Intelligencer.* That evening I found an ad by a Seattle stockbrokerage outfit called Renndag & Associates that wanted to hire some stockbrokers. They advertised $100 a week draw against commissions. That was more than I now earned at Riverside Lumber. Next day I skipped my brown-bag lunch and walked over to a nearby drive-in restaurant that had an outside pay phone. I called Mr. Renndag, and had to shout above the traffic roar.

"Mr. Renndag, I'm Jim Bradley from Riverside, California. I want to be a stockbroker. Is that spot you advertised up there still open?"

"We always have room for another good man. Send me your résumé."

"Do you want some background now?"

"Nope. Just send me your résumé and I'll consider it. Must go. Another call."

I sent my résumé, and waited in anticipation. I said nothing to Lois about my stockbroker ambition and immediate plans. It would take a real sales job to convince her, so I would say nothing until I had something arranged, a fait accompli. I searched the Northwest papers every other day, but the Renndag ad was all I found. Securities firms did not often advertise for brokers.

Summer passed. The chill of November air made puffs of steam as you worked. Tidler and I managed to stay out of each other's way. It was weary. I stacked lumber, filled orders and made deliveries, and neither of us said a word to the other. Matt sometimes helped me, but mainly I worked by myself. Matt always had the cushy tally job. He kept track of board footage, while Pat and Mike did the hard heavy work. I was a flunky who worked where I was needed. It all seemed a waste of time. I had greater ambitions than this. Mr. Renndag never responded to my résumé. Guess he found some local person for the position that he had advertised.

Mid-November, on the second Monday morning, I came to work. The faces of Pat, Mike and Fred were like they had been to a funeral. They moved like zombies. Matt sat on a half-pile of lumber with his bottle sack in his hand. He took nips openly. Pat and Mike were the only ones functioning, filling orders, and going about the boss's business. Neither of the Tidlers was around. Something was wrong. Mr. Tidler was always there first.

"What's wrong?" I asked Pat and Mike as they broke down a stack of lumber.

"Shit!" Mike said, "The old man got caught fuckin' that Maxwell she-bitch."

"What!"

Pat said, "Saturday night, Mrs. Tidler felt sorry for them, working so late. She came down to the office with coffee and some hot soup for them."

Mike added, "Mrs. Tidler was under the false impression that Irene was hired to keep books, not fuck her husband."

"Where are they?"

"They're down at the lawyers to settle things up," Pat said. "They're gonna split, I'm afraid."

"And Irene?"

"She went home with her husband," Mike said. "Hell, he knows when he's got a good piece. Shit, if I'd known she hankered for it, I could of taken care of her. Hell! Then we wouldn't have this mess."

"Wonder what's going to happen to the business," I said.

"It's gonna go to hell, I'm 'fraid," Fred said.

The preacher stayed away. The lawyers took over, his and hers. They liquidated the business. I never saw Mr. or Mrs. Tidler again. Mr. Tidler went back up north to Alaska, while they dismantled his business. Lots of mountains up there, time to sit and meditate on his sins. I could just see him on his knees out in the snow under a pine tree pleading, "God, please forgive me. I'll never do it again."

Three weeks later, the lawyers gave me my pink slip and final check. Most of the lumber had been wholesaled out at bargain prices. Riverside Lumber was to be no more. Uncle Jim dropped a hundred grand, and I desperately needed a new job. Yakima, Enumclaw, Tacoma, Snohomish, Snoqualmie, Seattle were the sounds that pounded in my brain.

SEVEN

Renndag had never responded to my letter and résumé. The last two weeks, I had tried three times to call him, but he was always out. Before I left for home from Riverside Lumber that last day, I tried once more. I called from the outside pay phone at the nearby restaurant. I didn't want to put up with Lois's fuss about the merits of my being or not being a stockbroker, not before I had a sure thing.

This time he answered the phone himself. It was after the usual business hours. "Mr. Renndag, sometime ago I sent you a résumé. I still want to be a stockbroker with you."

"Can you sell?"

"In college, I sold TV sets and even insurance policies, lots of them, through the screen door, before anybody told me that wasn't the proper way to sell. Those sales helped put me through college."

"Sounds like you might do okay. How's your finances?"

"Just sold my business interest in the lumber business, so I'm free. I'm ready to start right away."

"Just sold your business, eh?"

"Yes."

"If you're interested, I'd probably gamble a hundred bucks a week on you. By ten weeks you've got to show you can produce, or we part company."

"That's good enough for me. I'm on my way up."

"Call me when you get here, but bear this in mind, you don't have the job 'til I look you over. Got to see you first. On that basis you can come on up."

"I'm on my way."

I felt good. At last I'd be a stockbroker! Nobody would talk me out of it this time. I damn near jumped up and down, right there in front of the pay phone, I was so excited. Then, I thought of Lois, and slowly trod home. I still had to deal with her.

I stopped by a florist and picked up a dozen red roses.

"What's this for?" Lois demanded as I came into the kitchen.

"I just wanted to be nice." She had fixed her dad's favorite baked beans recipe, which I had come to like almost as much as my favorite meal of fried okra and spinach. She jammed the flowers in a vase, without trimming the stems.

I said to her, "I'm going to be a stockbroker. This lumber business has played out."

"That's a scam business. They cleaned out my grandfather."

"You mean he lost it in the '29 crash."

"He didn't lose it. They stole it from him."

"His broker couldn't help it. Everybody lost money then."

"They stole his whole fortune."

"I'm a stockbroker."

"I don't want to hear any more of this stockbroker crap!" She took the baked beans out of the oven and stirred them like she was mad at them.

"I think we need a change. Seattle sounds good to me. All the truck drivers tell me that it's beautiful country and it's growing."

"I like California."

"I'll settle for the clean air of the Pacific Northwest."

"You're not going up there in my car."

"Fine, you stay here and I hope you find it real cozy with your mother's car. I'll hitchhike up there."

"Then you're going to go?"

"Sounds like it."

"You're not going without me, asshole," she yelled, as she pounded the vase down on the kitchen table with a bang and a splash.

"Think how romantic! It'll be a second honeymoon," I said.

She gritted her teeth.

Next day we headed north with $395. We pulled the trailer that we had brought west with us. The back seat was loaded with dishes and linens, and two blankets, which we would use to keep warm. The rest of the bedding was used for packing breakables in the trailer. The open road felt good, and after this, my second encounter with the lumber business, I didn't care if I ever touched another board. The nearest I ever wanted to get to the lumber business again was to push a wooden pencil.

Lois was tolerable. We entered a forest of tall redwood trees. Deep in a forest on a side road we parked, just to soak up the majesty of them. Light streamed down from above, made it a sacred moment. I pulled her close and kissed her. A few more and the mood drove us further. We were ready to capture a sacred moment of love there in the forest. Then I heard a truck. It was a red pickup that came down a maintenance road. I quickly buttoned up, and we took off, a little shamefaced at the sacrilege of it.

Patches of blue ocean reflected the sky. Late that night, as we drove through a far northern California town, we heard music that came from a dark tavern. We stopped, went in, listened to music and watched people dance in old country costumes. I tasted my first pizza there, an onion and cheese affair. A couple of hours of this, and we headed on north again. I drove into the night, full and content, until sleepiness made us pull over and rest.

It was a grand trip, even better than our honeymoon. It looked like life could be fun again. Then hell dropped its bricks. Our car broke down in Centralia, Washington, something to do with the transmission. We waited two days for parts. When we left that town, we had only $30 to stake us in Seattle.

You'd think Washington had a special reservation on all the rain. From the state border it was rain, rain and more rain. When we reached Tacoma, it still rained. It was close to midnight Sunday, just thirty miles south of Seattle. Late November 1960 was almost over. The further north we went, the colder and wetter it got. On the radio we listened to "Elvis the Pelvis." In spite of Jackie Gleason's predictions, "He won't last! He won't last," Elvis was still there. He continued to dance with a microphone and his strong voice thundered over the airwaves and through music palaces. A back east liquor baron had just bought his son the presidency. The young upstart charmed the country, both he and his queen.

I found it difficult to find a motel room in Tacoma that we could afford.

I said, "Let's sleep in the car."

Lois said, "No way. I want a room."

We finally found an old hotel downtown that cost only four dollars a night.

My first question at the desk was, "What makes this town stink?"

The hotel clerk winced. "You are smelling the famous old ASARCO plant."

"Oh, I've read about that. American Smelting and Refining. Used to be owned by the Guggenheims."

"Yep," he said with pride.

"Thought that went out with the prospectors."

The hotel clerk ignored my stupidity, and pushed the key at us, "Room 205."

"Thanks. I'll see my wife up and be right back. I'm sleeping in the car to protect our stuff."

"Price is still the same for only one."

"I didn't ask for a discount."

Outside, across the street, two men looked in the window of our pink Plymouth, piled high with everything we owned. They moved away when they saw me. Tacoma was dark and it rained and it smelled like hell. ASARCO may be famous and a relic of the old Wild West, but that sure didn't make it smell any better. With Lois settled in her hotel room, I dug two olive drab blankets out of the household pile on the backseat. They came from my Dad's old army days. I stretched out on the front seat, used one blanket for a pillow, and the other one to cover up with. The dampness in the air gave the blankets the pungent odor of wet wool. Occasionally, late night cars roared past with a thunder as puddles splashed against the Plymouth. They shook the car like an unsteady boat. A streetlight maintained an all-night vigil. There was a red and blue neon sign. Flashy red "Drink" flirted with "Blue Brass Beer." The streetlight and the sign conspired to keep me awake, and they did so until my eyes would no longer stay open. It was warm and dry and comfortable. I felt safe, at least for the moment.

Seven a.m., I woke up, cramped and sore. Traffic moved all about me. It was still raining, foggy, cold and dark. I ached and I was hungry. It took several taps on the door to arouse Lois. Sleepy, she rubbed her eyes as she opened the door.

"What did you get me up so early for?"

"Let's move! It's time to get on to Seattle. I want to see Mr. Renndag this morning."

Her long red hair and freckled face blended with the light pink bathrobe, which gave her a sexy look. The robe, haphazardly hung open, exposed her pink nude body. We made love, which helped make the agony of marriage tolerable. Then I let her go back to sleep, while I shaved and showered at the community restroom down at the end of the hall. I put on my best business suit, in fact the only one I had, and polished my shoes with a sock that had a hole in it. Lois still slept. When I finally got her up again, the first thing she said was, "I'm hungry."

"We've got twenty-one bucks left, and I don't give a damn if it breaks us, let's have a good breakfast."

"I can call Mother for some more money."

"No. We won't do that. We're on our own."

"Breakfast," she said and she smiled. Her eyes sparkled like a Scottish sunrise over the hills of her ancestral home. "I'm all for that. Buy me a good breakfast, and I might even forgive you for this dump."

We found a restaurant in the old part of Tacoma on Pacific Avenue, called Iron Horse. We feasted on scrambled eggs, bacon and a pile of hash browns that made me think of Mount Rainier. It was like a last meal. We savored each bite, each morsel of egg, each fragment of toast, each mouthful of hash browns. Now I was ready to conquer Seattle. Breakfast cost two-fifty for both meals. That left us eighteen dollars and fifty cents.

I easily found Mr. Renndag's office. It was downtown in the Seattle Securities Building. Lois waited in the car, outside his office; that way she could move when she saw a meter maid. Mr. Renndag's office was not plushy, not shabby, just in between. There seemed to be no one there but his secretary.

"Hi. I'm Jim Bradley."

"Just call me Miss Shirley."

Middle-aged, blond-headed with flecks of gray, she fought the plumpness war, but she had a friendly smile.

"May I see Mr. Renndag? He's expecting me."

She looked at a steno pad. "I don't see your name on the list of appointments I canceled yesterday."

"I just came up from California. He said come on up and see him."

"You don't sound like a Californian."

"Originally from Oklahoma."

"Oh, that explains it."

"I'm to join your firm as a stockbroker."

"Ah, that's too bad."

"What do you mean?"

"Haven't you heard? Don't you know? State Securities just suspended our license this last Friday."

"What! I just talked to him last Thursday. Isn't he here?"

She peered up at me over her half-glasses and continued to type. "I canceled all of Mr. Renndag's appointments for today, yesterday. By now, I suspect he is somewhere between here and Canada. Said he had some business to do up there."

"He told me that he had a lot of brokers. Where is everybody?"

"They're all out looking for new jobs; something I shall do very shortly."

"He didn't say anything about securities problems when I talked with him."

"He probably didn't know. They just showed up Friday. When they left, Mr. Renndag just said, 'My license has been suspended.'"

"He must have had some kind of feel that he was in trouble."

"Maybe, maybe not. I suspect that he thought he could satisfy those people."

"What did he do wrong?" I asked.

"I don't know for sure. He didn't say. Probably overlooked some rule. Mr. Renndag always said that they have so many rules and regulations, there's not a single brokerage firm in the country that's not in violation of at least one securities rule all the time. They just put you out of business when they want to."

"You don't have the least idea what he did wrong?"

"Net capital, I suspect, but who knows? Mr. Renndag said they were out to get him ever since he got on their bad side."

"What could he have done to make them put him out of business?"

"Who knows? Mr. Renndag always did push the rules."

"You mean he broke some securities laws?"

"Who knows? Mr. Renndag said that they didn't like a piece of legislation he lobbied for. He called it revenge."

"Is there any chance Mr. Renndag will get his license back?"

"About as much chance as Noah sailing down Puget Sound in his ark looking for salmon."

"Sounds hopeless."

"Listen! Mr. Renndag is right. When those guys get on your case, you're dead! Why don't you try some other firms?"

"Thanks. I will. Any ideas who I might call on?"

"Not the slightest. The street is crawling with Mr. Renndag's brokers trying to find a spot."

"Should I come back to see Mr. Renndag?"

"No, why embarrass him?"

Outside the weather was as foul as Lois's reaction. "What do you mean? No job! You bring me all of the way up here to this soggy, smelly place. Even the ducks get waterlogged. We've got no money! We've got no place to stay! You put me up in a fleabag hotel. You can't even afford that tonight!"

"I've got just as good a chance to find a job up here as down in Riverside."

"Bullshit!" On and on she ranted. Froth came out of the corner of her mouth. It always did when she was enraged.

What could I say? How could I blame her?

"I've got to call on some more brokerage firms."

"We better find a place to stay!"

"We will, but not until after three o'clock. I've got to find a job. Then we'll look for a place for the night."

Lois stayed in the car to beat the meter maid. Dimes were too precious to waste on parking.

Moorbeck & Company was a name that sounded good. I found them in the yellow pages of the telephone directory chained to the pay phone. The address was nearby so I walked. Lois stayed in the parked car. Spots were hard to find.

"If you see a meter maid, move; just come back to this spot after a while," I said. "I should be back within the hour."

The reception area of Moorbeck & Company was modest. The gatekeeper was an elegantly dressed older woman, who looked like a drafted shopper.

"I'm Jim Bradley. May I see Mr. Moorbeck?"

"Which one?"

"Senior." I figured that was a good gamble.

"He isn't in today."

"Will he be in tomorrow?"

"He returns Wednesday."

"Do I need an appointment?"

"I am not setting up any appointments until he gets back. Give me your number. He will call you if he wants to talk with you."

"Thanks, but I will call back." What else could I do? I didn't have a phone number to give to the old prissy.

Back at the car, Lois greeted me with frown. "Forget this crazy stockbroker dream. Get an honest job that pays a salary."

I drove the car up to Capitol Hill, parked where there was no meter, and walked back downtown. Lois read a magazine, fumed and waited. Before three o'clock I made three more calls. The first one was out to golf, so I missed him.

The second great man let me sit in his reception area for an hour before he would see me. He wasn't interested. The third I got to see after a thirty-minute wait and maneuvering through an underling. Results in all cases were the same, lots of encouragement, keep your dukes up, young man, and come back and see us when you have some book. Maybe it would be easier when we got settled, and I had an address to give to them.

Most of the motels were on Aurora Avenue, or Highway 99, in the north part of Seattle. We found a five-dollar place, scrubby, but it was a place to spend the night. We parked the car right in front of our window. We had ten dollars left, after we bought a box of crackers and a small jar of peanut butter. We choked them down that night with our instant, tap water-heated coffee. We couldn't find our coffee pot in the mess of things.

The classified ads in *The Seattle Times* yielded three possible places for us to check out the next morning. I called and arranged a specific time to see them. I didn't want to spend the gas and not find them there. Once we had a place to live, I would have an address to give to the brokerage houses.

After a breakfast of more peanut butter, crackers and black coffee, we set out to find a place to live. Ten dollars separated us from poverty. How I expected to rent a place with no money, I didn't think about it. I'd worry about that when I found a place. I'd have to negotiate.

The first two places demanded a damage deposit, and the first and last month's rent. When I told them I was looking for a job, they looked towards the door and said, "Sorry."

The third place was a small shingle-sided house with bird shit on the shingles. The structure was set back from the road under some tall trees. Next to this small place was another house just like it. A man and a woman, who wore denim jackets against the cool morning air, sat on the front porch. They were spotlighted by small stream of sunshine that came through the trees. He smoked a pipe. Last night, when I called, they said they would expect us about eleven o'clock. It was five minutes 'til.

They stood up at our approach. The man was tall, thin, middle-aged and wore vertical-striped overalls, the type farmers wear. She was shorter and round. Together, they looked like a bean and a squash.

"Howdy, I'm Crawford Brown. This here is Hilda Mae, the one that fries the bacon."

She smiled and bowed slightly. "You folks must be the Bradleys."

"Yes, Jim and Lois."

"Proud to meet'cha," he said.

"Please 'cuse our appearance," Hilda Mae said. "We just cleaned up the other folk's mess that moved back east."

"Reckon they didn't cotton to this weather," Crawford said.

"It is a little rainy," I said.

"Jus' liquid sunshine, I calls it," he said. "I tells new folks just grow a little moss on your backs and you'll learn to love it here. Those folks just didn't give the moss time to grow. That's the trouble with them Easterners. Always in such a big hurry."

"He'll just stand here and talk all day if you let him," Hilda said. "Let me show you the place."

"Now, Hilda, I raised you better than that. Don't interrupt when a man's a talkin'."

She led us in. "See what a nice little kitchen, dining room and living room you have."

"You don't waste time getting from one place to the other," I said. The kitchen, the dining room and the living room were all in the same room. An enclosed back porch was the bedroom.

She ignored my comment. "See, what a nice little cookstove and 'fridge you have."

She saw me look at the kitchen table and chairs, which probably came from the Salvation Army.

"Look at these nice wooden cabinets," she said. "Crawford built them hisself."

The potbellied stove, at the edge of the living room area, caught my attention.

"That uses heating oil," Crawford said. "There's a couple of fifty-five gallon drums outside that feeds it. You have to dipstick it to be sure you don't run out. Full now, but watch it; next one is yours."

"We'll watch it," I said.

"Where you folks from?" Hilda asked.

"Oklahoma."

"Oklahoma!" Crawford exclaimed. "Well, I'll be darned. You folks is home folks. Hilda Mae here is from Eufaula. I'm from Texas, myself, Amarillo, and I'm damn glad to see all the rain I ken."

"I'm from Wewoka," I said. "That's the capital of the Seminole Indian Nation." I was proud of that. "Lois is from Tulsa."

"We've been out here twenty years," Hilda said. "Don't see many home folks. Guess most of them went to California."

"They'll be comin' along when they hear about all this rain up here," Crawford said. "Stay long enough and you'll grow to love it."

"How much did you say the rent was?" I asked.

"Didn't say," Crawford said. "Thought you'd never ask."

"Well, you've been asked," I said and gave him my biggest smile.

"Eighty-five a month. Utilities paid, 'cept for the oil. That's yours."

"That's fair," I said and dreaded what came next, "but we do have a problem."

Lois retired to the sidelines, busied herself looking about the kitchen, with her ears perked to hear how I was going to handle that one.

"You don't like the table and chairs?" Hilda asked.

"That doesn't matter, but I don't have any money. Our car broke down in Centralia. Cleaned us out. Cost us $300."

"You got a job?" Hilda Mae asked.

"Thought I did when we came up here yesterday morning, but I found out that the outfit had just lost their license, or had it suspended."

"Whose that?"

"Renndag Securities."

"Oh, yeah. I heard about them. Read something about them the other day," Crawford said.

"What did you read about them?" I asked.

"Paper made you think he was some kind of crook. Seems the owner was holding a friend's check that weren't no good, and counting it as part of what he owned."

Hilda Mae added, "I think the friend had written the check to do him a favor, knowing he wasn't going to cash it."

"Net capital problem. That's all it takes to put a stockbroker out of business," I said. "Too bad. Lots of us have that problem."

"Seems a shame to call a man a crook, just 'cause he don't have enough money," Crawford said.

Changing the subject, I said, "Say, listen, Mr. Brown, I've got an idea. I've never had any trouble finding a job. If you'll just rent the place to us, I'll pledge the car to back up the payment."

"That's asking a lot. If you don't get the money to pay, some night you can just load up and drive away in my collateral."

Crawford did not say anything further, just stood with his hands in his pockets, and looked out the front door. We were all standing up. In a few moments he turned around and looked at his wife. Their eyes talked. A frown crossed her face, and I just knew that meant the answer would be no.

"That's good collateral," I said. "You can't lose anything. I'll have a job pretty quick." I could see Lois look out the window, and I knew she held her breath, either in anger at me for pledging her car or in hopeful suspense.

Hilda Mae still had a stern look on her face. They looked at each other again, and their eyes spoke another mouthful. Then finally a smile cracked across her face, and she said, "Yes."

"That about does it, I guess. She's the boss."

"Thank you! Thank you so very much! I'll get the car title for you."

"Won't be necessary. If I had to have that, we wouldn't rent to you anyway. Your word is good enough for me."

"You've got it. I thank you with all my heart."

"Here's your lease." He stuck his hand out to shake.

As soon as they left and went back over to the other small house that adjoined, Lois and I explored our new domain. "Oh, look!" she exclaimed. "A money tree, that's a good omen. Now maybe you'll make lots of money." In the small garage out back, she stood over a ceramic pot filled with branches of dried leaves that looked like round silver coins.

"We'll hope."

In the back porch bedroom, I sat down on the bed and sank in the mattress almost up to my chin.

"It's a camel-back bed," I said, "but it beats the back seat of a car. How do you like the place?"

"It'll do."

We hiked over to a nearby grocery store to save gas. It was a small one-man family store just off Aurora. The man looked like a busted-up ranch hand, but was civilized with his white butcher's apron.

He smiled, waved a greeting and said, "Just yell when I can help you." He went on chopping up something. We picked up some eggs, a pound of bacon, bread, oatmeal, powdered milk, more peanut butter and crackers, and the little donut cereal that fed me in college. Then we unloaded the car. It felt good to have a home and a roof over our heads again.

"It was pure luck or God's help that we ran into some home folks from Oklahoma and Texas. That's probably why they rented to us with no money down," I said.

"Ha! They were just desperate for renters," Lois said. "Who'd want to rent this dump?"

Tuesday was shot. It took the rest of the day just to get settled in. Wednesday, we were up early. Lois fixed us a good breakfast of eggs, toast and coffee. We saved the bacon for evening meals. I rode the bus to town, far cheaper than downtown parking. We were down to five dollars and fifteen cents.

I first called on Moorbeck & Company. I approached with apprehension, as I didn't like the uppity old gal.

A different person was at the front desk.

"May I see Mr. Moorbeck Sr.?" This girl was much younger, and gave off friendlier vibes.

"And you are?"

"Jim Bradley."

"Shall I say your purpose?"

"I'm interested in becoming a stockbroker with your firm."

She reached into her desk drawer. "Mr. Bradley, why don't you fill this out, and I will send it in ahead of you."

I filled out a brief employment form, and returned it to her. She immediately took it in to Mr. Moorbeck.

When she came back, she smiled and said, "He will see you, but would like a few minutes to review your employment application."

"Thanks. There was a different lady here last Friday, wasn't there?"

"Oh, that was Mrs. Moorbeck. She filled in for me while I went to the dentist."

"She was a nice lady," I said, thinking of nothing else to say.

She gave me an "oh yeah" smile.

After a few moments, she took me in to see Mr. Moorbeck. He said nothing but continued to look at my application. He sat up straight in his hard-back chair, not the usual plush executive chair. He was a thin and elegant man with thick gray hair. He looked well-placed behind his modest wooden desk.

The old man finally looked up. "So you want to be a stockbroker?"

"Yes, sir, with all my heart."

"Any experience?" He knew I didn't have any, from my application. He picked up his pipe, packed it, lit it, and waited for my answer.

"I've studied books and read about the stock market since high school days. To get through college, I sold about everything."

"Like what?"

"TVs, car tires, cars, pots and pans, books, and even peddled newspapers."

"Any insurance?"

"Tried that too."

"How did you do?"

"Didn't like to sell death."

"Any other intangibles?"

"Guess not."

"Selling an idea is not like selling pots and pans."

"I sold books."

"Paper, glue and ink all bound up," he said. "You can see a book, not ideas."

"It's ideas that created the paper, glue, ink and bindings," I said. "Give me a chance and I'll show you."

He sucked on his pipe. I could hear the air rush through. He looked at me for a long time, and then said, "You have any resources, son?"

"I have a car. I have a wife. I have brains, energy and a determination to succeed. What else do I need?"

He smiled for the first time. "That sounds substantial if you have the last three in sufficient quantities. The first two are liabilities."

"Mr. Moorbeck, I'll pay any price it takes to become a successful broker. I won't let you down. Try me. You'll see," I said excited, feeling that I had a live one that might hire me.

"How long have you been in town?"

"Two days."

He discharged a puff of smoke and said, "Let me talk it over with Junior. He runs the place now. I'm just hanging around waiting for the Grim Reaper."

"I'll bet," I thought. "These old geezers never quit. They never trust their kids to run their business."

"What do you think his reaction will be?" I asked.

"I don't speak for Junior. You come back next week, and talk with him."

"Thanks! I will. Monday, be okay?"

"That'll do."

The rest of that day, Thursday and Friday, I made more calls downtown. Everywhere I got the same answer. "Get some book and we might be interested." Bus fare ate up what little cash we had left.

Friday, when I got home, Lois met me at the door. Her eyes blipped fear. She said, "Did you find anything today?"

I hugged her and said, "Nothing for sure, Hon, but it looks good for Monday." I had to give her some hope. I felt ashamed of myself to have put her in this position.

"Jim, we almost don't have any groceries."

"I know, Hon, I'll see what I can do."

I said nothing, didn't even think, just loaded up our old twelve-inch Admiral television set, and drove over to the store. The owner recognized me from our previous tiny purchases. We were alone in his small store. He sat on a high stool behind the checkout counter, adjacent to a covered white meat case. He was reading *The Seattle Times*. He looked up and smiled. Then he noticed the small but heavy TV set resting on my hip. His smile drooped to a frown.

"We're new in town. I was wondering if I could...."

"We're not a pawnshop."

"Okay," I said. "Thanks for your flexibility." I turned around and left. In my controlled rage I squashed my finger against the door frame, but I didn't show any pain.

I put the TV in the backseat. Pawnshop? I hadn't even thought of that. I had never pawned anything before in my life. I couldn't face Lois empty-handed. Her look of fear cut like a razor. I drove to First Avenue, downtown, where I had seen two or three pawnshops. I knew one of them stayed open late, or at least someone was there after hours when I walked by last week. Nearest place to park was a block away. The meter still had ten minutes left on it. I gambled I could make it back, or at least wouldn't get caught. About halfway there, the TV made itself known, so I switched it to the other hip.

That pawnshop was still open. I set the TV set on the wooden part of his counter. On each side were glass display cases loaded with watches, both wrist and pocket types. Two or three pistols were intermixed with the watches, and rifles were encased in glass against the wall.

"Does it work?" asked a youngish clerk.

"Yes, sir. Let me show you."

He plugged it in.

"Ten dollars," he said, as the picture of the young president-elect Kennedy came on with his Boston accent.

"Make it twenty," I said. "I need groceries." Shadows from downtown interference didn't help my bargaining position.

His eyes X-rayed me up and down for a moment, and then he said, "Ah, hell, why not. The old man will probably kill me, though." He made some notations on a ticket and attached it to the TV set, tore off a stub, which he pushed towards me, along with a whole twenty-dollar bill that looked as large as a pyramid.

I know my eyes must have sparkled. I could see it in his smile. "Thanks," I said. "I'll see you in a few days." I really meant it. I would not let this guy down.

Outside, I broke into a run. Had to beat the meter maid. The time had expired, I knew. I squeezed the twenty dollars in my pocket. I didn't know what the fine would be, but whatever it was, it would be too much out of that twenty. I looked at the windshield half a block away. I didn't see a ticket. Oh God, this was a good day. I would take Lois to the museum. It was too cold and rainy for the zoo.

Saturday morning, with twenty dollars hostage money from our TV, Lois and I splurged. We bought some gas and drove to the Frye Art Museum. It was free. This museum had been built by an earlier Seattle immigrant who had come to Seattle from Iowa and made good. With bravado, gall and tenacity, Charlie Frye had become one of the largest meat-packers on the West Coast. Looked down upon by the city elite because he was a meat-packer, this lover of art left the art museum to the people of Washington. One of his earliest art acquisitions was a picture of a country girl with some pigs—rather appropriate for a meat-packer. As a farmer's son, I found this a good omen. If this pig-peeler could succeed, why couldn't I? I would just have to press on. All that weekend I had hope. First thing Monday, I would go see Mr. Moorbeck and become a stockbroker. Sunday, we took in the big new downtown library that had just opened earlier in the year.

Monday morning I rode the bus downtown. I approached Moorbeck & Company with apprehension. Would Junior say yes or would they say no?

"May I see Mr. Moorbeck?" I asked the receptionist.

"And your name?" She had forgotten me already.

"Jim Bradley."

"Oh, yes. Mr. Moorbeck is expecting you."

She led me towards the back. I could see Mr. Moorbeck Sr.'s empty office. There was a young man about my age who sat at the desk in the other office of this two-man firm. He had just put the phone down.

"Mr. Moorbeck, this is Mr. Bradley."

"Yes, I've been expecting you. Have a seat."

I sat down and waited to be hired. I had not met young Moorbeck before. He seemed nice enough, but you could see he didn't have the power that the old man had.

"Mr. Bradley, my father and I have given a lot of thought to your situation. We would like to hire you, but it would take you at least a year before you could make any money. You are new in town and don't know anybody. We're a small firm and can't pay you a salary or any advances. Dad doesn't want to put you through a year of starvation. His conscience couldn't bear it. He suggests that you get yourself a salaried job, save some money so you can carry yourself a few months. Then, come back and we will reconsider the situation."

"I don't want to waste anymore time. I want to be a stockbroker now. I'll get a part-time job to help. I've never starved yet. Please hire me."

"No, I am sorry. Once the old man makes a decision, that's final."

"I thought you ran the place."

He smiled at that, but chose to ignore the statement. "Come back and see us when you have secured your position better."

"Thanks, but no thanks," I said as I left.

Outside, across the street, there was a little coffee shop, called the Horseshoe Cafe at the bus stop on the corner of Fourth and Pike. I ordered coffee and picked up a newspaper left on the counter. The classifieds were a magnet. I had to find something quickly. Bus fare and food, that twenty dollars was going fast, and still no rent money in sight. Maybe I had better expand my search to things other than stockbrokerage, at least for a while. Every brokerage house I went to had said, "How much book do you have, or come back and see us later, when you have some money." Maybe I'd better listen to them. Take any kind of job for a while and save some money first. That was everybody's advice. I bet Charlie Frye wouldn't have done it that way.

Jobs as accountants and bookkeepers were listed. I didn't want to be a bookkeeper again. I liked to make things happen. There was one bookkeeping job that looked interesting, though. New England Fish Company was interested in an accountant. I had visions of old New England whalers, Moby Dick, Captain Ahab. There might even be trips to Alaska to do auditing. Maybe I should give them a try. Montcalm was another listing. They were looking for a clerk buyer. Other jobs listed were dishwashers, janitors and waiters. That would be some comedown for a college graduate, but I could do that kind of work again if I had to.

EIGHT

The day was hardly spent, so I hit the New England Fish Company first. Their nearby downtown office was pretty fancy for a fishing outfit. The chief accountant interviewed me. He looked like a fat catfish with his long twisted mustache. He must have eaten more Danish pastry than fish. He was friendly, what you might call fat and jolly. I could feel that he liked me, as he studied my application.

He looked up, smiled from behind his big desk, that barricade that separates those who have and those who don't. "You have a good chance," he said. "Check back to see me in a couple of days."

"I will. I think I would enjoy working for you."

"Thanks. This would be a good opportunity for you. We're the biggest fishing company in the world."

"I bet you had to catch a lot of little fish getting there."

He grinned. "A few big ones too."

My next stop was Montcalm Machinery. They were four miles south of downtown, so I hiked to save bus fare. Montcalm had a big spread. There were several large buildings, employee parking lots, and a personnel office with a multitude of clerks. Industrial steel fabrication was their business. I could hear the pounding and stamping of metal out in the shops, even from the personnel office. I could see sparks dance from cutting torches through the doorway of a nearby building.

The clerk handed me an employment application and said, "Fill this out, and we'll have someone interview you."

I finished filling out the form, and then I sat and waited and waited. Most of the rest of the day went by. Finally another clerk interviewed me, an Ivy Leaguer. He was more of an audit clerk. "Did I fill everything out properly? What did I do on my last job, and the job before that? Why did it take me so long to get through college?"

I didn't like him, so I said, "I guess I was dumb."

"How could you be dumb? You made the Dean's Honor Roll."

"Maybe I was working. My old man didn't have a lot of money. I worked my way through college, plus I did a stint in the Air Force."

"Oh, I see. It's all right here."

I think he practiced on me so he could get to be a big personnel man. "I think you should talk to Mr. Sandlund," he said. "Here is a referral slip."

"Thanks."

I see why big companies get bigger. They never make bad decisions. They don't make any decisions. They pass it on to the next fellow.

Two hours later, a chirpy young thing took me in to meet Mr. Sandlund.

After we talked a while, Mr. Sandlund said, "That's fine. You come back and see Mr. Calvert in a couple of days. He's out of town today."

"Thanks," and I went home.

The next two days I went back to calling on stockbrokerage outfits, which I was about to run out of. I made another try at New England Fish. He said, "You come back again. We're still considering you."

Thursday, I was back at Montcalm. After waiting for hours, I met Mr. Calvert at last. The heart of the day was gone by the time he got to me. He didn't say no and he didn't say yes. "Maybe you should talk to Rhomely. I'll set it up for you tomorrow."

Ten o'clock, Friday morning, I was back in Montcalm's personnel lobby, ready for my meeting. Mr. Rhomely was a busy man. He let me wait three hours. It was one o'clock, and still he had not called me in. I walked over to the receptionist again.

"Is Mr. Rhomely really going to see me today?"

"I don't know. He's in a conference, and cannot be disturbed."

"Ma'am, I'm sorry. I don't have any more time to waste in your lobby. I must find a job. Here is my phone number." I gave her my landlord's number. "If you have anyone who is really interested in hiring me, please call." I gave her back the personnel packet and left. That company could go to hell. I was so mad, I pissed in their parking lot, and walked back downtown.

For the third time I called on the New England Fish Company. Fat Man said, "Try me again the first of the week. You're still in the running."

On the way back to the bus, I picked up a couple of pop bottles. With enough of them I could buy a package of crackers. I was weary, and it was dark when I reached home. There was a note taped on the front door from my landlord, Crawford Brown. Since Lois rarely answered the door, he must have left me a note.

The message read, "I want to talk with you." Oh Lord! That's all I needed now, to be out on the street again. Crawford had seen me come and go day after day; he would wave, and I was sure he looked at me with a questioning eye. Had I found something yet? I knew that's what he was thinking.

I went on in, and Lois was fixing dinner of canned pork and beans that she was sprucing up with some spice.

"Did you know there was a note on the door?"

"I didn't answer. I can't face them. We don't have any rent money."

"I'll go see them."

When he opened the door, Crawford said, "Come on to the kitchen." I followed. His wife stood by the stove. She poured me a cup of coffee.

"Have a seat," he said.

Oh God! This is it! He's just being kind. I knew he was going to say, "I'm sorry, but you'll have to pay something or move."

Crawford cleared his throat, and there was a serious look on his face. "Had any luck finding something?"

"To be quite honest, no."

"How does it look? Any prospects?"

"I don't know for sure. There's a fish outfit that hasn't said no. They keep telling me to come back, that I've got a chance. I've been back three times. I think he's comparing me with others that he has talked to."

"What do you think we should do?" Crawford asked.

"I don't know. I'm doing the best I can. I know I'll find something. I always have, but it's sure taking a long time for some reason."

"Maybe your luck has changed," Crawford said as a broad grin broke across his face. Hilda Mae had her hand up to her mouth like she was going to cough, and then she looked away.

"What do you mean?"

Hilda Mae started laughing. "Crawford, you're mean."

"That big machinery outfit, Montcalm, called today," he said. "The girl said they wanted to hire that kid from Oklahoma."

"You're kidding me!"

"Nope. She told me that one of their managers looked at your interview papers, and he said, 'Hire that kid from Oklahoma. He's got spunk to tell Montcalm to go to hell.'"

"Really!"

"That's what she said."

"I thought you called me over to kick us out."

"Naw. Not a chance. We noticed right off. You had that stubborn, don't quit look about you. Those guys always win, if they live long enough. You look healthy."

"Gee! I was really concerned. I was afraid you had changed your mind about our deal."

"Naw. The ol' lady and I was just funning with you. Doesn't hurt to keep you on your toes."

"That's a relief! Who am I supposed to talk to?"

He handed me a piece of paper, which had the name of Daniel Brewster written on it. I had not talked to that man.

"Whoever called, said that you were to go directly to this man."

Next morning I went in to see this Mr. Brewster. The personnel clerk gave me a temporary identification badge and told me where to go. It was a nearby flat-roofed industrial building. The inside was one broad, vast room. Desks were lined up like soldiers. Every so often, there was a cubicle, sticking up like a toad's stool.

Mr. Brewster was a man of small stature, reddish brown hair, and he was bucktoothed. He reminded me of the chipmunk that once bit me, when I was a kid. I found the chipmunk dead, or thought to be, and felt his front teeth. His corpse left with a bit of my finger.

Mr. Brewster was on the phone, and he motioned me to take a seat in front of his desk. When finished, he grinned and gave me a bucktooth smile. "I like Okies. Had some up in the woods. They knew how to work."

"I've worked in a lumber mill."

"Oh yeah, where?"

"Prineville, Oregon. Helped me get through college, worked in my uncle's lumber mill."

A disdainful grin flickered across his face. "Always up in the woods myself. That's where the real men are."

"Have you ever pulled the green chain?"

"Hell, no! You wouldn't ever catch me being a pond monkey. You ever work up in the woods?"

"No, sir. Just the mill."

"Who was your uncle?"

"Jim Gordon."

"Never heard of him. Must have been a woodpecker. My old man worked for Montcalm, when he was still in the timber business."

Mr. Brewster looked at his watch and said, "I see you have an education. Think you can handle a buyer's job?"

"Yes, sir." I answered like my dad would have.

"I see you have a major in business, and a minor in speech."

"Yes, sir."

"I think you'll do. You do the work and don't give me any lip. We'll get along just fine."

"I'll carry my weight."

"I majored in forestry myself," he said. "When Mr. Montcalm sold out, Dad and I followed him into the steel fabrication business."

I started to show some interest, ask questions, but he cut me short.

"That's your desk. Go get squared away with the front office. Come back and I'll give you something to do."

73

I went back over to the personnel office. Even if he was a crusty old bastard, I was so grateful to get a job, I could have hugged him.

Three weeks later, Montcalm's first paycheck was gold in my hands. I cashed it at a nearby bank, located on the company premises. I carried the cash home in my breast pocket, felt like a successful hunter. I was ever mindful of its presence as I jostled through the crowd on the way to the parking lot and home. I had driven the car in order to be right on time.

I opened the door and grabbed Lois up in my arms and swung her around. "Let's celebrate. I'll take you out to dinner. I got paid today."

Her eyes lit up with glee. "Let me get dressed."

She came back, dressed in her best blue with the low neckline. It was Friday night and downtown hummed. We celebrated with a steak dinner at the Doghouse. It was not a fancy place. The food was truck-driver style, plain and plentiful. The waitresses had been beautiful years ago. The place looked like it had been there for a while. Some called it a greasy spoon, others, a Seattle landmark. It was high-class and grand for us. It had been so long since we had seen the inside of a restaurant. The steaks tasted better than chocolate fudge, and you didn't need a loan from Seattle First to pay for them.

As they served us apple pie, almost as good as my grandmother used to make, I said, "Lois, tomorrow is Saturday. Let's take a drive down to the ocean."

Her eyes sparkled like when I first dated her. "That would be fun," she said as she squeezed my hand.

I was amazed at how excited you can get at little things, when you're poor. Lois had never had to live this way at home.

Six o'clock Saturday morning, we were on our way to the seacoast. It was foggy and rainy and dark. By the time we reached Olympia, it was daylight. From the highway you could see the Capitol dome poke its head through the fog.

"Let's visit Olympia," Lois said.

"Maybe next payday. Every two weeks let's do something different," I said.

"Please, let's do. This is such a great country to be poor in."

"We won't be poor always. Wait until I get into the brokerage business."

"Spoo!" She stuck her tongue out, and looked away.

"You wait and see. That time will come. Montcalm is only temporary."

"It paid for this trip."

"I know," I said.

There was only one motel at Ocean Shores. Off-season, it was a snap to get a room. They were so hungry, they gobbled us up. The room nearest the motel office was the project sales office. We poked our heads in, out of curiosity.

A slightly older, handsome salesman approached us. He was the only one in the office. "Hi, folks, I'm Michael O'Keefe. You can't go wrong if you buy a lot right now. This is the ground floor." He pointed to maps on the walls that showed roads and canals that were to be.

"Looks interesting," we both said at the same time.

"Not too busy. Give you a ride over the whole project?"

"Maybe tomorrow morning. We want to enjoy the beach today," I said.

"Cold today. Maybe the sun will shine tomorrow," he said. I noticed the old fart give Lois the eye.

"What sun? We haven't seen the sun since we've been here," Lois said.

"We left that back in Oklahoma," I said.

"Come spring, he'll be back. I guarantee it," he said with a smile.

"That's good news. You got a date tomorrow," Lois said. We waved goodby. We dumped our stuff in the motel room, and headed on to the shore to beach comb. We were still fully dressed. It was much too cold to swim. We took our shoes off to keep the sand out. The cold sand felt good as it squished between our toes. We got our feet wet a time or two as the waves sent a soda pop froth over them. We had to retreat. The water was so cold it made our feet ache.

We held hands and ran laughing as we dodged the cold tongue licks of water. Her hand was warm. I stopped and pulled her close, and kissed her hard. The return was like when we first met. Such days make memories. That night was the honeymoon we missed. Well spent, I said, "We must come to the beach more often." She squeezed my hand, and we went to sleep, listening to the music of the sea.

"Hop in," Michael said. He greeted us that morning like we might be his only customer that day. His olive-drab jeep had a canvas top, like the army uses. I took the back seat, and gave Lois the front. The back foot-space was cramped, and there was a briefcase of sales material on the other side. He must have known that we didn't promise a lot of potential as a sales prospect, but it didn't look like the kind of day he could be choosy. We were the only ones in the motel except for an older couple, who still held hands like newlyweds.

It was cloudy and cold. Patches of fog danced in the hollows. Bundled up against the cold, it was nice though. You could hear the sea gulls and foghorns in the bay out towards Westport. As we drove along, we passed beach grass that grew almost to the ocean, which was never far away. You could always hear it, but most of the time small mounds or tiny hills separated us from the view.

"Does it ever flood?" I asked.

"Not since I've been here."

"How long has that been?" Lois shouted above the roar and the wind.

"Two years."

"You sound like an old-timer," I said, but no one heard me above the ocean's roar.

"How long did you say?" I heard Lois ask again.

"I've been here two years, ever since I went broke up in Alaska as a building contractor."

"When did it last flood?" I asked again.

"I think the last time this land flooded was twenty-five years ago, when a tidal wave came in from the Pacific. Started way out in the ocean, caused by some earthquake. Doesn't happen very often. Maybe once in a lifetime."

"Let's hope it doesn't happen today," Lois said.

"I guarantee it," Michael said, as he reached over and squeezed her hand to seal the bargain. I thought that inappropriate, but allowed it to his Irish ways.

"How much are these ocean front lots?" I asked.

"Only $8,000, and you get a fifty-by-hundred-foot lot, right on the ocean. It's a steal."

I looked at all that lonely barren beach. "You could almost build a house for $8,000," I said.

"You could build a motel here and it would pay for your house."

"But who'd come?" Lois asked. The wind blew through her hair like a wild filly on the run. The side panels were down so we could see. The canvas roof was up to protect us from the mist. It was good to see her spirit, so wild and free.

"They'll come," the Irishman said. "You just wait and see."

"How much are the resident lots, back from the ocean?" I asked.

"I got a good one for $2,600, only $26 a month. Isn't that great?"

"How much down?"

"Ten percent."

"Two hundred and sixty dollars," I said.

"Yes."

"Don't have $260," I said, as we drove on.

He ignored my statement and pointed. "See that stretch over there. During World War II they strung barbed wire over that area in anticipation of a Jap invasion."

Down at the end of the peninsula, we came to a rock-filled causeway that led out through the ocean to a small island at its end. Midway, he stopped the jeep and we watched the high waves pound the large rocks and disappear in the cracks. It was a glorious stormy day as the wind and the waves whipped the rocks. At the barren island we turned around and came back.

"A fancy restaurant is in the plans for that island," he said.

On the way back to the motel we stopped by a small body of water, somewhat larger than a pond. There were two small rowboats pulled up on the shore.

"This is Duck Lake," Michael said.

"I don't see any ducks," I said. "Are there any?"

"Sure. Members of the Lot Owners Association can hunt them in season."

"And use the rowboats?" Lois asked.

"That's what they're here for," he said, "for members."

On farther down, Michael pointed with pride toward lines of orange flags, string markers.

"These will be canals, filled with water, when we get through," he said. "The lots along the canals will probably go for $5,000 or more, but I can get you one right now for $4,000."

Lois turned around and whispered to me, "Golly, it would be nice to have a place like this to come to."

I smiled and said, "Yes."

Michael O'Keefe was quick to pick up on our interest. "It's only 10 percent down."

"What if I pay you 5 percent down on that $2,600 dollar lot? That's $130, and we delay the balance of the down payment sixty days."

"I could probably do that."

"How about if I pay you $50 down, and we pay you an extra $10 a month until the rest of the down payment is made? I could handle $36 a month."

"You're pushing it."

"Why not? The land won't go anywhere."

"You drive a hard bargain."

"Let's look at that $2,600 lot you mentioned," Lois said.

We drove about another mile to the lot, which made it three miles down the beach from the sales office. It was already staked off. There were two layers of lots in front that separated us from the ocean. If you stood on the drift log at the back of the lot, you could see the ocean above the grass-covered sand dunes.

Lois paced off the lot like she owned it. She came back and said, "Let's take it." We both were excited to own a piece of Washington.

The salesman knew when to close. He used the assumption technique on us. He sped back to the office, dropped us off at our room, and said, "Stay put and I'll call the sales manager, and see if we can work something out. He's in Seattle."

"We won't go anywhere," I said.

Lois and I stayed in our room to await the news. I planted a kiss on her lips, and we romped around a bit. Hadn't had so much love since we first married.

"What a great place to come to on the weekends," Lois said. "It's going to grow. It's a good investment for us."

"I would rather buy one of those commercial lots, right on the ocean," I said. "But $8,000 is too much for us right now. Twenty-six dollars a month, plus the ten, we can handle."

There was a tap at the door. We scrambled to straighten things up. Michael was there with a smile on his face and the forms in his hands.

"Sold him," he said. "You pay the $50 down, and sign a separate note to me for $210. I'll loan you that part of the down payment."

"Done," I said, and we shook hands on the deal.

Just as soon as he left, we got in our car and drove back down the lightly graveled road to find our piece of Washington. After a frantic search, we finally found it again. We hiked around that fifty-by-hundred-foot lot like it was a plantation. It was a grand estate, our land. I found a tall bush and marked our territory. That afternoon, happy as perky kids, we headed back to Seattle. We owned a piece of Washington.

By the end of the fourth week at Montcalm, I realized why Mr. Brewster liked workers from Oklahoma. They were tasty morsels that he could devour. The first week or two he was tolerable. At the start of the third week, he looked and acted like he had just sucked on a sour lemon. By that weekend, I knew that I worked for an asshole. Each morning we'd have to stand in line, and wait our turn to be berated as he reviewed each buyer's previous day's purchase orders. He'd roar out something like, "You imbecile! What did you do that for?" Another time, "Dumb-ass, don't you know how to spell dollar? It's *ar*, not *er*. I'm supposed to make a buyer out of idiots like you? What are you trying to do? Bankrupt the company? Look what you paid for this. This vendor's no good. Cancel this order, you dumb-ass." This went on for at least an hour every morning until each buyer had been well-masticated.

One day I muttered under my breath as I left his office, "Who does he think he is, Bull of the Woods?" A fellow buyer heard me, and it went all over the office. One day Brewster overheard someone refer to him as Bull of the Woods. The bastard loved it. Everyone knew Bull of the Woods was out of line in the way he treated his buyers, but no one dared to cross him.

Brewster had let it be known that he was close to the family that started and still owned Montcalm. "I knew the old man from our logging days," he said. "He built a fortune, then sold out to a big eastern outfit, just before lumber prices tumbled."

My third month there, Brewster took a vacation. A contract came up for renewal on a special cleaning acid that the firm used in heavy volume. Negotiation for the new contract fell to me. One firm seemed to always get this contract. Their vendor representative had been a big football hero in his younger days. Brewster was a football nut, and he was buddy-buddy with this ex-football hero. I sent out requests for bids to three large, well-qualified supplier firms in addition to Football Jock's company. When the bids came in, Football Jock's price was the highest. I awarded the contract to a competitor at 40 percent less. `One of the other line managers, who filled in for Brewster, approved my selection of the new vendor.

When Brewster came back from vacation, he didn't say anything to me, but he looked like a boil ready to burst. Later, I saw Football Jock in his office commiserating with him over my evil deed. Brewster's attitude towards me became even more intolerable. He was livid with me. Every morning he found something to rave at me about. The other buyers benefited. By the time he got to them, his anger feasted on me, made his attacks on them milder.

"Dumb asshole," he yelled at me. "I don't know why I ever hired you. Look at this handwriting! It's worse than shorthand. Look at this spelling!"

"I'm a buyer, not an English professor," I said back to him.

His eyes bulged like a bloated fish. His teeth clenched and his face reddened, as he puffed up. "Damned shame he didn't have a stroke," I thought. Probably would have, if he hadn't had so much practice at being a bastard.

"You dumb-ass, sheepskin-totin' monkey, get outta my office." This went on every morning. Oh God! Why hadn't I taken the fish company job? They had called me a week after I took this Montcalm job. Smart-ass me, I told them they were too late, and felt smart about it. I should have taken that job or looked further for a brokerage connection. Anything was better than this hell.

Even though Football Jock had no business with the firm anymore, he still came around. He buttered up Bull of the Woods and always took him to lunch. Probably, they schemed for next year's contract renewal. I would, most certainly, not be the one permitted to handle the renewal.

At lunchtime, most of the buyers and the line managers mingled in little groups to play cards, mainly pinochle. Brown-bag lunch sandwiches, coffee and cards were spread out on their desks. Cigarette smoke hovered above. All the climbers played cards. I stayed out of their games. I read the *Wall Street Journal*, studied books on investments, and dreamed of the day when I would be a stockbroker.

The house we bought on the Eastside, in a section called Lake Hills, sucked money like a giant vacuum going over a crumb-covered rug. Furniture to buy, drapes to be paid for, plants for the landscape, and all the while, the debts built up. Frankly, I would rather have stayed with the Crawford Browns. They were so nice to us, but Lois said, "No! We must have our own house." The sad look in their eyes when we left still haunted me.

Yet, savings were vital. Somehow I must figure a way to save some money. How else would I ever get another stab at being a stockbroker? That dream burned brighter each month as the debts grew heavier with each new acquisition that Lois said we must have.

Monday was another bad day. Daniel Brewster was at his worst. He dumped the full load of his bile on me. At lunchtime, I buried myself deeper into the *Wall Street Journal*. It was hard to concentrate with all the laughter, the card calls, and good-natured joshing going on around me.

I heard my name called, "Jim."

I looked up, and Mr. Corrigan, a line manager, whose section was near ours, across the aisle, stood before me. He also played cards at lunchtime from time to time, but I had also seen him read at his desk in his management cubicle.

"I've noticed that you read the *Wall Street Journal, Baron's,* or some book on investments," he said.

"Yes, someday, I would like to be a stockbroker."

"Why not just make investments?"

"Guess I could."

"Jim, I've brought you a book to read. One of the best I've ever come across on investments."

· He handed me a copy of *Battle For Investment Survival* by Carl M. Loeb. "I thought you might like to read it."

"Thanks!" I said. "I'll enjoy it very much."

I had already read the book twice, but I didn't want to disturb the zest of his good wishes.

"You keep it," he said. "I've finished it."

"Thanks. I'll read it with relish." I was surprised that he would give away such a book. I hoarded good books like some people did money.

After that, Mr. Corrigan often loaned me other books on investments. Most of my lunch periods were spent studying such materials. These investment studies might help my future, but they certainly did not help me at Montcalm. It hurt my pride when those around me moved up, and I stayed on as Brewster's whipping boy. Maybe I was wrong to spend my lunchtime alone. The others had so much fun at their card games. They also bowled after hours and that created another set of heroes for them to talk about at lunchtime. Everyone became such buddies. I was left out. The sharper I got on investments, the more my work life deteriorated. I played with money I dreamed I had. I turned $10,000 into $200,000, all within two years. Only problem was, I couldn't spend this dream money.

Three more years vanished. I now made two-fifty an hour, up slightly from my start. There was never enough money. Bad things went on in Vietnam. President Kennedy was not well thought of in the business world.

"The nerve of that man, telling US Steel what it can charge for steel. That's a crime against private enterprise." I heard that again and again at lunchtime.

Then that day in November came. "President Kennedy has been shot," came over the company intercom. "That's all we have right now. We will post you as we get further news." You could have heard a butterfly's wing flutter by. All talk and activity stopped. Then the buzz of voices began again. After that day the critics toned down their sour remarks regarding him. Everyone said what a great president he had been.

Brewster was relentless in his tyranny. At last, all the studies of the lives and the stories of the men on Wall Street and their boldness bore fruit. The audacity and bold strokes of men in high places gave me some backbone. I decided I would take no more of Brewster's crap. I'd go to the top. I had never seen Mr. Montcalm in person, only pictures in the paper. Any man who could build such a large company as Montcalm would not want someone like Brewster stomping in his steel patch. I didn't care how well Brewster knew the family, I was going to see Mr. Montcalm. I felt sure Mr. Montcalm would not tolerate Brewster if he really knew how he conducted himself. I would go see Mr. Montcalm, and we'd discuss this old bull of the woods face to face. Maybe we could just turn the old bull out to pasture. Tomorrow was the day. At lunch break, I'd make for headquarters.

NINE

I had to move fast to catch Mr. Montcalm before he got away for lunch. My lunch break started at eleven-thirty. Headquarters was on the other side of the plant, half a mile away. I raced through the factory, watched the vast array of overhead cranes used to move steel from work-station to work-station. I had to be alert and quick to avoid all the lift trucks that scurried from place to place. Bangs and clangs of metal against metal would drive me nuts if I had to listen to it all the time. It was a mighty plant, and here I was on my way to see the boss of it all.

I didn't try to get an appointment with Mr. Montcalm. I'd gamble that I'd catch him in. If word got back to Brewster that I went over his head, he would finish me off as quick as a spurt of blood. He'd trump up something to get me out. I'd seen him handle troublemakers before. Company brochures said the Old Man maintained an open door policy, but I hadn't heard of anyone who had gone through it.

Headquarters was in a small two-story structure, dwarfed by the huge plant buildings at its back. I went in the side door at the end of the building. I hoped to avoid the first floor receptionist and approach the big man's secretary directly. I had once overheard a noonday conversation when a first-line manager described the place. He had once been in the headquarters building. I climbed up the steps to the second and top floor. Bigwigs always had their offices on top.

It was a fairly narrow hallway. Pictures of buildings constructed with Montcalm steel lined each side of the hall. Several had been put up by Halvorson Construction. It seemed so quiet like everyone had gone to lunch. The office doors were open and no one was inside, just like another world had snuffed them out. I passed a conference room door. Inside there was a large long table with leather-covered high back chairs all around it. At the head of the table was an old gray-haired man sitting alone. He was eating lunch from a brown paper bag.

"Sir, can you tell me where Mr. Montcalm's office is?"

He grunted and said, "What do you want to see that old buzzard for?"

"I have something important to tell him that I think he should know."

"Have a seat," he commanded as he pointed to a chair across from him.

My back stiffened and my muscles tensed. Was I in the presence of the old
lion himself? At closer look, I realized that he could be an older gray-haired model
of the younger man that I had seen pictures of in the papers.

"I am sorry to disturb your lunch, Mr. Montcalm."

"What are you doing here?" He pushed a sandwich towards me. "I always eat
lunch here by myself. Good time to think. All the ass-kissers go out to lunch."

He saw my discomfort. "Go ahead, join me for lunch. Bessie makes a good
sandwich."

I picked up the sandwich that he pushed towards me. I felt queasy. I didn't
like to squeal on a co-worker.

"What bugs you, son?"

"Sir, I like to work at Montcalm, and I think you have a great company."

"Cut out the bullshit. What's bugging you?"

"I don't hardly know how to begin."

"Well, lay it on the line. I've been listening to shit all my life." He took a bite
of his sandwich, and gave me a quizzical look, like he was enjoying himself, a cat at
play with a mouse.

"It's touchy. Everyone is afraid to say anything about a friend of yours from the
old days. He's a line boss who's a bastard, who runs roughshod over everyone."

"You've got to be a bastard if you are the boss. Never saw a wimp succeed at
anything."

"Employees shouldn't have to take that kind of treatment from anyone."

"Did the union send you up here?"

"What union? You don't have a union. They're all wimps."

"Well, tell me then, what does this old family friend of mine do?"

His eagle eye stared down at me from a massive picture on the wall. I felt
foolish, me a squealer?

"He thinks he has to have all his buyers for breakfast every morning. Calls us
imbeciles, idiots, dumb-asses, fuck-heads and whatever else comes to his mind. He
blares it out for everyone all over the place to hear."

"My, aren't we fainthearted? You should have been up in the woods in my
day. He sounds mild compared to the words we used to use out in the woods."

The old man just smiled and waited for my response.

"I don't think people should have to put up with that kind of stuff."

"Who is this old family friend of mine?"

"Daniel Brewster in the purchasing department."

He looked out the window, and seemed to be in deep thought. "Daniel
Brewster," he repeated slowly. "I don't believe I know Daniel
Brewster...Brewster...Brewster," he said as his mind searched the years "Wait a
minute, there was a John Brewster who was one of my woods bosses. Good man.
Remember him well. I think he did have a son. Danny, I believe, was his name.

John spent every dime he could get his hands on putting that kid through school. I thought Danny went into the forest service."

"No, sir, he works for you."

"Well, I'll be damned. Sounds like he picked up a few things from his old man."

I didn't say that I also suspected that he took bribes. That would be hard to prove. Maybe, if I got fired, that would give me another chance to be a stockbroker. "I've taken all of Brewster's dung that I'm going to."

"What did you say your name was?"

"Bradley, Jim Bradley, sir."

"I admire your spunk, young fella. Took guts to come here. You run along. I'll see if I can tone Danny Boy down a bit."

It was five minutes after the hour, when I got back to my workstation. "Where've you been?" Bull of the Woods shouted at me. You're late." He knew I always spent my lunch hour at my desk.

If I had a red handkerchief, I think he would have charged. I could have sworn I heard him snort.

I smiled at him and said, "I took a walk."

"You're late."

"Sorry."

"Don't let it happen again, dumb-ass."

I smiled at him again, and said, "Yes, sir."

Then mumbling something under his breath, he went back to his office cubicle.

Monday morning I went to work as usual. Brewster wasn't there. In four years, this had never happened, except when he was on vacation. He surely wouldn't have gotten fired, just on my say-so. About ten o'clock Brewster showed up. He didn't say anything to me, just looked in my direction with contempt. He chewed no one out that morning. He harassed no one the rest of the week. My fellow buyers thought he might be sick, but they enjoyed the respite.

The next Monday morning there was a letter on my desk from the Director of Purchasing that reassigned me to Mr. Corrigan's section. This was not the usual channel of change. Your immediate boss usually called you in, told you that you were being transferred, promoted, laid off or fired. I didn't say anything to Brewster. I just picked up my personal things and moved them over to Mr. Corrigan's section. I sat down at my new desk and looked back towards my old section. Bolts of Brewster's hate snapped the air between us.

I felt like I had just climbed out of hell. Mr. Corrigan was a good scoutmaster. If you screwed up, he did not bellow at you, but suggested that next time, this or that might be a better way. One day Mr. Corrigan caught me writing a letter in longhand to be typed by one of the staff secretaries.

"No, Jim, we don't do letters that way. You dictate them. Try it. It's much easier."

"I'll try."

The next day, I had an urgent letter to get out.

"I'm swamped with high priority stuff," our group secretary said. "Why don't you try the big boss's secretary? She always has time on her hands."

Humbly, I approached the secretary to the Director of Purchasing, "I have an important piece of mail to get out. Could you possibly help me?"

"Surely, have a seat. I have to stay here at my desk. Phone might ring." She pulled a steno pad from her desk drawer, sat with her legs crossed and the pad on her knee and waited. She looked sophisticated in her blue mini-skirt business suit. It matched her blue eye shadow. Her polished nails were so long I wondered how she could type. It was difficult to not look at her legs. Mini-skirts were new. I was shy in the presence of all of that bountiful womanhood. I started to say something, but nothing came out.

Finally, she smiled and said, "You haven't dictated much, have you?"

"This is my first time."

"Oh. I'm honored," she said. "I have a virgin here. Don't worry. Just take your time and we'll get through this together."

It took thirty minutes before I finally completed the letter. I actually enjoyed myself. Dictation wasn't all that hard. You just talked, and someone else wrote it down. They had to worry about the spelling and punctuation, not me. After that, I dictated all my letters, and wondered why I had ever gone through the chore of longhand. Across the way, Bull of the Woods was back to his old self again, and I watched in sympathy as his men suffered.

Pressures at home grew worse. We need this. We need that. Each paycheck was devoured. Even worse, rumors were that Montcalm might lose its major customer. That meant layoffs.

An ominous unspoken mood came over the entire plant in mid-'66. Everyone knew it. Layoffs were upon us. Mr. Corrigan stood up that Monday morning. His eyes peered over the office cubicle that floated like a sinking ship in a sea of desks. He tapped on the side panel to get attention. There was an immediate hush. Desk drawers clanged shut and phones clapped down. Any other day he would have had to bang to get their attention.

"We will have a brief meeting in the conference room," he said.

On the way there, behind me, I could hear Charlie Chaplin. That's what we called him. Small cropped mustache, high water pants, and a bit of a clown.

He yelled at Ralph, the buyer who was everyone's friend, "It's coming. One of us is going to get the ax. I know it." Charlie Chaplin repeated again and again, "One of us is going to get it."

The crew gathered around the long mahogany conference table with rounded ends. Mr. Corrigan took his rightful place at the head, and Charlie Chaplin at the other end, which he always managed to grab. Two maternal women in our group, mostly due to Mr. Corrigan's liberal outlook, poured us coffee and passed the cream and sugar around.

Some sipped the coffee from Styrofoam cups. Others nervously crossed and uncrossed their legs. Silence, nobody talked.

Mr. Corrigan finally said with a great solemnity, "You probably all know we've lost the Halvorson contract. They've declared bankruptcy."

"We thought it was just a rumor," went around the table.

"No rumor now. Just got the word. They've taken Chapter 7 bankruptcy. It will cost us a bundle." His usual smile was a face of gloom.

"I'll try to save all of our positions that I can, but I don't know just yet how we will come out. We'll get the department cutback figures this afternoon. I would like each of you to prepare a detailed report of your current activities: project name and number, and last month's purchase value you initiated for each."

"When you gotta have it?" Charlie Chaplin asked.

"Yesterday, but I will settle for tomorrow morning."

"That doesn't give us much time," Ralph said.

"That's all the time we have. Get something put together for me by morning."

Mr. Corrigan stood up and said, "We'll meet here at eight in the morning. I have an appointment at headquarters now."

On the way back to our desks, on and on went Charlie Chaplin, "I told you it was coming. I told you it was coming."

When I returned to the disarray of unfinished work on my desk, I thought of all my unpaid bills.

Across the room, Bull of the Woods was his old self. I wondered, would my job have been safer there? The old fart did have clout. He still blared out insults. His animosity had now turned on Mr. Corrigan at higher staff meetings. He undercut him whenever he could.

Friday morning, there was a note on my desk from Mr. Corrigan, "See me at ten." This could mean only one thing—the ax. My pay rate of $2.75 an hour didn't go far, but it was making a $125 a month house payment, furniture payments, department store payments, and payments on other debts that had been incurred, plus Ocean Shores. If I was out, what would we do?

I sat down in the lone side chair. Staccato chatter of the secretary's typewriter came from just outside the cubicle. There was a shadow of sadness in his eyes.

"Bradley, I think you have potential to become a valuable employee." He fidgeted with his tie clasp. Over the last six months, Mr. Corrigan had already gotten two dime-merit raises through for me.

"They've hit our group pretty hard, two out of eight."

"That's a lot more than the 10 percent that was mentioned."

"I know, but that's the way it is."

I thought of the spring vacation that Lois and I had looked forward to. The first trip back home after five years out West, and all of those monthly payments we had to make.

"You are my latest recruit, so you know that puts you on the low side of the totem pole."

"Yes, sir."

"Ralph retires at the end of this year, so I managed to stall one of the cut casualties until then. We won't replace him."

"Guess that leaves me."

"Like I said, Jim, I don't want to lose you. I think over the years you can become a valued employee." Mr. Corrigan rearranged some papers on his neatly organized desk.

His round moon face was all gloom. "Jim, they've tied my hands."

"That's what I was afraid of." This was the moment I dreaded. I remembered the two coke bottles I picked up that time I walked away from trying to get employed at New England Fish.

"Now, don't get any false hope up, because I can't promise anything."

I felt blood rush to my head. Then it wasn't all lost, just maybe.

"I've gotten John Stacker down at Stores to agree to interview you. He thinks he might be able to work you in as a grade 8 warehouse clerk."

"Right now, a job is a job," I exclaimed.

"Your grade status drops from 4 to 8. Probably a 25 percent cut in pay. Could you handle that?"

"That beats the street," I said, but I thought to myself, maybe with a part-time job we can survive.

"Do you really think they can work me in?"

"Stacker owes me a favor. He will, if he can."

"Thank you, Mr. Corrigan. I appreciate your efforts to help me."

"Now, Jim, as I say, this may not work out, but if it does, it won't be forever. When things pick up, I can probably bring you back in. So don't feel too put down by the low pay."

"Thanks, Mr. Corrigan. Thank you very much."

"That's okay. Just don't let Stacker down. He's doing me a favor, warehousing you for a while."

"I'll do my best."

"I'm pretty sure it won't be long. Terwitte will be back in the fall, and I'm sure he will back me, if I'm still here."

I could see Bull of the Woods look our way. There was a smirk on his face.

Mr. Corrigan glanced at his watch. "It's ten-thirty. If you hurry, you can catch the eleven o'clock shuttle down to Stores. Give John my best."

The bus wasn't there yet, so I lit a cigar while I waited. Cigars were a legacy of my lonely stay on Kwajalein as an airman, where there wasn't anything to do, except sun, midafternoon rain and old movies at night. No female company to take your mind off the loneliness. I had been too young to drink.

When the shuttle came, it was filled with shopworkers, office clerks, expediters on errands, and desperate ones such as me, looking for another spot. The small industrial shops and warehouses that we passed reminded me of Tacoma, that first night Lois and I had spent in the Northwest. Then, we were really broke. A car breakdown in Centralia, with only twenty-five dollars left, and not a friend within 2,000 miles.

All those stories I had read of rich brokers and their yachts, now I couldn't even afford to take my wife out to dinner. Five years had gone by. I was really poorer now than that first night, when I slept in the car. Then I didn't owe anyone.

Yes, I'd take that store clerk job in order to survive. But here I was, a college graduate with a BS degree in business, back down to a grade 8 warehouse flunky, and that was only maybe. I wondered if that degree I had worked so hard to get, was worth it. About halfway down to Stores, I thought of that song, *Wheel of Fortune*, that kept turning, turning. I wondered when on earth it would find me. It had certainly forgotten to point my way. Montcalm wasn't the answer.

Right that moment on the bus, I decided that it's got to be now. If I wanted to make a fortune, my waiting had better stop. Things were different now. No longer was I new in town. I knew lots of vendors, people with money. Most of them invested in stocks. I had given them thousands of dollars worth of business. Why wouldn't they deal with me?

Lois would never tolerate the uncertainty of a commission job. That was the only thing most of the securities firms offered. We had no savings. Miss a house payment or two, and we'd sleep in the car. Nothing ventured, nothing gained, as the old saying goes. Sink or swim, Lois or none, bankrupt or not, street or tent, I'd had enough of Montcalm and poverty.

The bus stopped at Montcalm's Stores. I got off. My step was light. The burden bore me down no more. I was a stockbroker.

I virtually ran into the warehouse. High ceilings, rows and rows of racks loaded with supplies, parts, and goods greeted me. Narrow passageways tunneled through the mass. Lift trucks whined and groaned. So this could have been my destiny, to spend my days here in Stores. I could see myself climb up ladders like a monkey, retrieve packs of paper, steno pads, paper clips, and all such things as needed by

Montcalm. All of this, just to earn my daily bread. I had worked my way through college, ate ten-cent bowls of Cheerios every morning in order to get an education, just for this?

Down the tunnel, off to the side, I saw a pillbox office that sat at the foot of the tall racks, like a fallen pine cone in the forest. I guessed that would be where I would find Mr. Stacker. I headed that way.

Suddenly, out of a passageway lunged a lift truck that almost got me. The driver trembled and cussed.

"What the hell are you doing out here?" he shouted.

He saw my company badge, but did not recognize me as one of his own. He yelled, "What the shit you doing in here?"

"Looking for Mr. Stacker."

"He ain't out here, goddamn it." He pointed to the shack where I had been headed.

"Thanks."

"Keep your goddamn ass out of my aisles if you don't want to get killed."

"I'll buy that," I said, and continued on my way down the aisle, but peeked up and down each row before I stepped out. So that character was to be my brother-in-arms. My decision to leave felt better all the time.

Mr. Stacker was a small man. Napoleon of the racks, I thought.

"You Mr. Stacker?" I asked.

"You must be Bradley."

"That's me."

"Come right on in. Corrigan spoke very highly of you."

I felt guilty, but couldn't back out this time. It was stockbroker or nothing, regardless of the consequences.

"Thanks," I said. "May I use your phone, Mr. Stacker?"

"Sure." He pointed to the corner of his desk.

I dialed Mr. Corrigan's office. Mr. Stacker sat down at other side of his desk and made busywork.

"Mr. Corrigan, this is Jim. On the bus down, I did a lot of thinking. You've known of my interest in the stock market."

"Yes."

"Well, I deeply, deeply appreciate your efforts to find another spot for me. I know it's dumb, but I've decided to become a stockbroker right now."

Mr. Stacker listened to everything I said, but pretended not to hear. There were piles of paper on his dusty gun-gray metal desk, weighted down by aluminum bolt nuts.

"Jim, I told you, I think you have a great future with Montcalm. The old man was impressed by you. That warehouse job is only temporary."

"I know, Mr. Corrigan, but there comes a time in the lives of men when a man has to stand up and do what he was meant to do."

"Jim, don't be hasty. I think you'll be sorry."

"I hope not, but this is a chance I have to take."

"Jim, you'll only be down there a couple of months. Why don't you keep your job and invest in the stock market on the side? That makes better sense."

"Thanks, Mr. Corrigan, but that's not the problem. It's now or never if I'm to be a stockbroker. Who knows, maybe one day you'll buy some stock from me."

"Good luck, Jim. Change your mind, call me."

"Thanks. I've burned my bridges. I don't need that temptation. There's no return."

"Okay, friend. Good luck," and he hung up.

Mr. Stacker stood up, stuck out his hand to shake. "Good luck. You've got guts. I've wanted to tell Montcalm to go to hell for years. My best to you."

"Thanks," I said and left. Now, to face the real music.

TEN

Outside, the morning sun had dribbled orange juice on the clouds. I took a walk along the Duwamish River. There was no sandy beach, just a few trees amidst several industrial structures along the riverbank. I walked like a king. Montcalm owned my soul no more. What a glory! I was on my way. I was a stockbroker.

The spring air was warm and pleasant. The rhododendrons blossomed red, blue and white along the riverbank structures. The flowering cherry and the dogwood trees were in bloom. I felt alive again. I was my own man.

Then like a rock from heaven, reality hit. I was unemployed. There'd be no more paychecks from Montcalm. I had to make a stock brokerage connection quickly. Lois would never forgive me for turning down that warehouse job, if she knew. Two hundred in the bank and a house payment due. Maybe I was foolish, but the right time to make changes never comes. You just make the time, and do it. I had already wasted five years at Montcalm. I would find a way. I would borrow money to get us by while I looked for a brokerage connection. I had contacts now. Why wouldn't a firm hire me? I now knew lots of people with money. Most of them invested in stocks. Why wouldn't they do business with me?

I left the riverbank and walked back up to the shuttle's bus stop, just in front of Mr. Stacker's warehouse buildings. Back at the main plant, I stopped by Personnel and asked them to process me out. Then I drove downtown to the main library and compiled a list of brokerage firms and the names of their chief executive officers, which I would work on tomorrow.

It was five o'clock by the time I finished the directory work. Zero hour approached. I dreaded evening. A den of vipers would be easier to face.

I stopped at the supermarket to pick up some milk. Spring daffodils were in bloom and cheap. Tempted, but instead, I bought a dozen red roses. The red would blend well with my blood, when I told Lois that I no longer worked for Montcalm.

I parked her mother's old pink Plymouth in the carport. Held the roses at my back. She was in the kitchen. The vegetable soup smelled good. She looked up from the pot, and saw the smile on my face and my hand behind my back. I handed her the flowers.

"Well! What'd you do?"

"What do you mean? I brought you some flowers."

She glared at me. "Well, who's the bitch?"

"What do you mean?"

"My dad always bought flowers when he played around."

"That's not my style."

"You must feel guilty about something to bring me flowers."

"Could be I love you."

"Ha! You don't love anything but that damn stock market dream." She grabbed the flowers and stuffed them into an empty vase. "Thanks."

It didn't seem appropriate to spoil the moment with bad news. I'd tell her in the morning. That way, maybe I can get a good night's sleep, and be fresh for tomorrow's job hunt. After the flowers, it might be a smooth sail. That night, she turned the other way.

Next morning, I shaved the face of an unemployed man. It was a man who had quit a real job to chase a dream. I wondered how we could survive my stupidity. Then I thought of that famous general who burned his ships so there would be no retreat. Find a job as a stockbroker or starve. I had no choice.

I went into the kitchen and sat down. Lois was up, which was unusual. She always let me get my own breakfast of cereal, or toast and coffee. She poured me a cup of coffee. She was in the midst of fixing a full breakfast. Bacon was frying and butter was melting for the eggs. Four brown eggs were in a dish waiting for the proper moment. I felt like a man at his last meal.

She smiled and said, "Would you please fix the toast?"

"Sure." I put the toast in the oven, the way I'd seen my mother make it in the Depression, when we didn't own a toaster. Browned in the oven, turned over and toasted with chunks of butter made it taste far better than that electricity-seared stuff. Since this might be my last peaceful meal, I said no more. I would wait until after breakfast. No sense to spoil such a meal.

"It's about time for you to get another raise, isn't it?"

"Not likely this year."

"Why not? You get one about this time every year."

"Don't think there will be one this year," I parried. So there was some reason for all this fine breakfast, so early in the morning.

"You better. I ordered some new drapes for the living room."

"I am afraid that will have to wait."

"I smell something burning!" Lois screamed.

"Oops! The toast."

"Can't you do anything right!"

"Sorry."

We ate in silence, and she glared at me as she ate her scraped burnt toast.

"There is something I should tell you," I said.

"What this time?" She chomped down on her last piece of charred toast.

"I am going downtown to call on brokerage firms today."

"What about work?"

"I no longer work for Montcalm."

"What! You got fired? Or, did they lay you off?"

"Neither."

"What!"

"I quit."

Her face went crimson. Her eyes, two red coals, flared out of the furnace of hate. "You what!" Her fists knotted.

"There comes a time in the tides of men when a man must either sink or swim. I decided that it was time to swim."

"Swim! Hell! You'll drown us both, asshole."

"Four years I have suffered the politics, passed over promotions and the threatened layoffs. No more. They cut my pay 25 percent."

"That's better than 100 percent of nothing."

"Four years at Montcalm, and we can still hardly make furniture payments."

"Some kind of salary is better than none. Dumb-ass, quitting is no answer."

"At least in the stockbrokerage business, there's hope that you can make some real money after a year or so. Only a dumb-ass would work where there is no hope."

She stood up and paced the kitchen floor like I'd seen agitated tigers do in the zoo jails. She pointed her finger at me. "You go right back down there this very minute. You take that reduction."

"We can't survive on that."

"You can get a part-time job and earn more money!" She stood there with her hands on her hips. Her tits stuck out like an angry Amazon. "Any decent man should be able to earn a living."

"I may get a part-time job, but it will be as a supplement to my brokerage career. That's final. I've got to go." I had the car keys in my hand, and headed towards the door.

"You are not!" she shouted as she yanked the keys out of my hand. "You go apply for unemployment and you get a job that pays a salary."

"Nope. I'm going to be a stockbroker this time."

"Then you're not going to drive my car downtown!"

"That's fine. I'll ride the bus." I was out the door before she could block my way.

My love stood there in the doorway of our little home and shook her fist. She shouted obscenities that could never have come from her Catholic upbringing. Neighbors looked out of their windows, as I walked down the street. I didn't care. My steps had a spring. I could smell the flowers above the gutter spew behind me.

J. Glenn Evans

It was fifteen miles to downtown Seattle, five of it to the nearest bus stop. My step was decisive all the way to the bus stop.

To file for unemployment was out of the question. I had not been fired or laid off. I had quit, so there would be a waiting period. That support source was out, at least for a while. That was another bomb to explode, when Lois realized that there would be no unemployment checks.

A large New York house was my first call. I had the branch manager's name from the list compiled yesterday. "I'm Jim Bradley. I'd like to see Mr. Youngston."

"Do you have an appointment?" asked this well-favored, but harassed brunette, between calls.

"No, but if he's busy, I'd like to make an appointment."

"I'll see if Mr. Youngston has the time to see you now." Her smile was seductive.

"Thanks."

Interrupted by two more calls, and then she had the big man on the phone.

"Yes, Mr. Youngston will see you if you can wait a few minutes." Her smile and boobs gave me thoughts I shouldn't have.

I acknowledged with a nod, and sat down on the expensive leather couch. There was a smorgasbord of financial magazines before me. I picked up the one that I could least afford, *Fortune*. We shared the next thirty minutes, and waited. Just as I began to feel guilty sitting there so long, Miss Pretty Tits said, "Mr. Youngston will see you now." She pointed to a glass-enclosed cubicle on the other side of the large room. I took a path through the bullpen of stockbrokers, busy with their chatter-bones made famous by Mr. Bell.

Mr. Youngston was hardly old enough to be a "Mister." A husky build, teenage-look, blond hair, blue eyes, and his face had a 'why bother me' look. He said, "What'd yeah want?" He sat behind a desk that was half the size his bulk needed.

"I'd like to join your firm as a stockbroker."

"We don't hire grandpas."

"Thirty-five is hardly over the hill."

"It can be in this business. Where you from?"

"Oklahoma."

"Good God! Another Okie, there aren't any prunes up here. You should head down south to prune pickin' country." He tried to imitate a Southern accent.

"I'm not looking for prunes, nor smart-asses. I'm looking for a stockbrokerage connection."

"How much book do you have?"

"None of your damn business! I wouldn't work in this prairie dog town, even if I was a hungry wolf."

94

"Don't think you'd fit in. Old farts like you would give us indigestion, when we chewed you up."

"You don't need men here. You need mammas to change your diapers." I wanted to slug the smart-ass bastard. Instead I said, "Okay, kid, I'll leave before you pee your pants." I symbolically dusted off my shoulders, turned, and left. At the front desk, Miss Pretty Tits gave me a smile.

The son of a bitch so enraged me that it took an hour and four cups of coffee at the Horseshoe Cafe to calm me down. The rest of that day and the rest of the next two weeks, I called on Big Board firms whose names were familiar to me. Always the same response. How much book do you have? You're too old to be starting in this business. This is a young man's game. A big change had come over the industry since my call on Mr. Balton in his fancy San Francisco office. It was no longer an old man's game.

Daily bus fare pecked at the crumbs of what little cash we had left. Monday I called on the branch of another New York house. Brokers Exchange, Inc. was the name still on the downstairs directory, which had not yet been changed. This successful independent had just been acquired by a New York house. The founder was the branch manager, and his son, Junior, the assistant. The old man was tall and had a distinguished look with his gray hair and mustache. He overshadowed his mousy son. The office, paneled in rich walnut wood, had solid mahogany desks, not tinny metal ones. What a great place to work! Nearly all their brokers were younger than my thirty-five years.

"You're a little old to start as a stockbroker, aren't you?" the old man said as his son slinked off to the side.

"Maturity breeds confidence," I said, looking him right in the eye, determined not to be cowered.

He studied me a few seconds in silence. Then he said, "Might give you a chance. How are you on tests? We have these new fandango tests this New York outfit thinks will tell us who we should hire and who we shouldn't. You want a ticket to their game?"

"I do okay on tests."

"Thirty years I operated a successful company, and never did ask a lot of silly questions."

"I guess they have their reasons," I said.

"They liked us well enough to buy us," he grumbled.

Then he shouted, "Junior, let's give Mr. Bradley the Chinese water torture. See how much he sweats." He looked at me and said, "I always let Junior make the final decisions."

Twenty-five year old Junior came back in, and took me into a smaller room that had a desk and chair. He smiled on his own, and said, "You shouldn't have any trouble." He left me with a stack of printed pages and a pencil. "You can take an hour."

"Thanks." I said, elated.

A lot of the questions were funny. Did I always pass people up on the freeway, or did they pass me? Did I finish eating first, or did other people have to wait on me? They asked a question in a certain way, and then the same thing in another way in a different place. I suppose they meant to test either my memory or my honesty. No, I didn't eat fast. I took my time and savored my food. No, I didn't speed. I saw no reason to beat everyone on the freeway. An extra five minutes wasn't worth the risk. I tried to be as honest as I could, so the double-checked questions gave me no problem.

After the test was finished in the prescribed time, Junior came back and said, "Come back same time next week. We'll have the results back by then."

The week passed slowly. The next Monday I was excited as I made my way back to the old Brokers Exchange. I was anxious to hear the good news. There was a big smile on my face as I was ushered into Junior's office.

Junior greeted me with a wilted hand. There was no smile on his face. He said, with a frown of self-disgust, "You didn't make it."

"What do you mean?"

"You must have given us a snow job. You didn't pass the test," he said with irritation. "The test reflects that you are not aggressive enough to be a broker."

"That doesn't make sense," I said. "I'll do anything as long as it's honest."

"Sorry, head office says no. Nothing more I can do. If Dad still owned the firm, I'm sure he would give you a chance. We can't help you now."

He stood up and dismissed me with a handshake. "Sorry. Good luck."

Outside, I felt like a wadded-up piece of paper. This job had been a sure thing. Continued calls on the other houses had just been to keep busy. Now, nothing, and no prospects in sight. My cash was gone. There were no more New York firms to call on.

The rest of that day, I called back on firms that had already said no. They had not changed their minds. "Too bad you don't have a book of customers." It was the same old flapdoodle they fed me when I first came to town. Or they said, "We don't have room for any more trainees." What they really meant, but didn't say, was that they had no interest in a thirty-five-year-old trainee, nor did they give any importance to my list of Montcalm vendors.

That evening I tried to hide my desperation from Lois. My continued calls on brokerage firms had netted nothing. Lois did not say anything about my prospects. She, somehow, sensed my despair and need for support. What now, ran through my mind. Maybe, after a good night's sleep, I might think of something. I was being unfair to put Lois through all this. Perhaps I should have accepted that low pay job at Montcalm. Maybe it was still available. Mr. Corrigan said to call him if I changed my mind. Perhaps that's what I should do. Maybe things had eased up by now at Montcalm. If not that, perhaps I should find another job that paid a salary.

It was no better the next morning. No great inspirations had come in the night. Lois was cheerful, and I appreciated it. I put on a smile and my usual enthusiastic front, as all salesmen must do, regardless of how they really feel.

"I'll go back downtown and tangle with the tigers today," I said, but we both knew that even pussycats would be a tough adversary that day.

Before I made any calls, I went to the Horseshoe Cafe at Fourth and Pike. It was the place where I calmed my rage after I left Youngston's prairie dog town. I ordered coffee. I was still benumbed with disbelief that I had not passed that test. I picked up a newspaper left on the counter. It was opened to the classifieds. Up to now I had not considered anything, but a stockbroker job.

Jobs as accountants and bookkeepers were still plentiful, but I had already tasted that. I didn't want to count other people's beans. Maybe a part-time job would work, help me to survive, and maybe make some useful contacts. I saw one job that might not interfere with my brokerage career, newspaper delivery. I swallowed my coffee and headed down to the *Seattle Post-Intelligencer*, better known as the P.I. It wasn't much more than a half-mile, so I walked to Fifth and Wall in the Denny Regrade district to their office. They hired me instantly.

"Be down here at four in the morning, and Don will show you the ropes," the circulation manager said.

Next day, I discovered that even this job had an apprenticeship. Don, who was headed back East to college, said, "The new man doesn't get the profitable apartment house routes. He ends up with routes like this, in the single-family residential sections. Tough to make a buck."

All that week, I was up at three o'clock in the morning. I worked for free to learn the route. Actually, I found the early morning work enjoyable. Sunups were wonderful. They seemed to wash away my misery. I had forgotten how beautiful it was in the early morning. Hadn't seen many sunrises since basic training. That first Sunday's work, when I lifted those heavy papers, I was reminded of my days as a lumber stacker. I skipped the Saturday collections with Don. I wanted to put off personal encounters as long as possible. I might run into some of those brokers who I had called on, or someone from Montcalm.

That next Monday, my second day of owning the route, I caught the bus downtown. I'd make my paper deliveries first, then call on more brokerage houses. I brought the yellow pages in my brown vinyl leatherette-covered briefcase from Woolworth's. On the bus the briefcase served as a lap-desk. I studied the list of brokerage firms again, mainly to see if I had missed any. All the Big Board firms, I had called on several times, always got the same answer, "No."

Then I spotted them. How dumb I was! Right there before me were listed ten over-the-counter securities firms that I had never heard of, never called on. My thoughts had only been on the big guys. Why not try these smaller firms? All the big guys had said they wanted brokers with book. Why not get started with a smaller firm? Once I had proven myself, the larger firms would be eager to hire me if I still wanted them. Why had I been so blind to think that Big Board houses were the only real stockbrokers? They all started small.

ELEVEN

I walked my route in a business suit. The milkman and a couple of people on their way to work looked at me with a curious eye. I rushed to finish my route by six. I gulped down a quick breakfast at the Horseshoe Cafe. Then, I almost ran to my first call, Barker & Company, the first name on my new list. Their office was on the top floor of an eight-story office building that bore the name of Joshua Barker Building. I learned from the receptionist that Mr. Lional Barker, who headed the firm, was the grandson of Joshua who had founded the firm at the turn of the century.

The office was richly furnished. On the walls were mounted heads of deer, moose and mountain goat. A tiger and a bear looked up at me from their spread-out skins on the floor. Mr. Barker looked down at me from behind his big desk. He was a big man, head full of neatly combed gray hair. He must have been in his eighties. With his Indian-like nose, he reminded me of an old hawk that looked down at a field mouse. "Well, young buck, what can I do for you?"

"Mr. Barker, I want to be a stockbroker with your firm."

"Why would you want to do that?" he asked.

"You have an excellent reputation at making money for people." My thoughts were, "How could he not be successful, surrounded with all this."

"Tiger spoor! I've listened to bullshit for fifty years. That tops it. Who've you talked to?"

"Oh, different people around town," I fibbed.

"You've talked to different people than I know. Most of 'em say I'm an old pirate."

"You're spoofing me."

"Now be honest with me, young buck. Why do you really want to be a stockbroker? Most of 'em are scalawags. Tell you anything to turn a commission. Who did you talk to?"

I thought a minute, and decided to level with the old hawk. "Mr. Barker, to be completely honest with you, I talked with no one. I got your name out of the yellow pages."

"I thought so, but you might make a good stockbroker, after all. You know how to bullshit. Now that we've skinned you down to the bare truth, why do you really want to be a stockbroker?"

"I want to get rich."

"Now you make sense, but there are a hell of a lot of easier ways to get rich."

"How?"

"You could run a whorehouse or be a gigolo. Both are a hell of a lot easier ways to make a living."

"That's against my principles."

"Principles? I thought you wanted to get rich."

"Honestly."

"Now that's a worthy ambition, but of doubtful conclusion. How'd you choose to call on us?"

"You were the first OTC house in the yellow pages."

"That's being honest, but why OTC? Why not the Big Board houses?"

"I've tried them, and they didn't bite."

"How old are you?" He was playing with a large ivory letter-opener.

"Just turning thirty-six at the end of the year."

"Any experience as a broker?" He knew I didn't have any, from my application. He took an expensive cigar from a polished humidor, lit it, didn't offer me one, just sat there and watched me as he smoked his cigar. It was how he might have stalked one of his game victims.

"No, but I've studied a lot."

"You're an aging buck. Big Boards want young whippersnappers who'll jump when they point."

"I thought a little maturity might help me in this business."

"Could be, but not so with the Big Boards. Older folks ask too many questions, especially about research."

"Is that really true?"

"Very much so. Those firms want action, not questions. Move stock. Stay on the phone and sell, write orders, that's your business. They don't want thinkers and philosophers."

"What would you suggest for someone in my position?"

"Tell you what I'll do," he said. "I'll have you talk to our trader. If you can sell him, I'll talk to you again."

"Is that a deal?" I asked. "You'll hire me if I sell him?"

He smiled. "I said I would talk with you again."

Mr. Barker took me into a nearby office. Here was another man of gray, but this one had lost most of his hair.

"Fred, this is Broker Jim. I want you to talk with him. See if he'll fit in."

Broker Jim, he said. I liked the sound of that. It reminded me of Joseph Conrad's Lord Jim.

I saw a slight grimace cross Fred's face, like this was not something new, but an expected routine. Fred seemed a kindly gentleman, almost old-worldly, while Mr. Barker was with us. But as soon as Mr. Barker left, he was all business.

"How much book do you have?"

"What do you mean?" I played dumb to make him tell me what he meant.

"Since you're not in the business already, how many people do you know who have money?"

"I know a lot of vendors from my days at Montcalm, which I'll turn into clients."

"Takes you too long. After you get established clientele, you come back and talk with me."

"I want to be a broker right now. I'll make the contacts."

"I know that may be the way you feel, but I just don't have the time to train you. You come back when you have some investors."

"Just give me a chance!"

"Sorry, but I'm just too busy to train a new man. When you get a book of clients or prospects built up, you come back and we'll talk again. We might be able to squeeze you in then."

He moved some papers on his desk like he had more important things to do.

"I'll work hard. I haven't failed at anything yet."

"When you get a book of clients, come back. We'll talk again." He stood up, and that was that.

I left the Barker & Company offices disappointed and angry at them for not at least giving me a chance. Mr. Barker had used Fred to do his dirty work, push me out the door. He remained the nice guy who had given me a chance. It wasn't his fault if I couldn't sell Fred. That was the trouble with these old men that had it made. They wouldn't give a man a drink of water out in the desert, unless they could make a buck out of it.

I made four more calls that day, but got no further. They fed me more of the same bullshit. Keep your dukes up. Keep trying. You'll succeed. Sorry, but we don't have a spot for you now. Come back when you have some book. I dreaded what awaited me at home. Even worse, I missed the bus and got home two hours late. It was dark. I was hungry. I had not eaten all day.

Lois met me at the door. There was no scowl and sarcastic comment such as, "Well, Big Man, did you set the world on fire today?" There was a smile on her face. She hugged me, then kissed me.

A glance at the dining room, I saw lit candles.

"What do you want this time?" I asked.

"Guess what?" She ignored my sarcasm.

"What?"

She held up a check. "A whole $380. Our income tax refund came today."

My sour attitude fell away like a splash of water in the sand. I hugged her, picked her up, and swung her around, elated. These funds would buy at least another month to look.

I reviewed my paper route list again that night. How awful it would be to run into some one from Montcalm, or one of these brokers I had called on. I'd rather deliver their paper free, than ask them for the price of a week's paper. I didn't see any names I recognized.

Next morning, after the route had been delivered, I killed a couple of hours, just walked around Madison Park and stopped in for a cup of coffee at a small cafe. I didn't want to knock on any doors too early on Saturday morning.

At nine o'clock I made my first collection call. She was a cheery, pleasant, elderly lady.

"Oh, my. You must be our new paperboy. Don said he was going back East to college. Would you like some hot chocolate and cookies?"

"Thank you so much. That's thoughtful of you, but really I've got to finish my collection calls."

She smiled and slowly counted out $1.75 in quarters and nickels. "I understand," she said as she sadly closed the door.

By the time I was halfway through my morning's collections, only strangers had opened their doors to me. I relaxed and began to enjoy meeting new people. Then I knocked on an unpainted door of a shacklike house that was so out of place in this well-cared for neighborhood. A stubby housewife answered. She saw my collection book and said, "What, you the new paperboy?"

"Yes, ma'am."

"You're kind of big for this, ain't you?"

"It's a living," I said. "I hope to take care of my family as well as your husband takes care of you." I think she got the message that I referred to her chubby appearance.

"How much do I owe you, sir?" she asked in a formal way.

"Dollar seventy-five."

She wiggled her shoulders; her big breasts bounced as she turned and waddled off to get the money.

"Thanks," I said as I gave her change for a five-dollar bill, and my best retail smile.

How sensitive I was to my fallen status, a paperboy again. I guess that's why a man with money in his pocket and a good job walks taller, even if he's a midget.

Then I came to a fenced-in, ill-kept lawn, littered with children's toys. How under this misty solemn gray sky could anyone leave toys out in this rainy country? I knocked. A young man dressed in a red T-shirt and black shorts opened the door. He looked familiar. Oh God! It was Youngston, that kid manager who had given me such a bad time at his fancy downtown brokerage office.

I looked at his kid's toys, and said, "Looks like Alexander does more than fight financial battles."

"What are you doing peddling papers?" he asked contemptuously, when he saw my canvas paper-bag and collection book.

"Making contacts and building up book, asshole." I turned and left him with his mouth ajar.

I'd send him a bill. He wouldn't receive any more personal collection calls from me.

The rest of the morning proved uneventful, no more embarrassments. Then, almost at the end of the route, a door opened, and there stood Ralph Hall, the buyer from Montcalm that everyone liked.

"What are you doing peddling papers, Jim?"

"It supplements my brokerage business while I build up a clientele," I fibbed. I didn't see any reason to let him know that I had no brokerage connection yet.

"Jim, I thought you'd be in big bucks by now. Aren't stockbrokers all rich?"

"I wish. Incidentally, Ralph, I'd appreciate it if you wouldn't say anything to anyone out at Montcalm about my paper-route."

"Not any of their business. Your secret is safe with me, Jim, but you don't have to apologize for honest work."

"This embarrasses me. I left with such big ideas and such high hopes, and look at me."

"Don't worry. Nobody from Big M will hear anything from me. I know how tough it can be. I sold magazine subscriptions for a while after I retired."

"How'd you do?"

"Not so well. Out of all of those Montcalm guys, even some of the vendors, how many subscriptions do you think I sold?"

"No idea."

"Well, three, to be exact."

"I guess they're not readers. They play cards at lunch and bowl at night," I said.

"Probably so. What they think doesn't really matter, Jim. Just do your own stuff."

"I know, but it shames me." He handed me a five-dollar bill, and I gave him change.

"Jim, stop in anytime. Have a cup of coffee with me. I get kind of lonely here, without my wife. You know, she died, just after you left Montcalm." Ralph shook hands and smiled. There was a sadness in his eyes as he said, "I miss the people at the plant. It doesn't take long for them to forget you."

Thursday afternoon, after paper deliveries and more futile calls on the brokerage community, I stopped at the Horseshoe Cafe, there on Fourth and Pike. It was a favorite spot to bring my spirits up. Coffee was good, and they didn't press you to buy more. Also, the horseshoe counter created a conversational community.

House payments behind, no unemployment checks, no savings, I was desperate. The income tax refund faded fast. On the way in, I had picked up a copy of *The Seattle Times* to go with my coffee. Another job might help me last a little longer. I spotted an insurance inspector job listed in the part-time classifieds. As I left, I called them from a street pay phone. They said come on in for an interview.

TWELVE

The Seattle Credit insurance inspection office was just a few blocks from downtown, so I walked. I was there by three-thirty. The stampede of typewriter keys sounded like hail on a plastic roof. Most of the inspectors were back from their field trips and now typing their reports.

The receptionist gave me a short questionnaire to fill out. That done, she took me in to see Mr. Sallisaw, the branch manager. Crew cut, blond hair and about thirty-five, he made a cursory glance at the application.

"College grad, normal typing speed, I think you'll do if nothing adverse shows up on your personnel report."

"There's no problem there."

"Okay, you're hired. If something bad shows up, I'll fire you."

"You sound like a man of action," I said.

That pleased him, and he smiled. He must have been desperate for help to hire me so quickly. "When do I start?"

"Right away."

He took me over to a desk in the far corner, and said, "Jim, you can work here. You'll share this desk with one or two other part-time inspectors."

"That's fine."

Then we walked over to another desk, where a man about my age banged away on an old L.C. Smith typewriter.

"Rosco, I want you to meet Jim Bradley."

He typed the rest of his sentence, then looked up at us.

"Jim Bradley, this is Rosco Tallon. He's one of our best senior inspectors. I'll put you under his wing." He put his hand on Rosco's shoulder, "You think you can make an inspector out of Jim?" he said.

"I'll kill him if he doesn't," answered Rosco.

The boss acknowledged his comment with a nod.

I shook hands with Rosco. He seemed a decent sort, short, wiry, black-headed and wore horn-rimmed glasses. He looked more like a professor than an insurance sleuth.

Rosco grinned at me when the boss left, pointed to a side chair and said, "Have a seat, Jim, and I'll show you the ropes. There're a few secrets to this business that the boss will never tell you about."

Each typewriter had its own distinct chatter. Some were low and quiet like the panting of a dog. Others worked up to peak like reaching the top of a roller coaster, a pause, and then the thunderous downward trip. Some slow, some fast, and some staccato. All together, they made talking about as easy as trying to carry on a conversation with a freight train passing.

"Let's go have a coffee and get out of this nut house," Rosco finally said.

"I'm with you."

Across the street there was an old-fashioned cafe with older women as waitresses, the kind that life had used up, not a cute chick among them. As we sat down at a four-place table, the waitress brought up a bowl of strawberry ice cream and set it before Rosco.

"Don't drink coffee," he said. "Bad for you."

"Who says that?" I responded.

"Me."

"How do you stay so thin, eating all that ice cream?" I asked.

"You'll see."

The waitress looked at me. "Coffee, like real men, or ice cream, like this nut who has it for breakfast, lunch and dinner? God! What some men do to get it up."

"Cream, no sugar," I said, and she went away. "Gather you like ice cream."

"You bet. It's the frozen milk of the gods," Rosco said as he dug in.

His brow creased with concentration. "Now, Jim, this is not a hard job if you use your head and your imagination. Like I said, if you do everything they tell you to do, you're up shit creek."

"How's that?"

"On a full-time basis, they give you fifteen or sixteen cases a day. You're supposed to visit each one's neighborhood, talk with two or more informants, and then when you get back to the office, call up and confirm their employment. Then you got to type up all the shit. All you get for this is $2.35 a case. You got to learn to calculate, even dream a little, if you don't want to starve to death. See what I mean?"

"I see why you're skinny with all that ice cream you eat."

"The secret is that you get the best information from the clients themselves, plus you get a look at them."

"I thought you were supposed to call on informants?"

"Sure, but a firsthand look tells you how much further you have to look. If they look okay, don't waste time on 'em. Spend your time on the problems. That way you'll survive, and help the company make money, and the insurance companies will love you."

"How's that?"

"Ah. You save some underwriter's ass. If things turn bad, he can always say, 'Inspection report was okay.' See what I mean?"

"I think so."

"If he looks okay, see one informant and move on. If you are suspicious, of course, dig deeper."

"Is that honest?"

"Beats starving."

"Guess so."

"It's a fun business, though," he said as he went on. He finished his ice cream and signaled the waitress to bring me more coffee. "The stories people tell on each other beats going to the movies, so you can't always believe negative reports. I once had an old man say his neighbor's wife stepped out with everyone on the block."

"Did she?"

"No! There wasn't a better, more faithful wife in the neighborhood. He was just sore because she wouldn't tango with him when her husband was off on a long business trip."

"How do you figure out who's telling the truth, and who's not?"

"Develop a feel. It comes with time."

"Hope I do all right."

"Don't worry. You're smart. I can sense it. You'll do fine. What made you try this racket anyway, Jim?"

"Need to make a few dollars while I build up a clientele in the stockbrokerage business."

"You a stockbroker?"

"Trying to be."

"God! You're lucky. Those guys make big bucks."

"How do you know?"

"Hell! I've done enough insurance reports on them. You should see the houses they live in. You could put my whole house in their living room."

"That's pretty big, isn't it?"

"You should see the cars they drive, and they're paid for. Which firm are you with?"

"Still out to make a connection, but I will, soon."

"Jim, when you get set, will you make some money for me?"

"I'll try."

Rosco reached for the check, but I beat him to it. I still had some paper collection money on me. We went back to the office, and he showed me the different forms that I had to fill out on the various types of inspections.

"I'm on the way home," Rosco said. "Come along and we'll do a couple stops to show you how field inspections are made."

"Thanks. I appreciate the help," I said. "Tomorrow, right after my Saturday morning paper route collection, I'll tackle some by myself."

"You do that too?"

"Got to make money to pay the bills until the big bucks roll in from the brokerage business."

"You must want to be a stockbroker awfully badly."

"That's what I set out to do. I won't stop until I make it."

"Why?"

"Don't know, just me, I guess. My mother and grandmother always said, 'Anything worth starting is worth finishing.'"

"Let's go, Jim," Rosco said. "Leave your car here; I'll bring you back."

"Where are we going?"

"Got a couple of cases close by, out in Snoose Junction, that I need to clean up."

"Where's Snoose Junction, what's that?"

"What! You been in these parts over five years, and you never heard of Snoose Junction?! That's Ballard. All those Scandahoovians used to dip snuff, 'cause they couldn't smoke in the sawmills."

"Oh, I see. My grandmother used to dip snuff. I didn't like it."

"You try that too?"

"Anything once."

"I haven't seen any sawmills in Ballard," I said.

"That was a long time ago. Back then, Ballard used to be the biggest sawmill town in the state, almost as big as Seattle."

"Why didn't it stay a town on its own?"

"I think Seattle snookered them."

"How's that?"

"Some big folks in Seattle wanted to absorb Ballard. Came time for the vote, a dead horse was found in Ballard's main water supply," he said.

"I guess Seattle had the horsepower."

Our first stop in Ballard was in a no-trash neighborhood of small wooden frame houses with neatly mowed and trimmed lawns. I followed Rosco up the steep steps to the first house. A thin, grandmotherly lady opened the door.

"Good afternoon, ma'am, I'm Rosco Tallon with Seattle Credit Reviewers. This is my associate, Jim Bradley. We're doing a routine insurance inspection on one of your neighbors, Mr. John Larson. He has applied for some insurance, and in order for him to get it approved, we must interview a neighbor or two that knows him."

"Did John ask you to call on me?"

"No, but he knows we have to make this neighborhood inspection."

"What kind of information are you looking for?"

"How long have you known him?"

"Maybe ten years, at least."

"Is he a drinking man?"

"Lord! No."

"Any hazardous sports."

"No, doesn't even ski."

"How many in his family?"

"Just him and his wife. Kids grown."

"I think that's all I need. Thank you very much, ma'am."

We next stopped at the client's house and after introductions, Rosco said, "Ma'am, Mr. Larson has applied for some insurance, and this is a routine insurance inspection to ascertain if we have the correct information."

"Isn't that what the insurance agent does?"

"We have to verify the information. You are Mrs. John Larson?"

"I wouldn't be here if I wasn't."

"You have lived here about how long?"

"About eleven years."

"Your husband fly, skin dive or ski?"

"Heavens, no! But he is a Russian bear hound."

"What do you mean?"

"He rushes around the table and bears down on a biscuit."

"Sounds pretty safe. No other hazardous sports at all?"

"Well, he plays poker with the boys occasionally."

"How's that hazardous?"

"If he loses, he has to deal with me," she said with a smile.

"Thanks a lot, Mrs. Larson. I appreciate your help."

Back in the car Rosco made a few quick notes that reflected his reactions and opinions, which had little to do with the actual questions that he had asked. "Jim," he said, "I don't see a problem here. You can learn a lot about people, just watch their facial expressions. The Larsons are no problem. Wish we had more of them."

The next case was about as simple, and when we finished, Rosco said, "Hey, Jim! We're close by. Why don't we stop by the house for a quick beer, and you can meet my family."

"Thanks Rosco. I'd love to, but maybe later. Right now, I better get on home, or I'll catch hell."

Rosco Tallon's smooth insurance inspections that Thursday seemed so easy. I was ready to tackle them myself Saturday. After collections, and a quick coffee with Ralph, I headed to the Eastside, where my cases were located. I felt shy to have to ask strangers all these personal questions.

Dudley Roundhass, an auto mechanic, was my first insurance applicant. His home was in Bellevue, a suburban and rapidly growing community east of Seattle. The Bellevue Chamber of Commerce grated at being called Boeing's bedroom.

Some of its members challenged the reference and that they would change all that, maybe someday surpass Seattle. Mr. Roundhass was not home, and neither were his neighbors on each side of his house. If this was the way I would find it on Saturday, it would be a hungry business at only two thirty-five a case.

When I knocked at the third house, a wisp of a dried-up old woman answered the door.

"Good afternoon, I'm Jim Bradley with Seattle Credit Reviewers."

"What're you doing over here? Don't you have enough deadbeats over in Seattle to keep you busy? Why bother our fine Eastside folks?"

"I'm not in the credit collection business. I do insurance inspections. Your neighbor, Dudley Roundhass, has applied for some insurance and to get it approved, we need to do an inspection."

"How much is he applying for?"

"I'm not at liberty to say. That's his private business."

"Private information, that's what you want from me, isn't it?"

"Not really. What I really need to know is, what kind of reputation does Mr. Roundhass have? Good? Bad?"

"At what?"

"Does he drink to excess? Take drugs, you know, that sort of thing."

"He never said anything to me about it."

"I wouldn't expect him to, but are you aware of it?"

"He keeps to his self. I've never seen any strange women. Fact, that's his problem."

"What do you mean?"

"Lack of nookie." The old woman smiled at her boldness and my embarrassment.

"Would you say he was a drinking man?"

"Never saw him take a drink."

"Does he smoke?"

"I've never seen him."

"Drugs?"

"How would I know?"

"Ever seen him act weird?"

She hesitated, then said, "Guess so, especially when he first moved in."

"How long ago was that?"

"Maybe five years ago."

"What happened?"

"Just being neighborly, I took him a nice freshly baked apple pie to welcome him to the neighborhood. I was younger and prettier then."

"What did he do that was so weird?"

"He practically threw me out. Said he didn't want any more predatory women around."

110

"What happened then?"

"I said, 'Screw you' and I haven't spoken to him since."

"Was that it?"

"Yes."

"Probably had a bad marriage," I said. "Anything else adverse that you can think of?"

"Guess not."

"Thank you very much," I said, and left.

The next informant was down the street two doors more. "Keeps to himself. Don't know anything about him," was all he would say.

Now that I had my two informants, I noted on Mr. Roundhass's worksheet, "Good middle-class neighborhood, no adverse information," and left Mr. Dudley Roundhass to his own business. I did note in my special notebook that Mr. Dudley Roundhass might be a good future securities prospect. Being single, he should be able to save some money.

My next two inspections were simple and fast. The fourth was an experience. Her name was Winona Flowerbell. She was single, and her beneficiary was an adopted son. Her home was the nicest in the neighborhood, located in an almost private cove. She came to the door after the second set of knocks. There she stood in the doorway on a Saturday afternoon, dressed only in a thin red nightgown. Light from the window across the room revealed a well-formed body, and over her shoulders hung long black hair. With that face and form, braves, a century ago, would have traded many horses for her. She was the sexiest lady that I had ever seen, probably no more than thirty. Her smooth brown face, dark eyes and goddess-like body would test any married man's conscience.

She smiled at me and said, "What can I do for you?"

"I'm Jim Bradley with Seattle Credit Reviewers. We're doing a routine insurance inspection on the policy that you've taken out on your son."

"Any problem?"

"Don't think so, but I do have to ask a few routine questions to verify information."

"Won't you come in?"

Ordinarily I would have stayed at the door. It was quicker, but in this case I made an exception. She opened the door wider and motioned me in. I followed her through a plushly furnished living room. We passed by a dining room with oiled furniture that you would find only in a well-heeled mansion. We continued down a lighted hall that was lined with expensive original paintings. She opened the door to her bedroom, and pointed to a dainty pink overstuffed chair on which I was to sit. She sat on the edge of her bed, and continued to polish her nails over a newspaper.

"Okay, Mr. Bradley, what can I do for you?"

Her low-cut nightgown, crossed and uncrossed legs, bewitched me. It was hard to concentrate. She remembered my name. "You're an American Indian, aren't you?" I asked.

"How could you tell?" There was an impish grin.

"I'm from Oklahoma," I said. "Had lots of Indian friends there. In fact, I'm one-eighth Cherokee, myself."

"Blood brother, eh?" When she smiled, her white teeth stood out against the brown background.

"What tribe are you from?" I asked.

"Osage. My father also was from Oklahoma."

I thought of the Osage Indians and of their oil. No wonder she had such a fine place; she probably had Indian oil money. "Do you have some kind of employment?" I thought I had better get back to business. There was no job listed on the application.

"Not really. I have an adequate trust fund from my father. Sometimes I work as a hatcheck girl at the Bardo Club, just to give me something to do, two or three nights a week."

"Oh, I see."

"I also write some poetry, but that's just for fun."

"I had an early ambition to be a writer myself," I said.

"Oh, even more blood brother."

"Any hazardous sports?"

"I don't ski, but there's always men," she added with a smile.

I thought to myself, "I'd sure like to be your hazardous sport." I slowly went on through the routine questions to confirm the correctness of the information on the inquiry sheet, and perhaps, to linger a little longer.

Business done, I said, "So you write poetry?"

"Yes, would you like to see it?"

"Love to," I said. I guessed she was talking about her poetry.

She left and came back with a three-ring binder full of hand-printed poetry. Her poetry subjects varied from sex to politics. There was one poem that caught my attention. It was an Indian poem about a picture of Wounded Knee. I liked it.

EIGHTEEN-NINETY

When the spring blossoms fell like winter snow
Thoughts came of the snow at Wounded Knee
There is a picture of Chief Big Foot
Lying frozen like a statue in snow
Body raised up, bundled against the cold
Looks alive, but lying there dead
In this white man's picture of a death pose
He is trying to rise but lies staring

Dead and frozen and all alone but for
A grazing horse and two men looking on
Gone are the Gatling guns and the soldiers
The two hundred fourteen dead Indians
Including hundred and seventy-seven
Women children which tidied up this scene

She watched me read and re-read the poem, and she said, "Chief Big Foot is an ancestor of mine."

"I thought Big Foot was a Sioux."

"My grandmother was Sioux," she said.

"I am honored to know one of his descendants. The white in me makes me feel ashamed to look back."

She smiled. "I wish there were more like you. Maybe it's the little bit of Cherokee that makes you feel that way."

"I'm impressed with your writing," I said. "As I previously said, I wanted to be a writer myself, but decided to get rich in the investment business first."

"I thought you were an insurance investigator."

"I am, but this insurance inspection business is just a part-time job, while I build up a clientele in the securities business."

"Oh! You're a stockbroker?"

"No, but I will be as soon as I make a connection."

"You should try Jones Bylor. I hear they're pretty good."

"Thanks. I will."

"You must give me your card," she said. "I make investments from time to time, when I don't spend all of my allowance."

"I'll mail you one as soon as I get connected."

"So you want to be a writer too?" she said as she looked up from her nails and smiled at me.

"Yes. I did publish some short filler stuff before I got out of high school, and I worked on the school paper."

"So did I. I wrote for my high school paper. Guess that again makes us soul mates," she said.

God, what an evil person I must be! All I could think of was, "I would much rather be your bed mate than soul mate." That made me feel bad. After all, Lois was my wife, even if she didn't act like one. I looked at my watch. Too much time spent here, I would not be able to finish my inspection and still have time to type up my cases if I didn't move on. It's a good thing she didn't say, "Take me." I'm afraid I would have. And maybe that's what her actions said.

Then I was rescued. A small Indian boy came in.

"This is my son," she said. "His reservation name is Little Blackbird, just call him John."

He was six or seven years old. He smiled and stuck out his little hand to shake, "Pleased to meet you."

"Guess I'd better move on," I said. "I have more calls to make and reports to type up."

She saw me to the door, even hugged me goodbye. I could have kissed her as her body pressed close to me.

Damn that Lois. She better change.

Winona Flowerbell said with a playful smile, "You be good, Blood Brother."

I hurried back to the office, typed up my cases, and then headed home to Lois. After only a week, I could do fifteen insurance cases a day for Seattle Credit Reviewers. Rosco's shortcuts really worked. To make catch-up bucks and survive, I found that full time at Seattle Credit Reviewers had crept up on me. Then I realized that soon I must get back to my brokerage firm calls.

My first screw-up at Seattle Credit Reviewers came after I had been a snoop for only three weeks. Mr. Sallisaw, the branch manager, called me into his office right after lunch, just as I started to type up my morning field investigations. His face was grim as I entered his cubicle office.

"Sit down, Jim," he said. "I have a problem with one of the cases you turned in yesterday."

"Which one is that?"

"This Mr. Rodney Becknor, the fireman. What are his duties?"

"The normal fireman's duties. He helps maintain the equipment and stands in readiness to fight fires. When the call comes, he goes and fights fires and helps to rescue people. You know, what all firemen do."

A slight frown crossed his face. "And, what does the conductor do all this time?"

My muscles tightened. "You mean, he works on a train?"

"I don't think he climbs ladders." He sat there with his hands folded across his lap with his head slightly nodding up and down.

"I don't know. I guess I misunderstood my informant."

"Informant or informants?"

"It won't happen again, Mr. Sallisaw."

"It best not."

I got up to go.

He grinned for the first time. "Other than that, you've been doing a pretty good job, Jim. Don't let it happen again. I might have to find another trainer."

Later, when I told Rosco, he said, "Good god! Jim, he could have fired you and me both. Be careful. You'll get us all in trouble."

"I know. Next time I'll make sure I know exactly what a man does for his living before I write up a report."

It was Friday before I got back to my brokerage calls. Almost every securities firm in town, Big Board and OTC houses, had heard my footsteps. Out of the nine over-the-counter firms, none had said yes. Unapproached was number ten, Jones Bylor & Company, which was the firm that Winona Flowerbell had suggested that I contact. I called for an appointment. The lady on the phone said that the sales manager was out of town until Monday. She suggested that I try then. She wasn't sure of his schedule, but she would try to get me in to see him. That gave me a whole weekend of undashed hope. If Jones Bylor didn't bite, I had to start all over again. I'd keep calling until someone said yes. Maybe I could wear one of them down. My finances were worse than when I first came to town. At least then, I didn't owe anyone. I was three months behind on our mortgage payments, owed friends, and everything we had was hocked. I just couldn't let my dream fade. That's all I had left.

THIRTEEN

Seven-thirty, Monday morning, after my paper-route, I called at Jones Bylor & Company. I planned to make this one call, then spend the rest of the day on insurance inspections. That, at least, would earn me a few dollars. Jones Bylor's reception room was small. There was a high counter that separated the customers from the reception area, almost like what we had had at Riverside Lumber. Jones Bylor, of course, was not a lumberyard. Their office was polished and first class, and not a nail in sight. An attractive, middle-aged lady, who had once been blond, but had lost the battle to gray, sat behind the counter. She plunked away at an old Underwood typewriter. She looked familiar. I had seen her before, but I couldn't remember where.

She smiled and said, "Well, if it isn't the stranded Oklahoma Jim. I thought I recognized your voice."

That was it. She had been the secretary at that Renndag Securities, that had promised me a job when I first came to Seattle, but had left me broke and homeless, because their license had been suspended.

"It's been a long time. Miss Shirley, isn't it?" I said.

"Then you do remember me!" She was all smiles.

"Yes. How long have you been here at Jones Bylor, Miss Shirley?"

"Ever since I left Renndag. I guess five years. I often wondered what became of you. Did you get in the brokerage business?"

"No. I starved out. Couldn't make a connection. New in town, nobody wanted to hire me."

"What have you been doing?"

"I've wasted five long years at Montcalm as a buyer."

"Still want to be a stockbroker?"

"You bet. I wonder if I might have a chance here."

She poured me a cup of coffee, and with a look, questioned, cream, sugar?

"Just cream, thank you."

"Have a seat. Mr. Hackett, our sales-manager, is in the morning sales meeting. He'll be out in about thirty minutes. If you can wait, I'll see if I can get you in."

Could I wait? Ha! My answer was a calm, "Thanks, I will be glad to wait."

Forty-five minutes later, Miss Shirley ushered me into Mr. Hackett's office. He paced around his desk like a caged tiger, tethered to the long cord of the phone in his hand. He was near forty, medium-sized and redheaded. He pointed to a chair, and continued his conversation for another five minutes.

"Look, Bob, don't bullshit me! What will you make this quarter? No shit. I don't believe it."

Finished, he sat down behind his desk, and looked straight through me like he could read my soul. "Shirley says you want to be a stockbroker, and that you are not the quittin' kind."

"That's right. I want to be a broker."

"Why?"

"That's what I set out to do."

"That's a dumb reason." He smiled and his Irish eyes sparkled. "I set out to get a piece of ass and ended up married."

"Don't we all?"

"Lots of easier ways to make a living."

"I've heard that before."

His phone rang, and he was up on his feet again. "Nope, won't do it. The deal's off. He won't meet our terms." Then there were two more phone calls that waited. With his free hand he covered the mouthpiece, and said, "Bradley, come back to see me at three o'clock on Wednesday."

I got up to go.

He nodded his farewell and jumped back into his deal world.

Outside, Miss Shirley said, "Mr. Bradley, if you have a few minutes, I'll show you around." She motioned for one of the clerks to catch the phones.

"We have seven brokers," she said as we started down a narrow hallway with offices on each side. The brokers were all busy on the phones. We came to Mr. Bylor's office. The name on the door said President. He was between phone calls. "Mr. Bylor, this is Jim Bradley. Mr. Hackett has talked to him. He wants to become one of our brokers."

He smiled and stuck out his hand to shake, "Let's hope you make it." The phone rang and we moved on.

On down the hall, Bill Tedmore was off the phone so Miss Shirley introduced us. Mr. Tedmore was in his late fifties. His office was immaculate and well organized. He was friendly, but we had only a second before his phone rang.

As we walked on down the hall, Miss Shirley said, "We call Mr. Tedmore, Old Spit and Polish. He's a retired navy captain."

The next broker, two doors down, was Elmer T. Campbell, about forty-five, thin and tall, sat like he had a board up his back. Only a minute, and he was busy again.

Outside, Miss Shirley whispered in my ear. "Mr. Campbell has lots of money. He made a fortune in chemicals. When he sold his business, he came to us for something to do. Now you couldn't chase him off."

"Sounds like a good recommendation for the firm."

"You'll like it when you get in."

"Thanks! I appreciate the *when*, instead of *if*."

She just smiled and said, "We've nicknamed Mr. Campbell, 'Jiggs'. You know, after Maggie and Jiggs, the comic strip. That's his life style, Rolls Royce, golf clubs and a big Airedale in the back seat. Not married, so he's a prime catch. All the girls would like to get their hooks into him."

"How about you?"

"Now, Mr. Bradley, you know I'm past that age." She smiled at the flattery, "But he does have a lot of money."

We completed the circle down the hall and back to the front. "Thanks for the tour. I'm supposed to come back Wednesday."

"I'll put in a good word for you," she said, as she gave me a big smile.

"I'd appreciate that."

That afternoon, Tuesday, and most of Wednesday morning, I worked cases for Seattle Credit Reviewers. Lustful memories of that close encounter with Winona Flowerbell haunted me. She was the most beautiful woman that I had ever seen, and to think I almost kissed her. I wondered if she would have slapped me. Midafternoon I dropped it all, and headed to Jones Bylor for my three o'clock appointment with Mr. Hackett. As soon as I came in, Miss Shirley said, "Please have a seat. It will be a few minutes. Mr. Hackett is still with some out-of-town people." She poured me a cup of coffee. An hour later I still waited.

Thirty minutes more, and Miss Shirley got off the phone with Mr. Hackett. Disappointedly, she said, "Mr. Bradley, I'm sorry, Mr. Hackett will not be able to see you today. He's still tied up with those out-of-town people. Can you come back same time Friday?"

"Of course."

Back home that night, Lois commented as I first came in, "Okay, big man, super-broker, where's all that money that's supposed to roll in?"

"I'll get there."

"I'd like to know where you're getting."

"I'll make a brokerage connection soon. It looks good at Jones Bylor."

She ran the vacuum cleaner and shouted over it, "I've heard that tale before."

I could see this was going to be another evening of bickering, so I went into the den to study for my brokerage test. I had a handout pamphlet that the state Securities Commission published on state securities laws. I got it from one of the stockbrokerage firms. The print was so small I used a magnifying glass to read it. I had already been through the book twice, and had a feel that the test would not be easy.

After dinner, I wiped the dishes. Strangely enough, later that evening Lois decided to be romantic, which was a surprise after all those weeks with the gate closed. You never know when you'll hit the jackpot with women. Take it when you can. We made love a second time. I thought of Winona, and that bothered me. I fantasized making love with her in a teepee a hundred years ago. Then, the securities business wouldn't have meant a damn to me. I visualized caressing those well-formed brown tempters.

Friday, at three o'clock, I was back at the offices of Jones Bylor. Miss Shirley was in a flutter. "Mr. Bradley, I tried to call you."

"I've been away from the phone."

"Your wife doesn't think much of us, does she?"

"Not much of the stock market. Her grandfather lost a bundle in '29. Why, what happened?"

"I told her that I needed to reschedule your appointment. Mr. Hackett had to go out of town today. She said that she thought stockbrokers only sneaked out of town after dark."

"I'm sorry. I guess what happened to her grandfather really soured her on the market."

"I won't hold her against you."

"Thanks. When can I see Mr. Hackett?"

"He said to try Tuesday about three. Three gives the Market time to close, and he would have more time for you then. Mr. Bradley, he's sorry about the delay. It just couldn't be helped."

"I appreciate your trying to call. Sorry my wife gave you a bad time."

"We'll forgive her," Miss Shirley said. "You'll change her mind about the stock market once you get in. You just wait and see." She smiled in sympathy.

I was a great deal more upset about this than I let on to Miss Shirley. Damn Lois! To say something like that to Jones Bylor.

That evening after dinner I said to Lois, "I didn't appreciate what you said to Miss Shirley about stockbrokers."

"That old bitch couldn't wait to tell you, could she?"

"Jones Bylor is about my last chance to get into the securities business. I don't want you to sabotage it."

"Big deal! Why don't you get an honest job that pays a salary?"

"I've told you I will be a stockbroker, and that's it."

"Why don't you go wallow in the mud with the hogs? You'd have better company."

"I'm sorry, but I don't see it that way. To be able to raise capital for small companies is important to me."

"I don't see why."

"My dear, in this world capital rules. Why should the big guys have it all? I think small business deserves a chance."

"So Big Jim will save the little world."

"No, but I think I can do something worthwhile."

"Why don't you make some real money and save your wife from poverty?"

"Lois, that will come in time."

"Like hell!"

She got up and went to watch TV and left the dishes for me to wash.

Tuesday afternoon, Miss Shirley ushered me into Mr. Hackett's office and left. Phone in hand, he paced around his desk. He turned and pointed his finger at me. "Bradley, I'm going to hire you. If you screw up, I'll fry your balls for breakfast! Now get out of here. Be back down at six in the morning for the sales meeting."

Back in the reception area, Miss Shirley was smug, like she knew all along. Then, she said, "Mr. Hackett told me that the only way he would ever get any peace was to hire you. Welcome to Jones Bylor. I knew you'd make it."

For a minute I thought she was going to dance the jig.

"I just know you'll be a fabulous success!"

"Thanks," I said. "I'd better do my best, if I know what's good for me."

"Let me show you your office. I'll introduce you to the other fellows that you missed the other day."

There was a big mahogany desk, and an executive chair that smelled of fresh leather. There were two side chairs and a four-drawer file cabinet. Each broker had his own private office, even cubs like me. Only vice-presidents at Montcalm had offices like this. This beat the big New York firms. There, all their brokers had desks in the middle of a bullpen. Only their execs had private offices.

Bill Tedmore, Spit and Polish, the ex-navy captain's office was to my right. Elmer T. Campbell, old Jiggs himself, was to my left. Here I sat between an ex-sea captain and a potful of chemical money, and me, three months behind on my house payments. I wondered if Jiggs would ever give me a ride around town in his Rolls Royce. Man! I was in deep oil. I sat down in that chair and smelled the leather.

Miss Shirley broke into my reverie, "Come on. We're not through yet."

She took me on down the hall and introduced me to John L. Lucas. He was a husky older man who made his chair seem frail. He may have been an old fart, but his handshake let me know he was no sissy.

Away from his desk, Miss Shirley said, "Mr. Lucas is an old rancher from Ellensburg. He said he put his foreman in charge, and came over here to the Coast to get in on 'the easy pickings.' That's his description of the stock market, easy pickings."

Miss Shirley then introduced me to a couple of younger men. Ralph Bailor was the son of the second largest stockholder in the firm, who had now retired. He came across as a smart chap. Then next was Jim Swenson. He was about my age, friendly, but there seemed an edge to his friendliness.

As we finished the tour, I asked, "Is Mr. Bylor in? I would like to express my appreciation for the opportunity to work in his firm."

"Yes," and she took me to his office.

Mr. Bylor was a short, somber, gray-haired man, who looked like he occasionally smiled. He sat behind his desk in an office twice the size of mine. He motioned for me to have a seat. After a brief moment, a smile swept across his face.

"Mr. Bradley, we're glad to have you aboard. We need to talk terms of your engagement here."

"Mr. Bylor, I was so excited that you hired me that I had not even given the matter any thought."

"Well, it's about time you did, if you plan to spend the next few years with us."

"What do you think is fair?"

"We pay our brokers 50 percent of the commission revenues they produce. You take care of your own sales expenses. We pay once a month. We can give you an advance against your production, since you've just started, at least for a while. Do you have any money saved up?"

"No. I spent it all just to find you."

"I figured as much," he said. "It'll be tough. It will take you a year to begin to understand what you are doing. After two years you might begin to earn a living, but not a decent one. After you've been here three or four years, you should make big money. Meanwhile, it's pretty lean. Can you and your wife pay that price?"

"We must," I said, but I wondered if Lois would accept this self-inflicted sacrifice.

"We don't want you to starve." Mr. Bylor continued in his solemn manner, "We will advance you $400 a month for the next six months. This includes $200 supplement, which you do not have to pay back. The six months that follow will be the same, except the supplement that you do not have to pay back, drops to $100. Six months after that, you're on your own, straight commission like the rest of us. Fair enough?"

"Sounds square to me. Thank you, Mr. Bylor, for the break."

"Just don't let the struggle break you," he said.

I thought as I left his office, "I can get by on this small income if I keep my paper route and continue to do weekend insurance reports." To catch up, I didn't know. I was still two payments behind on the house, behind on furniture payments, plus I owed money to personal friends. Some way, I would do it. I would make "Broker Jim" a name to be reckoned with.

FOURTEEN

"Lois," I shouted as I entered the door, "I made it! I'm a broker with Jones Bylor & Company. They hired me today!"

"That's ducky. Now we can starve a little slower."

"I think they were decent," I said. "Fifty percent commission on my production. They threw in an extra $200 supplement that I don't have to pay back on top of $200 a month advance against future income. That's fair. It gives me a chance to build up."

"Big deal! Why don't you get an honest job that pays a salary? Then you wouldn't need a supplement."

"Look, I've been on a salary for the past four years, and we've never been able to keep up with payments."

"We just begin to get ahead. Then, dumb you, you quit your job. You've loafed over three months now. We'll never catch up."

"When I learn this business, I'll make five times my salary at Montcalm."

"Yeah, I'll bet."

"We'll make it. I've got to go study for my broker's exam," I said. I refused to succumb to her negativism.

The next two weeks Lois went about her household duties, resigned to our fate of poverty. I studied twelve to fourteen hours a day for my broker's exam, eight of it at the office and the rest at home, yet still delivered my paper route and did some insurance inspections. I studied material on federal laws of the 1933 Securities Act, the 1940 Investment Company Act and the code of conduct rules of the National Association of Securities Dealers, commonly known as NASD. I studied for the NASD test, as well as my state securities license.

When test time came, I made an excellent score on the NASD exam. Their questions were straightforward, and they tested my knowledge well.

The state's test came after the NASD and wasn't so easy. Their exam was held in a large classroom at the University of Washington. At least a hundred people were there to take the test. People didn't talk, they just shuffled their feet and coughed. Finally, they handed out the test papers. The questions confused me.

Some were worded so that two or three answers could possibly be correct. Yet, the only correct answer was theirs. When people began to leave, I was a long way from being finished. I didn't have a good feel that I was choosing the right answers, the answers they wanted. It would be awful to fail at this late date. Another whole month would pass before I had another chance to take the test, and that would be in Spokane, on the other side of the state. To fail wouldn't set well with Jones Bylor. After all, I cost them $400 a month, and I couldn't do any business until I was licensed. Only four or five people were left, and I was not nearly through. This made me nervous and I worked harder and tried to be faster.

I finished the test second to last. The proctor said, "You will receive a letter in a few days that informs you whether you passed or failed."

While I waited for the test results, I studied annual reports and researched articles on specific companies. I wanted to be ready to sell, just as soon as I had my okay. I researched investment ideas at the office, and spent a lot of time at the public library, and studied at home. Still, I got up at three o'clock to deliver my paper route.

Every morning at six o'clock we had a sales meeting in Mr. Bylor's office. It was the only office big enough to hold us all. Sometimes Mr. Bylor was there, other times not. Mr. Hackett usually conducted the sales meetings. He or one the older brokers would give us pep talks to get us to move on favored issues. To stay awake, I pinched my leg blue. On the tenth day of this pace, after the sales meeting, Miss Shirley came into my office with a stern look on her face.

"Mr. Bradley, the test results are in. They came in this morning." Her facial expression seemed to indicate that I had failed. "Mr. Hackett said I should give you the results."

I felt crushed. I had failed.

Then the corners of her mouth slowly turned up, and a sparkle came into her eyes. "You made it!" Her smile was unrestrained.

"At last a stockbroker!" I shouted. "I made it! Miss Shirley, I'm going home to tell my wife and celebrate."

"Go for it. Give her one for me."

"I'll see you in the morning."

At home, I ran into the house. "Lois! Lois! I made it! I passed the tests. I'm a stockbroker!" I felt like a kid who had made his first A.

"Big deal. So I'm an underpaid housewife, which I'm tired of," she said. "I found me a job today. I'm a hostess in the bar at the Sherlock Motel."

"I'm not sure I like this."

"Tough shit! I start at four today. I'll be home sometime after twelve. Looks like you'll have to learn to cook or eat lots of canned soup, Mr. Big Shit."

"I'll manage," I said. "I hope you like your work, but it should not be necessary now that I'm on my way."

"Ha! I want money to spend. If I depend on you, I'll be so old I won't need it. This is my money. It won't go for household expenses. That's your problem."

"Four to twelve. That doesn't give us much home life."

"So? Big deal."

"I'm going to the den to work on sales presentations."

She bowed with a broad sweep of her hand, and pointed towards the den.

I sat at my twenty-five dollar, secondhand roll-top desk, and looked at the telephone. What was I supposed to say? How do you approach a total stranger that you've read about in the paper, or pulled his name from the telephone book, or you haven't talked to since you left Montcalm? My mind was an empty net.

"What on earth am I to do?" I said out loud to myself. Panic set in. How could I make a living this way?

I wrote on a scratch pad everything that came to mind. "Hi! I'm Jim Bradley. I'm a stockbroker with Jones Bylor & Company. Do you want to buy some stock?" Another pitch, not much better was, "Hi, I'm Jim Bradley with Jones Bylor & Company. We specialize in helping people with their investments. We do financial plans, and give you the results of our research. Could we set up an appointment tomorrow evening to discuss your program further?" I went on with three or four pages of this tripe.

About six that evening, I got up enough nerve to pick up the phone and call someone. His reaction was quick, "Not interested."

I tried again and again. Those canned pitches choke on the way up. They sound so artificial. "Hells bells!" I muttered. "I'm supposed to make millions? I can't even earn cigar money at this rate."

The torture continued at the office the next day. I had to keep on the phone. I couldn't just sit there, and look at it like I did at home. To recoup from a sharp rebuke, I even called Time and pretended no one answered. Otherwise, management and people walking down the hall would think I was loafing.

After three or four days of this, it did get a little easier. Some people were even courteous to me. I began to enjoy the calls once I got over my fear of first approach. I tried all kinds of pitches. Some worked and some didn't.

One day Mr. Hackett passed my door and heard me say, "This investment won't lose you any money."

God! You would have thought that I had committed blasphemy in a Jewish synagogue. He backtracked, stood at my door and towered above me like a thunderhead.

He shouted, "Look, Bradley! People don't invest money—NOT to lose it. They can leave their money at home under the pillow, or put it in the bank and not lose it. They want to MAKE MONEY. That's the game. MAKE MONEY! MAKE MONEY! That's what you emphasize."

"So that's the secret?"

"Just common sense. Get their attention first with something dramatic or some personal tie. Sell them on the idea quick, you can make them MONEY. Then, you save your own ass by cautioning them that they can also lose money if things don't go well. When they're convinced and enthusiastic, don't worry. They won't pay any attention to your negative statement. But the fact that you brought it up might save our ass later. Get it?"

"I got it. Thanks."

That sounded like good advice. I kept that principle foremost in my mind. After a month of this phone practice on strangers, I did a little business. I felt ready to tackle face calls on my old Montcalm contacts.

My first visit was to the office of Sam Huston, vice-president of the large steel distribution company. I had purchased many thousands of dollars worth of steel from him, while at Montcalm. The receptionist recognized my name, and I got in to see him right away.

"Mr. Huston, I wanted to make you aware of my new connection."

"I wondered what happened to you. Someone else calls me from Montcalm now. They sure don't do the business they did in the past."

"I know. One of their major customers got into financial trouble." I handed him my card and said, "I'm with Jones Bylor now. Maybe sometime we can do some securities business. I'd like to make you some money."

"Could be," he said.

I gave him a company brochure and another booklet on investments. "When I come across a good investment idea, I'll give you a call."

"Sure. That'll be fine."

"Don't want to take up your time today, so I'll give you a call when I've got something specific that I think you'd like."

He smiled, we shook hands, and I left.

I called on most all my Montcalm prospects. I'd let a week or so pass, then hit them with my best investment idea. A week later, I'd do the same thing, give them full blast of my enthusiasm. Over and over I did this. Some of the ideas I gave them did well. But not one of them bought stock from me. Not one bite. I made no progress. These Montcalm contacts shunned my bait. They didn't even give me a nibble. I think some followed my advice, because when I called back, two or three months later they told me they already had some of that stock. They hadn't mentioned it the first time. I picked up some business from strangers and new contacts that I called on, as I made my way between Montcalm calls. I couldn't understand it. I had given these Montcalm vendors thousands of dollars worth of business. Yet, they wouldn't invest $100 with me.

Six months later, with little or no results from these calls, I went to see Sam Huston, the vice-president of the steel distribution firm. I came right out and said,

"Sam," I called him Sam by now, "What's the score? Do you think we will ever do any business?"

He said, "Look, Bradley. I will probably never buy any stock from you. I've done quite well with my own stockbroker of many years. I don't think you should waste any more of your time or mine."

"Thanks for finally telling me," I said. "I could have bought steel from others."

"You did! But, you bought most of it from me, because I had a top product and the best price. I see no reason to change stockbrokers and buy stocks from you, just because you were a good steel customer. You get back in the steel-buying business again, and we might do some business, but not in stocks."

"Thanks for your honesty, even if it is tardy," I said and left. I was angry. I was hurt. Then, in my heart, I thanked him. That was it! That's why these people did no business with me. They didn't think of me as a stockbroker. To them, I was a clerk buyer from Montcalm. I had wasted a whole six months on these people. I went back to my office and tossed all of my Montcalm prospect cards in the trash basket. They wouldn't waste any more of my time.

After that, I called on new people. I'd send a short introductory note with some free investment information, maybe something about their own company that I had seen in the press. Then, I'd call them up in three or four days and say, "Hi, I'm Jim Bradley, a stockbroker with Jones Bylor. I mailed you some information the other day. From time to time we uncover some good investment ideas. Okay to call you next time I find a good one?"

It worked. Most would say, "Fine, give me a call when you get something really good."

I always managed to have something that I strongly believed in when I called them back. Some of them must have thought that I spent all that time just looking for them. If they didn't buy, I at least had their attention when I called back. I always emphasized the words, MAKE MONEY, and that always got their interest. I should have realized that sooner. After all, I was in the money game.

While walking down the street one day, a character caught my eye. She was dressed in a garish orange blouse, a purple skirt, brown oxfords, and her face was covered with wrinkles of seventy-plus years. We waited for the light to change, and exchanged a casual greeting. She identified herself as Mae Belle, and gushed with friendliness.

When the light changed, people dashed here and there. This strange lady walked beside me and perkily asked, "What's your business?"

"Minding my own," was what I really thought. But she was so friendly and her eyes sparkled with mirth when she smiled, so I replied with pride, "I'm a stockbroker."

"Oh! You're just the man I want to see. I have some properties that I need some help with. Can you come out to my place this evening? I'd like to discuss them with you."

Now here was a genuine new prospect, right off the street, who had actually asked me to come and see her. She had a lot of properties. She must be a wealthy eccentric. I had heard that Seattle had lots of these kinds of people. She wouldn't get away from me, no sir.

"Yes," I said. "I'll be delighted to come out to see you."

"Seven this evening," she said and handed me a business card. Then she hurried off in a different direction as the traffic signal changed at the next block.

The address on the card was 13th Avenue East in the Capitol Hill District. There was a picture of two rats running across the bottom of her card.

At six-thirty I walked out to Mae Belle's place. I thought with a quick stop, I might get an idea of her needs, tell her that I would call her back later with some recommendations, then get on home before Lois had dinner ready. Her home, a dilapidated old house, was painted a faded red, and sagged like a run-down farm barn. Large maple trees surrounded it in a seasoned neighborhood of old mansions, which once had been the place to live. She opened the door, and I followed her in. Coffee brewed on an old potbellied wood stove in the living room. It was a graniteware coffee pot with grounds and water mixed together, and it smelled good.

"Have a seat," she said, as she poured me a cup of her brew, grounds and all.

I sat on a frayed couch that looked chewed on. Her other furniture looked like it came from Goodwill. She used a kerosene lamp with a smoky globe, even though electricity was readily available. Where she obtained the kerosene these days was a guess. Her potbellied stove was the only heat in the house, except for an old wood cookstove in the kitchen, visible from the front room.

Mae Belle pulled up a cane-bottom chair, and sat in front of me. I felt a scratch on my thigh. I looked down, and there was a big rat on the couch, and another one appeared at the other end. I started to jump up, but Mae Belle cautioned with her hand to sit still.

"Don't mind them," she said. "It's only Minnie and Moe. They're my only family. I raised them from babies. They are orphans. They lost their parents in the same mine cave-in that took my Joe."

"Gee! That's unusual. I've never seen pet wild rats."

"Shush, you'll hurt their feelings if you call them rats. It happened this last fall. I guess Minnie and Moe have kept me from going crazy. Joe and I worked one of his claims up near North Bend."

"I thought all the North Bend miners gave up gold mining at the turn of the century," I said.

"No. There's still a few of us squirrels around looking for golden nuts."

When I thought about her age, I said, "Joe must have been a bit old for hard-rock mining, wasn't he?"

"Goodness, no. After Labronski, I liked my men young," she said. "Joe Hadoff was my last one. He worked the mine by himself, except for what little help he could get from me. He was killed in the cave-in," she continued. "I discovered Minnie and Moe when I grabbed up a loose timber to pry off some of the bigger rocks that had caved in on my Joe. Their nest was under the timber. There were five of them, but Minnie and Moe were the only ones that lived."

"Sorry to hear about your husband," I said. "Guess these little fellows have been a lot of company to you."

"Yes, they are. Joe was a good man. Not a kinder soul walked this earth. I lived with him ten years. We never got around to making it legal. 'A waste of dollars, a license and a preacher,' Joe always said. 'Price of that'd buy a lot of coffee or terbacker,' he'd say."

This chitchat went on and on and it got late. I'd be here all evening if I didn't press. There'd be trouble when I got home. "Mrs. Belle, what can I do for you?"

"Labronski," she said. "That's my last name, but just call me Mae Belle. I don't want to be reminded of Labronski. That was the name of my last legal husband. He was the biggest scalawag of them all. Couldn't get rid of him 'til he died. Not like today's shack ups that you can just dump like old muck, or just move out."

"Well, Mae Belle, what can I do for you?" I dreaded the hell when I got home late. I forgot to call Lois and tell her I had an appointment. There was no telephone here.

"I have some mining claims, and I need somebody to help me develop them. You're a stockbroker. I figured you might know an honest geologist or mining engineer. You might even help me raise some money to develop them."

"Have you tried Canada? They do lots of mining finance up there."

"Too many of those Canadian brokers just mine the public. They don't move any muck."

"We don't deal in the mining stocks, but one of my associates might know someone who does. I'll ask."

"Would you, please?"

All the while, Minnie and Moe climbed all over me, across my legs, over my shoulders, around my neck, and down my back. It was most disconcerting, but I showed no sign of it. I acted like they were old friends, but I secretly yearned for the sight of a nice big tomcat.

"Mae Belle, I'll see what I can do. Incidentally, would you like to put some money in the stock market?"

"Me? Don't trust them fellers that play with other people's money. They cleaned Labronski and me out in the thirties."

"Did you and Mr. Labronski invest in stocks then?"

128

"Didn't everybody? Didn't you?"

"I wasn't old enough then," I said.

"Your folks?"

"We didn't have that kind of money. We were farmers."

"Well, shove me down the shaft! I thought everybody gambled in the stock market 'til the bust."

"Did you lose everything?" I asked.

"No. Old Labronski always knew when to pull up stakes. He got us out in time."

This was going to go on all night. "I'll see if I can find you a geologist," I said. "I'll call you. If you come into some bucks and want to make some money, let me know."

"I have a little money in the cookie jar I'll let you play with." She got up, went into the kitchen and came back with a coffee can from which she counted out $1,000 in tens and twenties.

"She was for real," I thought.

"Help me dump one of my properties and you've got some big money," she said.

"I'll try." When I stood up, Minnie and Moe scampered for the hole at the end of the couch.

With all that money in my briefcase, I kept a wary eye. It was after eight and already dark when I reached home. Lois met me at the door. This was one of her nights at home and she had said she would fix dinner. "Where in the hell have you been?" she demanded. If eyes could spit flames, I would have been burned.

"Had an evening sales call." I was proud of my sale and was going to tell her.

"I've already eaten and cleaned up. If you are hungry, tough shit. That'll teach you to get home on time."

"I can survive a night without a meal," I said, not even mentioning my sale.

"Look what came in the mail today! Look! Another dun from that mortgage outfit. They say if you don't catch up on those payments, they're going to take our home. When that happens, Buster, I'm gone." She frothed at the mouth. "Don't expect me to pay any part of it out of my money. That's your problem, Big Man."

"Give me the letter. I'll go by and patch it up with them."

"Patch it up! Hell! Money is all they want."

I took the letter, looked at it. Yes, I had to do something soon.

Morning paper deliveries, Saturday insurance reports, even with my brokerage income, there was never enough money. It had started so easy. Buy some small item, write a check for an extra twenty dollars, then cover in a couple of days. Finally I was making as many as seven stops an evening. I floated $150 between brokerage paydays. I would clean up on the first of the month, and it started all over again by the fifteenth. It got so bad it was costing me two hours an evening for this nonproductive work. It was not only a waste of time, it hurt my conscience. What if something happened to me? How would it get paid back? I knew bankers floated money. Big financiers and smart money managers did it all the time. They called it shrewd money management. I did not feel shrewd, just desperate.

If Jones Bylor got word, I was finished. Personal integrity and fiscal responsibility were the watchwords there. You handled other people's money. I felt like a man who zigzagged down river rapids with high banks on each side, no chance to turn back, just forward. To survive, avoid the next rock. To fail now, I would drown.

FIFTEEN

Thursday morning, soon as I got to the office, I knew something was wrong. Miss Shirley looked sad when she said, "Mr. Bylor wants to see you right after the sales meeting." Her dispirited voice sounded like she had received news that someone close had died.

"Fine," I said.

No pinched legs to stay awake that day. What did Mr. Bylor want to see me about? Had somebody complained? Had he become aware of my evening financial foraging? Mr. Bylor conducted the sales meeting. Mr. Hackett was out of town. He gave us details on a forthcoming local utility company offering. He was also one of their directors. His occasional glances my way gave no clue. I could feel disaster that waited to eat me up.

The underwriting sounded like a good investment for my clients. It paid a 6 percent dividend and had growth prospects. Funds would be used for expansion into additional communities within the state where they had obtained franchises. That company had a great future, but I was more concerned about my own.

When the meeting was over, I rushed to my office, and buzzed Miss Shirley on the intercom. "I'm out of the meeting. Please let me know when Mr. Bylor wants to see me."

With formality she said, "Mr. Bylor is in his office and ready for you now, Mr. Bradley."

I stood at his door. This short, orderly man, with a well-trimmed gray mustache, was almost engulfed by his huge mahogany desk which looked like a fortress. Stern and unsmiling, he motioned me to a chair.

"Mr. Bradley, I have had some bad news about you."

"What's that?" I dreaded the worst.

"Yesterday evening your mortgage holder called me at home. He said you were several months behind on your house payments."

"Only three."

"He's ready to foreclose."

I breathed a little easier. He didn't know the worst. "I know I have a problem," I said.

"As a broker, you have a responsibility for other people's money. This is a trust. If you cannot handle your own affairs, you should not be in charge of our clients' money."

"I'm doing everything I can to catch up."

"Your progress has been good here, but we cannot tolerate this situation. I will take the matter up with the executive committee. If your predicament cannot be alleviated, your relationship with this firm will be terminated."

"Mr. Bylor, this job is my life."

"The well-being of this firm is my life, Mr. Bradley. The executive committee meets Friday afternoon. A decision will be made then. You'll be informed of their decision Monday."

I could see that his mind was already made up.

"Mr. Bylor," I said, "I think you know how important this position is to me."

"That is not the primary concern now. You will be advised of the executive committee's decision the first of the week. I suggest that you take the rest of the week off. I don't want you to talk to any more clients until a decision has been made."

I stumbled back to my office, put a few things in my briefcase, without knowing what, and left. I needed to drive, to think. After that executive committee's meeting, everything that I valued would be gone. I drove for hours. I stopped at high points that overlooked Puget Sound. The view, the water, the boats, large and small, did not soothe my soul.

By midafternoon, I started towards home. Then I thought of Mr. Rice. He was the man who controlled the mortgage company and had complained to Mr. Bylor. It had been my intention to call on him after work that very day to see if I could work something out. Why couldn't he have waited? He would have been paid. Now he's spoiled everything.

This was my first time to visit his office. Joseph Rice had been a gruff voice snarling on the phone. Mr. Rice sat at his desk in the corner, separated from the rest of his staff by a portable panel. Collection clerks at the four other gunmetal gray desks scattered around the open room had no panels to hide them from the boss. They were on the phones berating other late payers. The receptionist was doing busy-work.

"Mr. Rice, I'm Jim Bradley. You called my employer and told him I was behind on my house payments."

"Thought that might get your attention."

"Mr. Rice, do you want the house back?"

"I want my money that's due."

"Unless I can get this resolved, I will lose my job, and the house is yours."

"Pay your bill, and you won't have a problem."

"I can't. I don't have the money. There's no place that I get that kind of money in time to save my job. It's yours, unless we can work something out, right now."

"I don't see much chance of that, unless you bring your mortgage up to date. Do you have any other property you can sell?"

I hadn't thought of our lot at Ocean Shores. I had already tried to sell it, but had no luck. Many others were for sale, as development had been slow. Still, maybe I could trade my equity to Rice to catch up.

"Well?" he said, as he waited for my answer.

"Mr. Rice, I have a lot at Ocean Shores. It cost $2,600 and I have paid over $1,500 into it. I'll trade you my equity to catch up on the house payments."

"How much do you owe on it?"

"Two thousand." Interest had taken a big chuck of my payments.

"Now what would I do with a lot down there? Your house I can sell. A lot down at Ocean Shores, I couldn't give away."

"You are also in the real estate business. You have salesmen who could sell it," I said.

"Hey!" He boomed out to the clerks in his office. "Any of you guys want to buy a lot down at Ocean Shores?"

One guy shrugged his shoulders. Another said, "No," and then another clerk said, "Too far to drive."

"Not much of a market for your lot," Rice said. "But, tell you what, you come up with $200 more in cash, throw in the lot, I'll help you out. We'll call the back payments square on the house."

"You'll give me $400 credit for a lot that I have paid in over $1,500, and you call that help?"

"I didn't ask to buy your lot."

"The equity should be worth at least $2,000 with all the development down there. Why do you need $200 more from me?"

He shrugged his shoulders. "Go sell it for two thou'. Pay me the $600 and you are fourteen hundred smackeroos ahead. Take it or leave it."

"Okay," I said. "I'll take your deal, but I'm getting scalped."

"If that's your attitude, I'm not interested."

I cringed to humble myself before this pompous bastard, but I said, "Mr. Rice, I'm sorry. Please accept my apology."

"Okay, bring in the legal description, the $200, and we'll draw up the paperwork."

"I have the information at home. It'll take me a couple hours."

"All right. Just bring it right back."

What I really needed the two hours for was to go float some money. It was right after the first of the month, so I was clean at the moment. God might have to help me about midmonth. This on top of the usual shortage would be rough to cover. It'd be the guillotine if Jones Bylor didn't go along with me.

It was a quarter 'til four when I reached home. As I drove up, I noticed a shiny black Cadillac parked at the curb on the opposite side of the street. Behind the wheel sat a man, perhaps ten years older than myself. He had a grin, a mustache, and a look in his eye that would attract women. He nodded as I drove by.

Lois was just ready to leave for her hostess job. In her low-cut dress she looked sexy. She had disciplined herself to lose weight and was almost as pretty as when I married her.

"I've made a deal to trade our Ocean Shores lot to clean up the past-due house payments," I said.

"Who cares?"

"I need to run the legal description back to Mr. Rice, so he can get the papers drafted up for our signatures. You'll need to sign when they're ready."

"I'll think about it," she said as she scurried to the door. The motel lounge where she worked was half a mile away. She usually walked.

"I'll drive you," I said, as I opened the door for her.

"That's not necessary. A friend will take me today."

She got in the black car and they drove off. On top of everything else, just what I needed, to be made a cuckold? I could be mistaken. Perhaps it was truly just an acquaintance who had given her a lift. I couldn't think about that just now; too many other things pressed. I closed the door.

Two hours later, after making the grocery store rounds, I was back at Mr. Rice's office with the legal description and $200 that I raised by writing my checks for more cash than I had purchased. Rice took my cash and had a clerk type up a form.

"Both you and your wife sign this warranty deed before a notary and bring it back to me," he said, as he handed the document to me.

It was Friday afternoon before I could get Lois out to sign the deed before a notary. I took it back to Mr. Rice, and he said come back at 3:30, and we will have the assignment and settlement agreement drafted. Get that signed and the deal is done. I then rushed it back home before Lois left for work. She signed it reluctantly and I took it back to Rice. With this news, I hurried down to the office. Mr. Bylor might still be there. He sometimes worked late on administrative matters after an executive meeting. Besides, he was going to be out of town Monday. He was still there in his office. Everyone else had gone home.

I tapped at his door and said, "Mr. Bylor, I've got the problem solved. I've got the house thing squared away."

"That's nice, but it's too late to have a bearing on the matter. The decision has been made, but as I said, you'll be informed Monday morning."

"Sorry to bother you."

I went back to my office and sat down, too stunned to think. I just sat there in the dark, staring straight ahead of me. Finally I heard him leave and I was alone. It got dark and the city lights came on. It started to rain outside. I could see the raindrops on the glass. I got up and went to the window, and looked down seven floors. There were night people on the street; the workers had all gone home. With the lights off, I sat back down and closed my eyes. What had happened to my world? My job was gone. I didn't have a marriage anymore. It seemed so hopeless. You work so hard, and you fight for every inch of ground, and for what? At that moment, I didn't care if I saw the morning. Tears came into my eyes as I sat there in the dark.

It was late. I sat there with my eyes closed, not knowing, not caring. Then behind my closed eyelids a shadow appeared, a hump-shouldered figure, not unlike my dead grandmother. The figure said nothing, just stood there before me, but a feeling of peace came over me. I could almost hear her favorite words, "When you've got problems, press on." Then the figure went away.

I got through the weekend, and was there on Monday for the sales meeting that started at six o'clock. When I first came in, Mr. Hackett said, "Bradley, I want to see you in my office after the meeting."

"Yes, sir," I said with the enthusiasm of a man who has just been told to put the blindfold on.

Mr. Hackett conducted the meeting. Mr. Bylor was out of town this time. Bylor was the type who would let Mr. Hackett do his dirty work.

After the meeting I gave him a few minutes to get settled. When I went into his office, Mr. Hackett was on his feet and pacing around with the telephone in his hand. He pointed to a chair. When he finished, he motioned for me to close the door. I would see what he had to say, and then ask if my new deal with Rice would help straighten things out.

"My friend, Broker Jim, here is a check for $2,000. I want you to go to Frederick & Nelson and buy yourself a new suit. I want you to catch up on your miscellaneous bills. I want you to get your ass in gear and become the broker I know you can become. This is an advance. You will pay it back with interest, when you make the money that I know you will."

Shell-shocked, I started to say "Thank you." He put his hand up to silence me. "And furthermore, I want you to quit all of those pissy-ass, part-time jobs you've been doing. Devote your full time and energies to the brokerage business! Is that clear? The only excuse for time off is when you screw your wife. If you can't handle that, call me," he said as he broke into a smile for the first time.

"Thanks, but I don't think I need any help there." As I left his office, I walked on air.

With this new reprieve, I went back to my office so filled with exuberance that I generated ten transactions. This made it my best day's business since I had become a stockbroker. I was eager to get home and share the good news with Lois, but had to wait until five-thirty for the bus. Lois kept the car that day.

I splurged and took home a big bouquet of red roses. These past months had been difficult for her too. "Golly! I'll even take her out to dinner tonight," I thought. She had told me that she had this Monday off.

SIXTEEN

As I walked up the driveway, things did not look right. It was twilight, and there were no lights on in the house. Then, as I put the key in the lock, something else dawned on me. There were no curtains in the windows. Now why would Lois send all the curtains out to be cleaned? She knew how meager our money supply was. She did not know about our good fortune. I hadn't called her. I wanted to surprise her about the $2,000 from Jones Bylor.

When I opened the door, there was no living room furniture. The same thing in the bedroom, the dining room and the kitchen. Our place was totally cleaned out. There was nothing left in the house that not been carted away. Our clothes were gone, closets empty. If Lois had left me, why had she taken my clothes? Where was Lois?

Perhaps I should check with the neighbors and hear what they say. I hesitated. We were not friendly with them. Lois always squabbled with them about something. Out of desperation, I called on Mrs. Belinka to our right.

"Have you seen Lois, or anything unusual today?"

"No, I've not seen your wife. There was a moving van with two hefty men who loaded up your furniture. Are you moving out?"

"Not that I know of."

That's all she could tell me so I went to the lady on the left side. She said, "Nope, haven't seen her. Thought she was inside and supervised your move. Hate to see you leave the neighborhood. Don likes you. Your wife is something else! Let us know if we can be of any help to you."

The lady across the street said, "Yes, I saw her in your car high-tailing it after the moving van. She leave you? Count your blessings! Gripes is all any of us ever heard from her. Guess you got the same."

"Thanks," I said, and went back home.

I wandered through the empty rooms, tormented by thoughts of what our lives could have been if I had made more money sooner. I passed the bathroom. There, stacked in the middle of the floor, were all my clothes. An empty molasses jar sat on the counter. Its previous contents covered my clothes. She had even taken the hangers.

A finger dipped in sorghum left a message on the bathroom mirror, "Good-bye, shit-head broker. You've just been shorted."

At least she left with a sense of humor.

I remembered earlier days, the trip to the Gulf of Mexico with her brother and his wife, before we were married; then the honeymoon trip west. Parts of that trip were good. There were fun times, when we explored the West on weekends, while I was still in the lumber business. I had hoped to make up for the bad times, when the money rolled in. That opportunity was gone. Lois had obviously found someone else. It hurt. Most likely it was the man in the Cadillac. She had already made the divorce settlement. She had all the goods, and I had all the debts, which included the mortgage.

Rice could have the house. I'd find an apartment in town. No more commutes for me, besides I had no car. There was a chill in the air. It could even snow. I started walking toward Rice's office, three-quarters of a mile away. The yellow lights that came from my neighbors' windows were warm and homey, and they made me lonely. What backbreaking work I had gone through to move all of those rocks from the yard, tub by tub, so we could put in a green lawn and flower beds. Somebody else would enjoy them now. After tonight, I would no longer live here.

Rice was still in his office. He had said that he often worked late. That was the best time to catch deadbeats.

"Mr. Rice, let's work something out. My wife has left me. I don't think I can handle the house by myself." He gave me a look of concern. This seemed to strike a hole in his armor.

He said, "We'll just call it square. You keep your lot and I will keep the $200 as a clean-up fee. I've been to the same place you are now."

"Thanks."

He smiled for the first time, and shook hands. "Lucky you don't have any kids. I miss mine."

My next stop was the motel bar where Lois worked. It was a good place for couples on the sly to rendezvous. There was an imitation plush that was dimly lit.

"Do you know when Lois Bradley will be in?" I asked a lady behind the bar.

"She isn't here anymore, and I don't care if she never comes back!"

"Is Mitzie in?" I asked. She was one of the co-workers that I had heard Lois mention.

She pointed to an attractive young lady who had overheard me ask for Lois.

"Mr. Bradley, I am terribly sorry, but I don't have any idea where she went. With no notice, she quit her job last night. She told me she was leaving town with Michael."

"Who's Michael?" I asked. I knew in my heart that he was the old guy who had driven Lois to work that day.

"Michael O'Keefe is a contractor that she's been going with. He came into the bar one night, and they acted like they knew each other."

So that's who it was, Michael O'Keefe. He was the guy who had sold us the Ocean Shores lot. His hand had lingered on Lois's hand longer than it should have. That's why that guy in the Cadillac looked so familiar. He had grown a mustache and gotten a little more gray.

"Do you have any idea where they might've gone?"

"I think she mentioned Michael had gotten some kind of subcontract work up in Alaska."

"Thanks, Mitzie. I appreciate your help."

"Mr. Bradley, I just feel terrible about this. I knew she played around on you, but it wasn't my business."

"Thanks again, Mitzie. I appreciate your honesty. That old man probably did me a favor." I shook her hand. With her brown eyes and long dark hair, I suspected that under all that make-up, she was a natural beauty. The touch of her hand sent a charge through my veins. She was elegant, and certainly didn't look like she belonged here.

That night I slept on the floor, curled up on the rug before the fireplace. I covered myself with a garment that had somehow escaped the molasses. Next day I salvaged my better clothes, took them to the cleaners, and tossed out the others. I skipped the morning sales meeting. My first stop was Seattle's prestige department store, Frederick & Nelson. I bought a pin stripe, blue serge business suit, two new white shirts and two ties to match. This fulfilled my commitment to Mr. Hackett to spend part of my advance money on clothes.

I left my purchases at the store to pick up later, and walked down Fifth Avenue along the Monorail track. Four blocks from the office, on Blanchard and 5th, I saw a For Rent sign in the window of an old redbrick apartment house.

The manager, a middle-aged lady, said, "I have a furnished bachelor apartment on the third floor which rents for $65 a month, utilities paid."

"I'll take it," I said.

She handed me a key, and said, "Go look at it."

As I puffed up to the third floor, I understood why she hadn't come with me. There was a pull-down bed in the living room and a gray overstuffed couch weary from the weight of far too many heavy bottoms. The kitchenette had a gas stove with an oven that a chicken would fit in, but never a turkey. There was an oilcloth-covered table and one chair. The kitchen was dark, except for the natural light that came from one small window. Once-white lace curtains from long ago covered the two narrow windows in the combination bedroom-living room. Beige pull-down shades shielded the place from the night eyes of a bay of apartments across the courtyard. It was cheap, warm and out of the rain.

I gave the landlady Mr. Hackett's name as a reference, and handed her $155 in cash. That covered the first and last month's rent and a $25 security fee. Two more bus trips over to the Eastside, I moved the rest of my personal things that I wanted to keep. I gave Mr. Rice the keys to the house, and left the old neighborhood with a light step.

I kept a small amount of the advance for groceries and walking-around money, enough to last me two months, and then divided the rest up equally among the numerous people that I owed. I sent a short note, thanked them for their patience, explained the token payment, and that there would be more as soon as possible.

The next two weeks I worked longer hours and harder than I had ever done in the lumber business. I still got up at three o'clock in the morning. Instead of delivering newspapers, I went to the office, did research, wrote letters, and sent mail-outs to prospects. By day it was every minute on the phone, or out to see a client by foot or bus. When all this burned me out, I went to a movie. The Colonial Theatre charged only a buck. The place had been a grand theatre at one time but now people who seemed to have no other place to sleep took up most of the seats. Nevertheless, amid the body odors, the snores, and the smell of popcorn, I enjoyed the movies, especially Clint Eastwood's spaghetti westerns. They were all new to me, as Lois and I had not gone to many movies. We watched television.

Money was still difficult. One time towards the end of the month, I ran out of grocery money. I took my watch to the same pawnshop where I had taken my old TV several years ago. The same kid had grown older and developed a crust.

"Ten dollars," he said.

Here I am in my business suit, trying to hustle up grub money from a pawnshop. "Look, I only need the money until the end of the month. Can you make it twenty?"

"Fifteen."

"Done."

Then I went back to the office and stayed late. I worked on mail-outs for the morning's mail. I was alone most of the evening, except for distant janitorial sounds. Suddenly there came a loud bang at the front office door.

I heard a voice yell, "Mr. Bradley! Mr. Bradley! Are you there?"

I opened the door. A peewee person—too big to be a dwarf, too small to be a man—stood before me. I'd say he was about eighteen.

Peewee grabbed my hand and shook it. "I'm Benjamin Ergstein. I met this weird lady on the street, and she said I must come and talk with you. She said you worked late and helped people make lots of money."

"Sometimes I do," I said. "I work late because it's tough to build a clientele when you only work from seven to three."

"Will you help me make some money?"

"I'll try." I led him back to my office.

Hesitating, he said, "I don't have much money, and I want to make a lot of money, but I don't want to lose my money either."

"Sounds like you're going to be an interesting challenge," I said. "Let's see what we can do."

Benjamin, dark-haired, mild-mannered and Jewish, was twenty-five years old, not eighteen as I had first thought. After I filled out his new account card and had him sign it, I said, "Mr. Ergstein, how much do you want to invest?"

"I have $100."

"Do you plan to add to it?"

"I believe I can invest an additional $15 per month."

His account card listed a spouse. "Do you want this to be a joint account?"

"No, my wife has her own money."

"Mr. Ergstein."

"Call me Ben."

"Well, Ben, I believe a mutual fund that you can add your $15 a month to makes good sense for you right now. Later, when you have saved up maybe at least $500, in addition to your mutual fund program, we can look at some individual stocks."

I gave him promotional materials and prospectuses on three different mutual funds that I thought might fit his needs. Questions and more questions and two hours later, he still had not made up his mind where to drive that $100 stake. He couldn't decide which of two mutual funds he would risk his money on. With so much work yet to be done on my mail-outs, I was losing patience with him. The man exercised more caution on this $100 decision than most clients spent on a $5,000 commitment.

Just as I started to say, "Ben, why don't you sleep on it, make up your mind and then call me?" he suddenly jumped up. He excitedly pointed his finger at a mutual fund prospectus.

"I want this one, the Dow Theory Fund! That sounds familiar."

By that time, I would have agreed with him on Satan's Desire. "You won't go wrong with Dow Theory," I said.

"Will it make a lot of money?"

"With a $100 investment, you certainly won't lose a lot. By the way, Benjamin, who was the lady who sent you in?"

"I'm not sure. I think she said her name was May or June or something like that."

"You must mean Mae Belle?"

"Yes! That's it. She was an odd one."

"Ben, don't you know talking to strange women on the street might get you into trouble?"

"She's too old for that, but I think she gave me good advice to come here," he said as he shook his head up and down. "I've been to other places, and they didn't want to spend any time with me."

"Gosh! I wonder why?" I asked.

He handed me a well-caressed $100 bill, and I gave him a temporary receipt, marked on the back of my business card.

"The office will mail you a more official receipt."

"Thank you. I'm sure we'll do lots of business," he said as he left.

I worked on my mail-outs for another hour. Finally, I was so disgusted with myself to have wasted so much time for so little, I just had to get out of there. If I did much business with that man, I'd go bankrupt. Only a fool would spend three hours on a $100 mutual fund sale that netted him only three bucks. If I never saw this Benjamin Ergstein again, I would consider myself blessed.

I had had enough of brokerage business for that day, so I headed home. As I approached the Colonial, I saw the title of another Clint Eastwood movie that I had not seen, *Hang them High,* or something like that. I thought this might get Benjamin Ergstein off my mind.

There in this house of the lost and lonely, I sat down with a bag of popcorn to enjoy an evening of Clint Eastwood heroics. I chose the balcony. Deeply engrossed in Clint's problems, I suddenly felt a hand on my leg. An old man, gray-faced in the movie light, held up an open sack. "Here, son, have some candy."

"No thanks." His hand stayed there. I pushed it away and got up and left. I had lost my appetite for spaghetti westerns that night.

The weekends were the most lonesome. I'd bring a stack of library books home. They were my company. I had read and reread all the volumes of Carl Sandburg's *Lincoln,* stock market books and biographies of great financiers from J. P. Morgan to Daniel Drew. Four bare walls were not much company. After so much reading, you burn out. Going to movies alone wasn't much fun either. I needed a woman. I missed Lois, even with her bitchy, bitchy ways. What I really needed was a good screw, but it had been years since I had courted a girl.

Somehow I got through winter. Spring and summer had passed and it was fall again. Sunday afternoon, I walked out to Seattle Center, the site of the World's Fair, that Lois and I had visited a couple of years after we had first come to Seattle. I sat on a bench and looked up at the Space Needle. It was a warm fall afternoon. Squirrels skirted about and tried to con you out of handouts. Two crows in opposite trees talked to each other.

A pretty girl, somewhat younger than me, came and sat down at the other end of the bench. Out of the corner of my eye, I could see she was dressed as though she had come from church.

"Surely is a beautiful day, isn't it?"

"Yes, it is," she said.

"This your home town?"

"No."

"Where you from?"

"Back east," she said.

"Isn't this Space Needle something?"

"Yes."

She crossed and uncrossed her legs, which were nicely formed. They were covered with brown hose and she had on black high heels.

"Have you ever been up to the top?"

"No."

"Would you like to take a ride up and have a cup of coffee?"

"No." She stood up, and left without a look my way.

I watched her rhythmical movement until she disappeared around a corner. My girl-hunt technique needed improvement, I could see. The problem was, how do you meet nice girls? Guess I could go to church. Right now, though, I wouldn't care if the girls weren't so nice. There didn't seem to be any of those old-fashioned public dance halls like they had back home. There, you had an excuse to cozy up to a pretty girl at least for a few moments. I had grown shy. How do you approach a woman? I'd lost the touch. It had been almost ten years since I had actively tried to catch a strange girl's attention.

I'd never made commerce with a woman in my life. I needed a wife. One thing for sure, though, before I settled in with another woman, I decided that she must have character, brains and beauty, in just that order, and she'd better like to screw. I had to find her soon.

Eight o'clock, Monday morning, a man of Norwegian descent came to see me. He was a short man of stocky build, with gray hair, and about fifty-five. "Sven Nordoff," he said, as he extended his hand. "Mae Belle said for me to get my bottom in here to see Jim Bradley. She said that he was a genius who makes people rich. You Jim Bradley?"

"I don't know about the genius part, but they call me Jim Bradley. So you've met the mining lady. Did you meet her two little friends?"

"You mean the rats? No, but I've seen them on her card. She told me about them. Poor little orphans, she called them."

"They are friendly little cusses, but a bit nosy on close acquaintance."

"Mae Belle told me you coached $1,000 out of her cookie jar and turned it into two."

"With a helpful market, we made a lucky move."

"I like that action. You know that woman's a walking billboard for you. She's convinced that you are some kind of genius. The market has nothing to do with it."

"I'll take my accolades from wherever they come. Sometimes we get lucky. Say, I'm curious. How did you meet Mae Belle?"

"Last Sunday afternoon I was out at Seattle Center. I watched this little old lady feed the squirrels. I was impressed. How friendly the animals were toward her. I finally moved over and joined the fun."

"Mae Belle does attract people as well as rats," I said. I wondered how I missed them Sunday. They were there when I had my near-sexual encounter.

"Anyway, Jim, I've got five grand. Let's see what you can do with it."

"Let's first fill out a new account card. Have to be able to see what risk you can afford to take."

"Don't worry about that," he said. "I like your record. I can afford to lose it, but you better not."

"That's what most folks say," I said. "I see you work for Boeing as an engineer. How about some Boeing stock? I like that one."

"Why Boeing? They're going to hell in a hand basket."

"I think you might be too close to the runway to see the planes."

"You like Boeing?" he asked.

"I think they have a great future and should be bought right now."

"You're the expert. I'll take whatever you recommend."

"I think Boeing will make you some money with little risk. But since you don't seem to mind the risk, let's see if we can make you some real money. I've another company I think you should take a piece of. High risk, but I think the potential outweighs it."

"That's what I'm here for," Mr. Nordoff said.

"Well, let's put about half in Boeing and the rest in Bing Resources. This is a speculative oil company that I believe will do well. They've started to raise partnership money from the public. They've got a good story and I think the stock will go. They have brought in some big people on their board."

"You're the boss 'til you screw up."

"What happens then?"

"Remember, Jim, I'm a Viking. You know what they did to screw-ups."

"Not sure, but I've heard that they did pluck a lot of blonde flowers in England."

He ignored this. I then wrote up two tickets, putting approximately $2,500 each in Boeing and Bing Resources, and took the tickets to trading to be executed.

When I got back to my office, he was on his feet and all smiles, "Let's celebrate our new friendship and my first excursion into the stock market. I'll treat you to a Viking dinner at my place this evening."

"Sounds good. I'll look forward to it."

Seven o'clock that evening I entered Sven Nordoff's place on Capitol Hill. He met me at the door with a raised mug of beer in his hand.

"Skoal," he said as he handed the beer to me.

The aroma of fresh homemade bread permeated the small, but well-kept apartment, much neater than mine. On the walls were many original works of art, pictures of ships at sea, forest and farm scenes.

"Come, have a seat while I finish up," he said as he guided me to a seat at the kitchen table.

First he served pickled herring, and then a stew you could fight a war on. I had read somewhere that Napoleon moved his whole army on stew. His fresh bread and stew was a feast. Just as I finished pigging out, he came up with a couple of Havana cigars and more beer served with another, "Skoal."

This mild-mannered Norwegian truly had the spirit of a Viking. I could just visualize him on the British coast pursuing English flowers and plunder.

"I like good music, good food and my women not so good," he said as he raised his beer mug for another, "Skoal."

I returned his "Skoal."

"Vietnam is a capitalist war," he said. "Dirty Dick is out to make more money for the Republicans."

As he talked on, his political opinions and anti-war statements I could tolerate, but his anti-religious attitude and constant disrespectful reference to J.C. disconcerted me. But I liked him in spite of his imperfections. While under the influence of much beer, I invited him to go sailing with me on my yacht. He accepted.

"I would suggest that you wear a bathing suit," I said.

"Sure, I like to swim."

I didn't tell him that my yacht was an eight-foot plastic board with a small red sail and push-down keel.

There was gusto at Jones Bylor. Work was exciting and there always was something new. Daniel Lews was a new broker, hired just three month after me. I liked him. He was from Utah, but wasn't Mormon. His folks were small farmers. Right off, we became friends and shared ideas and tales of struggle. He used the same strategy that I used to get in. He kept coming back. When they hired him, Miss Shirley told me that Mr. Hackett had said to her, "Guess I'll hire that Lews. He's as bad as Bradley. Won't give me any peace."

Jim Swenson, nine months ahead of me, was more competitor than friend. He seemed to resent my progress. His monthly gross was usually 10 to 15 percent above mine. I nudged him though, and occasionally outgrossed him. He resented Mr. Hackett's support of me.

Ralph Bailor, slightly younger, just plain didn't like me. I wasn't much competition to him. He had two years on me, in the business. The thought filled me with ecstasy, that some day I might surpass him in gross. He was conservative, self-assured and damn prissy. He had an answer for everything that came up. What made him such a bastard, he was usually right. Another thing Ralph had going for him, he was the son of the second largest shareholder of Jones Bylor. Ralph not only stood to inherit John Bailor's stock, but had already taken over the old man's long-established clientele. He had me skunked, but I kept at it.

Of the older men, John Lucas was my favorite. He gave straight answers and played no games. If he liked you, he liked you and if he didn't, you were shit. I wanted his advice one time and went to his office. He looked up from his work as I stood at his door.

"Mr. Lucas, I notice that you don't buy any Bing Resources. Anything wrong with it?"

"That company is like wiping your ass with chigger grass. It'll bite you," he said. "Only way I would touch that son of a bitch would be with a red hot branding iron up his ass."

"Why do you feel that way?"

"Son of a bitch's got no pea under his shell."

"Can't argue with the tape."

"You'll see."

It also made no sense to argue with John Lucas. You wouldn't change his mind, but it might be wise to listen. He was never wrong. I waved a thank you and started to leave.

"Why'd you want to know?"

"Thanks. You answered my question."

Wednesday afternoon, I walked down Fourth Avenue, headed out to an appointment close to Seattle Center. It was a warm fall day and the tiny leaves of the mimosa trees had begun to turn golden. A man approached from the other way. He looked familiar and then I recognized him.

"Hi, I'm Jim Bradley. Remember, we chatted at the Montcalm water cooler from time to time."

"Sure, Jim, I remember you. I'm Saul Carlson. I don't think we ever introduced ourselves out there at Montcalm."

"Probably too busy dodging old Brewster's verbal arrows," I said.

"That son of a bitch."

"Let's have a cup of coffee," I said. "Have an appointment, but I've got an hour before I have to be there." I walked back two blocks towards downtown with him.

With cups of coffee in heavy mugs, we settled down in this elegant old place whose walls were covered by mirrors. Lowell's cafeteria on Fourth Street, once a popular lunch place, was now frequented mainly by senior citizens with time on their hands.

"Where've you been?" he asked. "You aren't at Montcalm anymore, are you?"

"No, I'm a stockbroker now."

146

"Wow! In the big bucks?"

"Hardly."

"I got axed," Saul said. "A year after I quit seeing you around."

"I quit."

"Come on now, Jim. Nobody ever quits Montcalm. They either die, retire or get canned."

Saul was a six-foot-three, rugged, blond, handsome Scandinavian. Women turned around to take a second look at him. He was a friendly cuss, but not overly bright. I noticed an attractive brunette who looked our way.

"No, Saul, I really quit, so I could become a stockbroker. What do you do?"

"Got a lawn maintenance job at the golf course."

"Sounds nice."

"Lots of sunshine. Get to play all the free golf I want, when I don't have to work. Beats working in a stuffy office with some asshole yelling at you."

"Did you ever tangle with Brewster?" I asked.

"That son of a bitch. If I ever catch him out on my golf course alone, I'll club the bastard to death."

"I guess you knew him well."

"Let's don't talk about such unpleasant fuckheads. How's the wife and kids?"

"Don't have any. Wife took off with an older fellow with more money."

"Just proves it."

"What?"

"They're all whores. What're you doing for snatch?" His smile was bigger than a country kid looking at a whole watermelon he just busted out in the field. The brunette, two tables down, raised her eyebrow.

"Doing without," I said in an undertone.

"That's kind of dumb."

"I guess."

"Why don't you come down to the Young Republicans Club with me? There's lots of young stuff there, and some old biddies that aren't bad. Some of them still like to screw."

"I thought their business was flags and apple pie, motherhood and conservative stuff like that."

"I find 'em pretty liberal when it comes to sex. They talk a lot of politics, but it's a damn good place to meet fuckin' gals."

"Might be fun."

"There's a cocktail social hour this Friday night at seven o'clock. You want to come?"

"Sure, why not?"

"Where do you stay? I'll pick you up in my truck."

"That old apartment building on the southeast corner of Fifth and Blanchard."

"See you at six-thirty. God! You must be rollin' in dough to live there," he said, and grinned.

"See you Friday, Saul," I said and looked at my watch. "I'm tired of Clint Eastwood spaghetti westerns."

"Stick with me, and I'll get you under the covers with a Pretty before you know it."

"I'm not out for that."

He gave me a quizzical look and then said, "By the way, Jim, you might also want to go to the German Club with me. They have a dance every Saturday night."

"Oh."

"Yeah, lots of snatch there too."

"I'm not German."

"Neither am I, but those frauleins can't tell the difference in a German dick and a Scandinavian one," he said in an undertone and nudged me with his elbow as we walked away after paying our coffee check.

"Six-thirty, Friday," he yelled as he started in the opposite direction. Then he stopped, turned around, and went back in Lowell's.

I supposed that he went back to check out the brunette. I wondered if this was the type of company that I wanted to keep. Oh well! I didn't have to act like him. There's bound to be some nice girls in these places too. I just didn't want to tango with any more women like Lois. If I ever got married again, my hormones wouldn't pick the maid. That got me in trouble last time. This time it had to be a woman with character, brains and beauty.

SEVENTEEN

Thursday morning, seven o'clock sharp, the big plunger, Benjamin Ergstein, the Dow Theory man, appeared at my door. The receptionist must not have come in yet, because he just came on back, unescorted. When I saw him, I thought, "Oh God, my day's shot. He'll take up the whole day." Before I could say anything, a three-hundred-pound man followed him in.

"Mr. Bradley, I want you to meet my father-in-law, Mr. Edwin Toola."

Mr. Toola smacked his lips and said, "The kid says you're smart, and he likes the way you do business!"

He plopped himself down into one of my two side chairs like a three-hundred-pound bag of cement. I secretly blessed that chair for its sturdiness.

"It's a bit early to judge," I said. "We've only had one transaction and it's too soon for results."

"Bennie's smart. He says you're the best, and that's good enough for me. I got twenty grand I want you to play with."

Twenty thousand! That made him my biggest client yet. "That's great!" I said. "We'll see if we can make you some money."

"I want to make a hell of a lot of money and fast. Don't bother me with details."

"There's risk, but you can make a lot of money."

"That's what I want to hear."

"What if we lose some?"

"That's your problem. I gotta lotta tough boys who can measure your shoe size!" Then he let out a belly laugh that resounded down the hall.

"I don't need a new pair of shoes," I answered back.

"Just want to keep you on your toes."

"What is your line of business, Mr. Toola?" I asked. "I'd rather not have any of those black limousine boys as clients."

"I drive a red Cad," he said. "I'm a longshoreman."

"That sounds better."

He picked his nose, and said, "I don't do much physical work anymore. I'm a union boss. Labor official in polite society."

149

"Mr. Toola, this market is not for the fainthearted. If this is money you can't afford to lose, you would be better to keep it in savings, or let's put it all in blue chips."

"Oh, you mean grandma stocks. I don't want to wait that long for action. Make me some money fast."

"I'll try, but there is some risk."

He smiled and said nothing.

"Let's put half your money in aggressive stocks, and the rest into something conservative—at least until I find something better."

"Sounds good enough to me."

"One of the speculations I think we should go for, is Bing Resources," I said. I still liked the company, even if John Lucas didn't.

"A-OK with me, if you think it'll make money."

I gave him a couple more suggestions, and he said, "Go ahead."

Mr. Toola then raised his bulk with the agility of a young deer. "Benjamin," he said, "let's go. Mr. Bradley's got work to do."

Benjamin had hardly spoken all this time. He stuck out his hand as he got up to go. "Thanks for your time, Mr. Bradley."

That next week Bing Resources went up five dollars a share to twenty and another of Mr. Toola's speculations was up almost as much.

He called up, exploded with glee. "I told you Bennie was smart! Say, I been talking to my bridge partner. She's got fifty grand she'd like you to work on. Here's her number. Give her a call. Jeanne Tremble's her name."

Soon as he was off the phone, I called this Mrs. Jean Tremble. She told me her husband was a Boeing engineer.

"This is my own money," she said in a voice that sounded like melody of the gods. Her voice buzzed through my head like a rendition of *Franz Josef's Waltz*.

I asked questions, just to hear her voice. How this gracious middle-aged lady came to be a bridge partner with such a gruff old union boss as Toola was something I couldn't fathom. Her son was in college, no children at home, and she was bored.

"I have my conservative investments elsewhere," she said. "This is my play money, so Mr. Bradley, let her roll!"

After a couple of good stock moves, this voice of the gods wanted her friends to meet this stockbroker with the quaint Oklahoma accent. Ultimately, she brought me fifteen new accounts, even larger than her own. She was a first-class gambler. And to think, I almost told Benjamin Ergstein to take his $100 investment and go to hell.

Friday, Saul picked me up right on time in his dented-up old gray Ford pickup truck. Elegantly dressed in a banker blue suit, white shirt and dark tie, he put me to shame. I felt like a bum, dressed in my brown tweed jacket and sport shirt not so well matched.

This particular Young Republicans Club meeting was held in a rented hospitality room of a local hotel. The lights were subdued. The hum of conversation sounded more like a bumped beehive than a stand-up cocktail party. Everyone seemed to have a good time. People circulated from group to group. Their heads swung back and forth like someone playing a pinball machine, not to miss a thing, to see who came and who went.

I didn't quite know how to break in, so I watched Saul for a cue. You would have thought he was a politician, not a golf gardener who drove a junk truck. One group, when there was a break in conversation, Saul butted right in with a loud voice.

"Ladies and gentlemen, I have a new member for us, a good Republican voter. Let me introduce Jim Bradley, and if you don't know me, I'm Saul Carlson of the Chicago Carlsons." With that, he moved right in on the discussion he had interrupted and added his own opinion.

Saul wandered off and left me with the group. From the snatches of conversation that I overheard from nearby coveys, the talk held little interest to me. It was mostly political gossip, what liars the members of the other party were, and who was doing what to whom. I had little to say. A few quick glances around, I didn't see any girls that caught my fancy. Some women were attractive, but most were not. Some were fat with pretty faces, some just fat. And the lean ones seemed to calculate what they would say. Most everyone was in clumps and seemed deeply engaged in conversation with others they already knew, and I hesitated to break in on them. I moved out on my own.

I saw a young lady alone across the room and started towards her. Before I got there, someone else had already moved in. I noticed a waiter who moved through the crowd, and asked him where the restroom was. That got me out of the room, so I kept on going. I walked back towards my apartment. This much, I realized. Stand-up political cocktail parties were not for me.

It was a warm night, and a light breeze caused the leaves to fall. It was still early. As I walked past the Colonial Theatre, I noticed there was another Clint Eastwood spaghetti western on that I hadn't seen. I started in, but stopped. No thanks. I'd had enough of that place.

Being Friday night, there was no urgency to get to bed. Saturday, I didn't have to get up early. Thought I'd go to the office later and work on more mail-outs.

I fixed coffee and settled down for an evening of Carl Sandburg's *Lincoln's The Prairie Years*. I looked around my shabby apartment and felt a certain kinship with young Lincoln, who spent nights in rugged inns as he followed judges around on their circuit courts. I sat there alone, and I wondered if somewhere in town, there was a lonely girl looking for me.

Eleven-thirty, I heard a lady's giggle in the hallway. A man's voice shushed the female to quiet down. Then came a tap on my door.

Saul's voice whispered, "Jim, open up!" With no security lock on the front door, anyone could come right up to your room, wanted or not.

I put Lincoln to rest, and quickly opened the door. Saul was with a chubby middle-aged lady. He pushed his way past me, and she followed.

"Jolly's got to pee," he said.

He guided her into the bathroom, which was adjacent to my front door.

"Fine," I said, "make yourselves at home," as she closed the bathroom door.

While she was in there, I could still hear her drunken giggle. I hoped that she would not wake my neighbors.

Before she came out, Saul said, "I need to sober her up before I take her home. She says her husband'll kill her if she comes home drunk."

"Oh? Why isn't she with her husband?"

"She says he don't like politicians, so she has to go alone."

"If you brought my wife home in that condition, I'd kill you in the bargain," I said.

"Don't worry. Give me a pillow and a couple of blankets. I'll let her sleep it off in your bathtub. I don't want to keep you up. She shouldn't take too long."

I wondered why I let this character into my life. I owed him nothing. I pulled my bed down, and gave him my only pillow and a sheet and a blanket. I hoped she wouldn't puke on my dad's old army blanket. That left me with a sheet and the mattress cover.

Saul joined her in the restroom. I heard the toilet flush and more giggles. From the crack under the door, I saw the light go off. I went to bed and tried to sleep, but all I could hear was more giggles and shuffling on the floor.

"Shush, you guys. You'll wake up my neighbors."

They answered with more of her giggles, and then I heard rhythmic movements, heavy breathing, and then it all was quiet. After a while, I heard them again. I would have a talk with Saul. There would be no more of this. They would get me kicked out of my apartment. The landlady and her husband lived downstairs in the first apartment by the front door. They may have even heard them come in, with all the noise they made. The landlady had forewarned me when I moved in. "Don't bring any pets or girls up to your apartment, or out you go."

I tried to sleep. It was uncomfortable. I rolled up a pair of my blue jeans for a pillow, and that was better. About four o'clock I heard them going at it again. Then it stopped, and I heard more giggles. Saul shushed her. Light from under the door showed again. I heard them stumble around as they got dressed in the close quarters. The lights went off again, and I heard the bathroom door open. They sneaked out the front door. Once they were in the hall, I heard her giggle again as they left.

Next night, Saturday, Saul came by at seven to pick me up for the German Club dance. He sat on the couch and smoked a cigarette, while I put my tie on.

"Saul," I yelled from the bathroom. "Don't you ever pull that on me again."

"What're you talking about?" he asked innocently.

"I will not have you turn my apartment into a whorehouse."

"Jolly's no whore. I just let her sleep it off before she went home."

"I know what the hell you were doing."

"Look, dammit, if you wanted a piece of ass, why didn't you come on in? I'd a shared her."

"No more! Never again."

"Okay, if you feel that way. I won't bring anybody else by, unless I got one for you too."

"No thanks."

"Okay, if that's the way you want it. But dammit! Think how much fun we could have. Your place is so close by."

"I'm sorry."

"Okay, if you say so, but you'll miss some good ass."

The German Club was in an old red brick building. It thundered with thumping feet. The vigorous German music was generated by a drum, an accordion and strings. Three men, dressed in Alpine shorts, colorful shirts and fancy red and green hats, made up the entire band. They made a lot of sound for only three people. I felt like I was in an old German beer garden. The dance floor trembled from stomping feet. Yet there were long tables filled with people, drinking pitchers of strong black beer. Mostly blond Teutonic people, but there were a few dark heads who didn't look German. The band members were the only ones dressed in costume; the rest wore street clothes.

We found a couple of vacant chairs and blended in quickly. Saul went over to the bar and came back with a pitcher of beer and four glasses. He was all prepared to share beer with a couple of blond beauties who sat across from us. They acted like we weren't there.

When the music stopped, and the band members took a rest-break, people scattered. Tables and chairs shuffled. Some dancers went to pee and some left, probably scored for the evening. Others returned to their tables to rest before the next onslaught, when the band would begin to play.

After another round of stomps, three unattached men came and sat down at the other end of our table. One carried a large pitcher of beer and the others carried mugs. All were flushed from their strenuous dancing, and reflected an exuberant happiness like there were no problems in the world. Time was only for this moment. They greeted Saul and me and acted like old friends. They offered to top off our beer mugs from their pitcher. For a brief time before the band resumed its play, a lively discussion ensued about Vietnam. Two of the happy fellows finally raised their mugs and said, "To hell with it, we're going to Canada." The music killed further conversation.

Spurned by the two well-stacked frauleins across our table, Saul and I left them alone, and danced with others. I ended up with a jolly German girl, a big-boned blonde that I had to look up to. "Bette," she called herself. What Bette lacked in looks, she made up for in an exuberant personality. We danced maybe four dances together before I took her back to her table to rest, and maybe give someone else a chance. I danced with her off and on all evening. Bette was popular, in spite of her big raw-boned body. Often she was taken away before I got her back to her table; so I would dance with her friends, Jeanie and Carol. They were nice girls too.

A time or two, Saul and I sat it out, and talked with one or two of the three friendly fellows, who also had missed out on girls. There were more men than women.

With an aside to me, Saul said, "Looks like you're making out with that big German pussy."

"She's a nice girl."

"Make a damn good lay. Man, to hump that! You'd never hit bottom." He raised his beer mug in a toast.

I said, "She's a nice girl."

He leaned over and whispered, "They make the best fuckin'."

I said nothing. This was the last of Saul Carlson for me. Next time he called, I was going to be busy.

As the evening wore on, Saul beat me to Bette one time. She danced with him the first time, just like her two friends, Jeanie and Carol. They all turned him down on his second tries. On my next dance with Bette, she said, "Your friend is an evil man."

"What do you mean? Should I say something to him?"

She frowned. "No, let's drop it. I don't care to talk about him. I certainly won't dance with that creep again."

She smiled at me, and then was back to her jolly self again. I danced with her three more times, and then it was time to go.

"Bette," I said, "May I have your phone number?"

She squeezed my hand and said, "Maybe later. Just for now, let's keep it to dance. See you next week?"

"Sure."

Bette left with her two friends, Jeanie and Carol. I looked for Saul, and saw him nowhere. I guessed he had made a connection in some motel or deserted place in his pickup. He knew he was no longer welcomed to bring his trollops to my place. It was only a mile, so I'd enjoy a midnight walk home. The moonlight on the trees made the world seem good again.

In spite of Saul's dirty mouth, I did appreciate his bringing me back into the lively world of women. At the German Club I danced with girls prettier than Bette, but none had her wholesome personality. She had the character and brains and the beauty was underneath, where it counted. I wanted to see her again. I would go there next week by myself. I didn't need Saul to show me the way

Saul called me once on Wednesday afternoon, and then twice on Thursday, to join him for a coffee. Each time I told him I was busy and couldn't meet with him. Friday morning, he called again. Said he wanted to run by for a few minutes. I said I was tied up.

"Go fuck yourself," he said and hung up.

Thursday afternoon, Sven Nordoff came to my office with a man who looked like a cross between a football tackle and Paul Bunyan. I could also visualize him with a horn-hat charging into some quiet British coastal village, with rape and plunder in mind.

"Jim, I'd like you to meet my brother, Stidem. He's a steel worker. He helped build the Space Needle," Sven said with pride. "He wants to buy some stocks from you."

"Looks like if I'm ever to get any peace again," Stidem said, "I've got to buy some stock from you."

Sven chuckled and looked out the window.

"I don't have the time or like to fart around with this stock market. I'm no crapshooter. I want you to take this $3,000 and see what you can do with it." Stidem handed me six $500 bills. "Maybe now, Sven will give me some peace. He says you're some kind of genius."

"I wouldn't bet on it. We've had some lucky moves."

He ignored my statement and said, "I'll let you and Olga worry about which stocks to buy. That's my wife. I'll send her in. Well, little brother, guess we had better be going."

With that, old Blue Ox's friend was out the door. Down the hall I heard him yell, "You comin', little brother?"

Sven Nordoff stood up. The palms of his hands beckoned heavenward in resignation. "That's my big brother."

"He's an interesting fellow."

"But a bit trying," Sven said as he followed his brother out. At the door he turned back. "Jim, there's a young lady my family has sort of adopted that I want you to meet. I'd like to see you make her some money like you did for me."

"When would you suggest we get together, Sven?"

"How about Wednesday of next week after she gets off work?"

I looked at my calendar. "Suits me."

"I'll set it up." Then he chased after his brother.

Friday morning, Olga came in. She was a husky woman, almost as tall as Stidem, but her head rested on slightly humped shoulders. She was dressed like a farmer's wife, catalog print dress. Her wholesome country look suggested she'd be more comfortable in a dairy barn than in a stockbroker's office. Her demeanor said she was not afraid to tackle anything. I liked her instantly.

She suddenly said, "Stidem is a pain in the ass."

This surprised me. From Stidem's comments, I had assumed that he was laird and master, and that his wife was a submissive woman.

"How's that?"

"I don't want to manage his stupid stock account. Every time I sell something, I'll have to get his signature. He'll make a big fuss about it. I know him. If I make money, I'll be creating taxes for him and if I lose money, I'm bankrupting him."

"What would you propose? Should I just give him back his $3,000?"

"No. Let's just put his money in something super-safe, so I don't have to buy and sell all the time."

"We could do that, but do you think that is what he would really want?"

"I don't care what he wants. Besides, he won't know the difference. Sven tells me you're pretty good. I've saved up a couple thousand dollars of my own money that Stidem doesn't know about. Let's buy stocks with that, and we'll put it in my sister's name. I don't want him raving about taxes. I'll settle up on taxes with her. We'll just let Mr. Stidem stew in his own income juice, while we make some real money. How's that?"

"Sounds like fun to me. I'll join your conspiracy."

"Good. Let's have some fun."

I said, "Why don't we just put Stidem's money in a good safe convertible bond that will pay him current income and have some gain potential?" I felt sure this would be a good choice for him.

"Suits me, if I don't have to kiss his behind to get his signature."

"Nope. It's not likely that we would have to make any changes. He could spend his income."

"Ha! Him spend money? That old tightwad still has the first dollar they paid him to shovel cow shit back in South Dakota. I like your idea, though."

"Let's do it," I said. "Now we'll see what we can do to make your money do more than a two-step. That okay?"

"Just what I want to do. Let's have some jazz." She counted out $2,000 in small bills. I gave her a receipt, an account card for her sister to fill out, and a power of attorney form that appointed her as the one who would make investment decisions. She stood up, pushed out her hand to shake on our bargain. "You pick 'em, I'll buy 'em, Sonny. We'll show him," she said.

"Fine, Olga, let me give some thought to your account, and I'll call you."

As she left, she turned and said, "Let's don't say a word about our little arrangement to Stidem or Sven, okay? When I'm gone, I'd like to leave Stidem a little surprise." She waved 'bye as she left.

Olga reminded me of a farm lady who I fondly remembered from my childhood days, the mother of my two friends, the Jolson boys that I swam with in Wewoka Creek.

Saturday night, I walked up to the German Club by myself. I looked forward to seeing Bette again. Her enthusiasm would add a spark to a lonely weekend.

EIGHTEEN

Bette wasn't there like she said she would be. Saul wasn't there either. Thank God for that. About halfway though the evening, Bette's two roommates, Jeanie and Carol, came in and sat down on the other side of the room. They didn't see me. During the music-break, I went over and asked Jeanie, the small, dark, pretty one, if she would like to dance. She was shy and not so full of life as Bette, but it was nice to dance with her. For once, the German band played some soft music.

"I haven't seen Bette," I said. "Didn't she come?"

Her face clouded over with concern. "I don't know what happened. Last evening Bette went for her usual walk after dinner, but she didn't come back. You know we are roommates, don't you?"

"No. Just thought you were friends. Did you call the police?"

"Of course, but when we told them of her impulsiveness, they said they would put her on the missing person's list if she didn't show up after forty-eight hours." She looked toward Carol, who had sat out that dance and was drinking a glass of beer with some fellow who sat across the table from her.

"Any idea at all what has happened?"

"She may have just gone home," Carol said.

"Wouldn't she have said something?"

"Not necessarily. Bette does things on the spur of the moment when the mood hits her," Jeanie said.

"Did you call her home?"

"No. We don't know for sure where her home is, except that it's somewhere in Minnesota. She had just moved in with Carol and me two weeks ago. We met her here."

"I'm concerned. I wonder what might have happened to her."

"We just don't know. The police said they will put out an all-alert if she does not show in forty-eight hours."

I tried one more dance with Jeanie, but this piece of news killed my interest in dancing. I took Jeanie back to her table and went over to my pitcher of beer. I finished it off, listened to the music, just stared out at the dance floor, and then left.

On the way home, I wished that I had gotten Jeanie's phone number so I could check back on Bette. I guessed I'd see them next week.

When I got home, there was a note on the door from my landlady, Mrs. Henshaw. It was worded quite formally. They usually called me Jim. The note said, "Mr. Bradley, you will come down to our apartment, no matter how late you get back."

It was half past midnight when I knocked on their door, apartment number 101. They must have been in bed as Mr. Henshaw was in his bathrobe. He looked hard and angrily at me. "I don't want your friend to come back here anymore."

"What do you mean, Mr. Henshaw?"

"Your friend, that tall blond bastard you hang out with. He was here after eleven, drunk and bellowing up to your window from the courtyard. He wanted you to come down and fight."

"Doesn't sound like a friend of mine."

"Don't get smart!"

"Sorry, I didn't mean it that way."

"Threw rocks up at your window, so damn drunk he broke the window next to yours."

"Did he leave okay?"

Mr. Henshaw grinned. "Yeah, after I gave him a piece of my mind and told him to scram before I called the police."

"Sorry he gave you a bad time. I won't see him anymore. I've already written him off as a bad case."

"Says you're his only friend."

"And he wants to fight me. Ex-friend, you mean. I'll tell him how you feel about his coming around, if I ever see him again."

"He knows how I feel," and gave me that grin again.

I wondered what that was all about.

Monday morning at nine-thirty, Saul rushed into my office in a fury. He didn't clear through the receptionist at the front, just stormed his way back. His hulk engulfed my whole doorway. Dressed in dirty blue jeans and a red-checkered lumberjack shirt, he just stood there and looked at me with a scowl.

"You tell that goddamn son of a bitch landlord of yours to go to hell."

"Sounds like you already did."

"Tell the son of a bitch I'll get even with him."

"What's so upset you, Saul? You were the one who was drunk and causing a ruckus."

"That son of a bitch pissed in my face."

I burst into a belly laugh, and didn't calm down until I saw the hate in his eyes. Then I said, "Sorry, Saul. That just struck me as funny." It also explained Mr. Henshaw's grin.

"You can go to hell too, you son of a bitch." He turned and stomped his way out as fast as he had come.

Miss Shirley, steno pad still in hand, had hurried to the shouts. Spit and Polish was there at my door.

"What was that all about?" Tedmore, the old navy captain, asked.

"Not much," I said. "Just an ex-friend from Montcalm bidding me farewell."

Miss Shirley went back to her business as soon as she saw that everything was all right.

"What was he so angry about? That man sounded dangerous."

"I don't think so. Saul is just mad at life. He came by my place late Saturday night, drunk and hollering up at my window for me to come down, but I wasn't there."

"What happened to make him so angry?"

"My landlord tried to quiet him down. They argued and Saul must have thrown up some nasty insults. It scared the piss out of my landlord, because some of it landed in Saul's face."

"I'd be mad too." Then the old sailor muttered, "Such friends you have!" He went back to his office, shaking his head.

Just as Bill Tedmore left, the phone rang. Miss Shirley said, "Winona Flowerbell is holding for you."

Flowerbell...Flowerbell? I didn't know any Flowerbell. Then I remembered. She was that pretty Indian girl I had met on my first day of insurance inspections. She had invited me into her bedroom for the interview on her insurance policy, while she finished her nails. She was such a beautiful thing, sitting there in her thin nightgown. How could I forget her?

"Hello, this is Jim Bradley."

"Mr. Bradley, this is Winona. Remember me?"

"How could I forget my Indian soul mate? I met you when I was doing insurance inspections."

"You were going to call me after you got your brokerage connection."

"I forgot." Really, I just didn't want the temptation.

"Well, I've gotten married since then."

"Congratulations to the lucky fellow. I hope you'll be very happy."

"A little too soon to know, Mr. Bradley, but what I called you about, I have a quarter of a million dollars that I'd like you to help me manage. Can we get together to discuss it?"

"Be delighted."

"I'd like to have you meet my husband. He's a logging contractor. Are you available for dinner Wednesday night?"

"You bet." Then I remembered Sven Nordoff had set me up that night to go out with him to meet his young family friend.

"We'll be by to pick you up at eight. You still live at that place on Fifth & Blanchard?"

"Yes," I said, but I wondered how she knew that.

"See you then," and she hung up.

I called Sven Nordoff. You don't stall a quarter of a million dollar account. "Sven, could we possibly reschedule our appointment with Sonada McLean for Friday night rather than Wednesday?"

"I'll try. I hope you haven't screwed me up. You know, I've worked on her for months to get her to agree to see you."

"I'm sorry, Sven, but it can't be helped. Something has come up Wednesday that I can't get out of."

"I'll try."

"Thanks, Sven, I'd appreciate it if you can reschedule."

"I'll see what I can do."

"Thanks."

Promptly at nine-thirty on Tuesday morning, Miss Shirley escorted a Beau Brummell in a business suit to my office door. His courtly manner had bowled her over. She had not even called to see if it was convenient for me to talk with him. She just brought him on back, she told me later.

"Mr. Bradley, I am Bill Riley. You handle my wife's account, Clara."

Her name was like a clap of thunder. This woman had lost a big chunk of money. She had listened to me at first and made a bundle. Then her self-confidence had outgrown her senses. She boldly started making her own investment decisions. Now I was in trouble. He was going to blame me for her losses.

As he sat down, he said, "My wife has a gambling problem. You surely knew that. She is a compulsive gambler."

"I've noticed those tendencies and tried to temper her action."

"It looks to me like you've been churning her. Buying and selling just for commissions."

"No, I have not, and I've kept a diary of our conversations."

"I don't blame you. I'm sure you've covered your tracks."

"Not really. I know the regulators frown on brokers taking advantage of their clients, but mostly, I thought it would be useful to remind her of our past conversations, hopefully to temper her risk-taking."

"Well, what was her reaction?"

"She didn't remember the conversations. She did tell me that you didn't know anything about her investments. Said you didn't need to know, since it was her own personal money."

"That's not entirely true."

"She said you didn't see her confirmations," I said.

"I found where she hid them."

"Well, it looks to me like we both know what we're dealing with," I said. "What can we do about it?"

"She's so distraught about these losses that I'm afraid she might try to kill herself."

"If she'd give me a free hand, I could probably make it back for her," I said, and sincerely believed that I could.

"I have to somehow put a stop to this."

"Did you want to close her account?"

"No. I don't think that would be wise. If she finds out that I know what she's done, it might drive her over the edge."

"Mr. Riley, we both know we have to get her out of the securities business," I said.

"Just call me Bill. I think so too."

"Bill, I've told her that I think the stakes are too high for her to be in the stock market. Dollars are too big, and that for kicks she should play bingo."

"How did that go over?"

"She was insulted," I said.

"Do you have any ideas of what we can do?" he asked.

"Yes, I've thought about it and I think her gambling instinct goes pretty deep. You may not be able to take it away all at once," I said.

"What do you mean?"

"Bill, I know she's been very concerned about your reaction if you found out about her losses. She's told me so. Now that she's broke, she might be more humble. Maybe she'll listen to reason."

"What do you have in mind?"

"It's still a gamble, and you could lose more money."

"If it will save my wife, I'm interested."

"Let's do this," I said. "If you can put up some cash, I'll make her think that I've loaned it to her personally to help her catch up. But, I'll only do that for her if I make all the moves, and she promises to stay out of the market after I get her even. No more security trades. I'll suggest she take up church bingo. She can't get hurt much there."

"Jim, that sounds good to me. I came in here ready to slug you, or even sue you, for taking advantage of her weakness, but I think you're square."

"Thanks."

"Let's do it," he said. "I think this little conspiracy just might work. How much do you need?"

"I'd say five should do it."

"Jim, let's make her suffer just a little, not make it back too fast. Give her time to get used to bingo," he said.

"I'm with you."

162

He wrote a check made out to me personally for $7,500, and then wrote something on the back of it. On the endorsement side, he had written, "This is a six-month no-interest bearing loan."

"I'll trust your integrity. If you lose a little and don't make it back, I won't hang you. Just do the best you can."

"Fair enough."

As he left, I wondered if his wife really knew how lucky she was to have such a rare man as a husband. I knew she'd jump at the deal. I had seen the desperation in her face the last time she came in to see me.

That evening, as I came in the door of my building, the landlord's door opened. Mrs. Henshaw was there, her face all puffed up and red like she had been crying. I had come to like them. They were friendly again, since Saul hadn't been back.

"Is anything wrong, Mrs. Henshaw?"

"Mr. Bradley, you haven't heard what happened?"

"Heard what?"

"Yesterday afternoon, Charlie was up on a ladder to fix that third-story broken window. He must have lost his balance and fell."

"Is he in the hospital?" Probably a dumb question, with her crying and all, but I didn't know what else to say.

"No. He died this afternoon."

"I'm so terribly sorry. I hadn't heard."

She wiped her eyes and said, "Charlie hit his head on the sidewalk. Went into a coma and never regained consciousness."

"Mrs. Henshaw, please let me know if there is anything I can do."

"Thanks, Mr. Bradley, I will."

I went on up to my room. Mr. Henshaw had been especially nice to me. When I first moved in, he had made special efforts to make me feel welcome. He had somehow sensed that I was at a low point. He even took me fishing with him a few times, until I had gotten too busy to go out with him. I had caught my first salmon with him. I was sorry that Saul had given him such a bad time.

On Wednesday evening at ten minutes to eight, a six or seven-year-old Indian boy came to my door. "Mommy's in the car. She sent me to get you."

"And you are?" I asked.

"Mr. Bradley, I'm George."

"Well, George, my pleasure," and I shook his hand.

I saw this astonishingly beautiful woman in the car. Winona smiled and motioned for me to get in the front seat, and young George jumped in the back seat. I got in and sat beside her. She was dressed in a long, sleek green and red dress that fitted snugly and made her look more like an Oriental beauty, than an

American Indian. She would put Aphrodite to shame. I saw no husband. How could he let something like that run free?

"I'm so glad you could come. We have a lot to discuss."

"I appreciate the invitation."

As we drove toward the restaurant, she volunteered, "Rod did not feel well, so he stayed home."

"I'm sorry," I lied. "I looked forward to meeting him." I wondered how a husky logging contractor would pass up a steak dinner and allow his beautiful wife go out to dinner with another man, just because he didn't feel good. Maybe he was drunk and passed out. Those guys sometimes were heavy drinkers.

"We'll get along just fine without him. At least you've met my son, George, who has come back from the reservation to live with me. He sometimes stays with his grandmother."

"How did you know I lived at Fifth and Blanchard?"

"Jim, I know a lot about you. You don't just turn over a quarter of a million dollars to a stranger to manage. I found out that you are most well-regarded at Jones Bylor."

"Who did you talk to at Jones Bylor's?"

"I think it was a Miss Shirley."

"She's the first person I met in Seattle."

"I also found out that you had an unhappy marriage that ended when a foolish wife ran off with an older man."

"Doesn't sound like Miss Shirley left much untold."

"She wasn't the only person I had talked with. I also found out that you most always make money for your clients."

"Not everything turns out."

She smiled and said, "The only thing I don't know, Jim, is how long it takes for the market to rise and fall." She glanced down at my lap.

I blushed and got down to business. "Is this conservative money you want to invest, or speculative, or is it both?"

"Just show me some action."

"I'll do the best I can for you."

"Do it well and maybe I can direct some of the tribe's money your way. They have a much larger investment fund that comes from mineral extraction."

"That would be wonderful."

"Enough about business for now. George and I are taking you to Rosellini's 410."

After we were settled in at the plush restaurant that belonged to Governor Rosellini's cousin, I tried to make conversation. "Winona, how did you meet your husband?"

"Met him at the Club 99. Used to be the hatcheck girl there."

"You worked there?" I knew it was a girlie place, and I wondered if hatcheck work was all she did there.

"Oh, part time when I got bored. Rod used to come in with his lumber cronies. I've told you he's a logging contractor."

"Yes, you mentioned that. I wonder how a husky lumber contractor really feels about me out with his wife at night."

"Don't worry about it. I've got my son with us."

"Guess a girl does get to meet a lot of interesting people at that sort of job."

"Not always the best people, lots of propositions, but the tips are good."

Young George paid no attention to this conversation, but looked around at other people in his quiet stoic way.

"Guess that gave you lots of choices."

"I never went out with any of them, but Rod always gave me such lavish tips, and he kept trying, so I finally dated him."

"Persistence pays off."

"I think he was looking for an easy lay."

"Well?"

"Certainly not! But, you should have seen how shocked he was, when he found out that I, a hatcheck girl, could buy and sell him several times."

"Such a good catch should have pleased him."

"Not so. I think an easy lay would have pleased him more. His ego can't take it. He likes to be the big man."

"He should count his blessings. A rich wife is one hell of a lot better than having one who always nags for money."

"When he's in a pinch, he gets angry when I won't advance him any money."

"Don't blame you for being careful."

"After I married, I found him out. He's a heavy drinker and a compulsive gambler. I should have known that, the way he always came to the bar so much."

"That his trouble tonight?"

The waiter came up. Winona ordered salmon for herself and young George and I ordered a T-bone.

"No," she said as soon the waiter left. "The bastard said I could take my stockbroker and go to hell. He was going down to the whorehouse where there were real women."

"Sounds like you picked a good one."

"I could have done better. I didn't know you were available."

I smiled at her and said, "Timing is everything."

I didn't want to get involved in this triangle. She was a married woman. Even with his silence, little George's presence helped relieve my discomfort of being out with another man's wife. I had not had a woman for over two years, one as a single man; the other, a year of Lois's rejection. I felt somewhat like my dog, Blacky, must have felt when I was a child. Restrained behind a fence, he could only watch the other fellows go.

I changed the subject. "Tell me about yourself. You didn't make over $200,000 as a hatcheck girl. That would take a lot of tips."

"Hardly. I'm Osage. My family came into some pretty good oil money."

"You mean the lawyers and judges didn't get away with it?"

"No. My father was a smart chief. He had trust funds set up for all his children."

"You're lucky to have a smart father. Where I came from, the lawyers and trustees ended up with most of the Indian money."

"I know. And I won't have some pale-face logger steal my money either. Will we, George?" She tried to include him in the conversation.

"I guess not," George said and continued to look out the window.

"Did you grow up in Oklahoma?" I asked.

"Yes, and we were very poor, until they struck oil on our land. When that happened, I got to spend time in Rome, Paris. Even attended some college in England."

"Sounds like your life sure beat chopping cotton or that of a poor reservation Indian."

"We were fortunate," she said.

After a dinner of lively conversation and too much red wine, we headed home. To my surprise, she did not drop me off first. My apartment was only four blocks from the restaurant, but instead, she headed to her place in Kirkland. She noted my puzzlement and said, "It's so terribly late. George is sleepy. Let's drop him off and I'll bring you back."

"Okay," I said, but it seemed strange.

At that late hour the misty lights on the floating bridge sparkled. I could hear foghorns on nearby Puget Sound behind us. When we reached her palatial Eastside home, the same place where I had interviewed her for the insurance report, she nudged young George awake. "Run on in, Honey. I'll be back home in a little while."

On the way back to Seattle, she again went into her woes with Rod. His impulsive gambling had required her to rescue him many times. She had picked up his markers from some rather ruthless people. Rod, when sober, was a fun guy, but when drunk, he was a loser. She did not know what to do. She was so unhappy with him.

"Dump him if he's that bad. Myself, I wasted ten years with the wrong woman. I wouldn't do it again."

There was a chuckle. "I'm not quite ready to commit suicide."

We reached my place. She parked in front, and turned off the motor.

I said, "Thanks for a great evening," and started to get out.

"No, don't go." She grabbed my hand and held it. "I want to talk," she said. She continued to chat about this and that, and seemed to say almost anything to make conversation.

I knew what I was supposed to do. I could just visualize how it would be to make love with her. Slowly unzip that sleek gown and remove her bra. Then I remembered, I had not made up my bed that morning. In my haste to get to work, I had just folded it up into the wall. What a mess.

She, obviously, was in no hurry to go home, even if it was early dawn. Such a temptress—why did she have to be married?

Thirty more minutes of this idle conversation. Her brown eyes, her breasts, so round and firm, pulled like a magnet. I said, "It's almost two. Hadn't I better let you get home? No telling what he'll do to you." I started to get out again.

"No! Who cares what Rod thinks?" She grabbed my arm. "Don't go yet. I want to talk some more."

I thought of Zorba the Greek, and his philosophy. Don't ever refuse to bed a woman when she wants it. Then I thought, that don't count if she's a married woman. After a few more minutes I started to get out again. She grabbed my arm again and said, "No! Don't go yet." She smiled and leaned over closer against me. I could feel her warmth, her breasts were in full view. I could kiss them so easily. Oh, how I wanted to! Oh God! Why do you do this to me? She's a married woman! I want her!

This brown treasure was all mine. All I had to do was, take it. My shoulders trembled in anticipation, at the very thought. If I didn't, I'd lose a client. That's always bad business. She'd be my biggest one. I could have a lover and a client too. She was there, just waiting for me, this beautiful woman. All I had to do was say, "Come on up and I'll show you my apartment." She leaned over again and still held my hand. I kissed her breasts. I thought of Zorba the Greek and his philosophy. A man who denies a woman is not a man. I felt my arms squeezing her up close to me and burying my face in her bosom. So beautiful, so easy, yet I mustn't. I'd never done this with another man's wife. It was against every principle that I had ever learned from talks with my grandmother, my mother, all those Sunday school classes at the First Baptist Church. No! I could not rob another man's bed.

I pulled away. "Sorry, Winona, I can't. I want to, so much. You're married. I've got to go." I got out of the car. The streetlight fell on her face like moonlight as she looked up at me. I could see her bewilderment slowly turn to rage.

"Son of a bitch," she said.

She dug out with a roar that awakened people two blocks away. I stood there, some moments, just looked down the street where she disappeared. There went a quarter of a million dollars, the most beautiful woman that I had ever met. Both could have been mine.

I climbed up, one step at a time, the three flights, as though I climbed to the gallows. I pulled down my messy bed, and flopped on it. Disgusted with myself, I muttered, "Damn prude, damn fool, damn stupid prude! Look what you missed. You could have had her right here, now, on this bed. Instead, Boy Scout, you've lost the biggest client you ever had."

Hell! Why did I have to have principles? Might as well have done it, I did it in my mind. Zorba the Greek would have kicked my ass. I needed my own woman, a wife, and I needed her now. That was clear. Bachelorhood wasn't much fun for a man with morals. Where was she? Where did she hide, this girl with character, brains and beauty? Winona had the brains and beauty, but she was not free. Her character, who knew? If she'd play around with me, how long would she be true to me? Where is this true goddess I seek? Does she exist on this earth? Oh, God, please help me to find her soon. Don't tempt me again. I might not be so stupid next time.

NINETEEN

It was two-thirty before I got to sleep. There was work to do at the office in the morning. I needed to be fresh. I finally resolved the matter in my mind. What would it matter three years from now? The pleasure would be forgotten. Yet if I had slept with another man's wife, it would haunt me 'til the end of my time.

It seemed that I had hardly gone to sleep when I heard a knock on my door. I looked at my watch. It was four-thirty. Who would call at this hour? I went to the door.

"Who is it?"

"Saul."

"What the hell are you doing here this early?"

"Open up, Jim," he whispered. "I gotta talk to you."

It had been over a month since I had seen Saul Carlson. I opened the door. A shaggy three-day beard covered his face. He had on the same dirty blue jeans. His lumberjack shirt was torn. He looked like a tramp with sunglasses on. There was a large trunk on a dolly. He was slightly out of breath. He had manhandled that large trunk up three flights of steps, pulled the dolly up one step at a time.

He whispered, "Jim, I gotta ask you a favor."

I had not invited him in yet. "How did you know I would be home?"

"I figured you'd be here at four-thirty in the morning. You're too damn holy to shack up with anyone," he said with a sneer.

"Saul, you look a mess. Are you all right? Come on in."

He wheeled the huge trunk through my doorway. "Jim, can I leave this trunk with you for a while?"

"Why?"

"Got to leave town for a few months. Job out of state. My truck broke down, so I have to travel light. Trunk's too big to take on the bus."

"I guess so, Saul. What's up?"

"Got fired."

"How did you get that trunk all the way over here from your place without your truck?"

"Only a couple of miles. I used the dolly."

"You must be exhausted. Sit down and rest a while."

"Thanks, Jim, but gotta go. Bus to catch. Where do you want this?"

"Put it over there by the window. I'll use it for an end table and lamp stand."

"Thanks, Jim. I really appreciate it. You'll be long remembered for this."

He waved and was gone. It was a large metal steamer trunk, about eighteen inches high when on its side, and was well secured with a thick padlock. The trunk made a nice place to put the table lamp I had picked up at Goodwill in my days of poverty.

Friday evening, I drove my green Volkswagen beetle up to Sven Nordoff's place on Capitol Hill. Sven had squared it away with his friend. She had agreed to meet me. It was one of those rare Seattle winter evenings when the air was crisp and a light snow swirled on the ground, pushed by the wind. It was a good night for a brisk walk, so we hiked the few blocks on over to her apartment.

Sonada McLean hurried us in, so she could close the door against the cold. Her hair was dark; she had brown eyes, a noble face, and a shape that blended well. Her beauty was awesome. She wasn't dressed up, just a black sweatshirt and blue jeans, but she did wonders for the jeans and the sweatshirt. Her apartment was modest, well-kept, but looked lived in. There were two works of art on the wall, a Northwest coastal scene of an old boathouse with a boat in front of it and a Picasso print from his blue period. Books of literary quality overflowed the shelves and were stacked against the wall. She had a record player and her classical records stood upright on the floor supported on each side by small statuettes of elephants. Elephants were everywhere.

I said to her, "Elephant hunter?"

"Not hunter, lover." She corrected me with a Mona Lisa smile.

"You a Republican?"

"God, no! Don't insult the elephants."

She introduced me to Robert, a blond-haired, blue-eyed man about her age. Sven seemed to already know her boyfriend. Sven had said nothing about her being married. I did not see a ring on her finger.

She then introduced me to Bonné, her standard poodle. Robert didn't say much, just sat off to the side. He served us coffee and made a comment or two to Sven about the weather and asked how things were at Boeing.

Sven became animated and charming. After the preliminaries, he said, "Jim, I've tried for months to get this gal to this meeting."

"He certainly has," Sonada said to me. "Almost every time I've seen him, all I hear is, 'You've got to meet this financial genius.' So! Here we are. Okay, Genius, show me your stuff."

Sonada, somehow, looked familiar. Where had I seen her before? How could I forget someone so beautiful?

"I'm afraid Sven may have oversold me. We've had some lucky moves in a strong market."

She gave that impish Mona Lisa smile again. "Trying to set me up just in case you lose my money, eh?"

"If you decide to invest, I want to see only the money you can afford to lose."

"You do cover your tracks, don't you?"

"No, that's not my intention, but I do want you to know that there are risks. Stocks do go up and stock do go down."

"My! You're profound."

Then, we heard movement in the next room, a bedroom I presumed. A young voice said, "Mother, can I have a drink of water?"

Sonada left and when she came back, she led a sleepy four-year-old child. "Mr. Bradley, this is David, man of the house."

I received a shy, "Hello." Then his eyes brightened up, and a big smile came when he recognized Sven. Satisfied with his drink of water, David went back to bed.

The conversation ranged from art to the war in Vietnam. Her attitude shocked me. She said, "I don't think Ho Chi Minh is so bad. He's the Abe Lincoln of Vietnam."

I wondered. Was she a Communist? She didn't like Republicans.

Then Sven Nordoff added a couple of nasty comments about "Dirty Dick." He meant Nixon.

Was I in a bed of lefties? Since I never discussed religion or politics with clients, I changed the subject. I asked her, "How did a dark-haired, brown-eyed girl get a Scot name?"

"My grandmother married a Scotsman, who was a miner. She was Croatian and they came over here and settled in the Pennsylvania coal mining area. My father did that kind of work too. Guess I'm a coal miner's daughter."

"So that explains it."

"Well, just tell me," she said, "How did a Jim Bradley get red hair?"

"I'm a mongrel, Scot-Irish with a bit of Cherokee Indian."

"Oh! Native American."

"Most every Oklahoman has a little Indian," I said.

"How'd you get your Indian? Raped or slumming?" the Norwegian said, trying to be funny.

"Not sure, but my great-grandmother was half-Cherokee," I said. "I grew up with Indians, some of them classmates. They were fine people."

Robert seemed bored. I didn't want to overstay our welcome. Since this was only a get acquainted meeting, I didn't think we should stay long. Certainly, I shouldn't discuss any investment specifics. Personal finances were her private business, not to be discussed in the presence of these other two men.

171

After our second cup of coffee, I said, "Sonada, let me give some thought to your investment situation. I'll get back to you with some ideas. We can talk some more on the phone." With that, we left.

Outside, as we walked back to Sven's place, I said, "Her husband is a quiet one. He didn't say more then five words all evening."

Sven laughed. "That's not her husband. That's her brother."

"Oh," I said, and faked disinterest. But, I walked with clouds under my feet. Here was a true CBB, character, brains and beauty. I'd get to know her better, even if she was a client.

"Wait 'til you get to know Robert," he said. "Then you won't be able to shut him up."

I had already forgotten about her brother. "Sven, she seems like such a nice person. I would certainly like to make her some real money."

"Just don't lose it. She doesn't make that much as a dental technician."

"I'll do my best."

"She is like family to us," he said. "We've kind of adopted her as our own."

By this, I later found out, he meant himself, his brother, sister, and their elderly parents, with whom his sister lived.

It took a couple of weeks to find investment ideas on which I was willing to risk Sonada's money. Such a commitment had to be safe, yet have pizzazz enough to move. Of the $500 she committed, I decided to put half of it into a small electronic company, and the rest into a San Diego financial conglomerate that everyone talked about.

It was Friday evening, after she had time to get home from work, that I called. I wanted to advise her of my investment choices, and let her think about it over the weekend. I could execute the orders first thing Monday if she went along. Before she answered, while the phone still rang, I got smart. Why blow this chance to get better acquainted? Why give her advice over the phone?

"Sonada, this is Jim Bradley, Jones Bylor. I've given some thought to your investment situation."

"I thought you had forgotten me and my trivial account," she said. "I'm such small potatoes."

"No, of course not, I wanted to find something really good for you. Say, by the way, are you free for lunch tomorrow? Like to go over some ideas with you."

"What if I don't like your ideas?"

"You can always say no."

"What time?"

"Noon okay?"

"Suits me."

"Shall I come by for you?"

"No, I'll meet you at your office. That way I can see the lion in his lair."

"Great, then I'll see you at noon." At last, I'd have her all to myself. It was a whole night and half a day away.

Saturday morning, noon, and she still hadn't come. I hadn't done much work that morning. My mind was on Sonada and how I might convert her into a date that evening. I had the office all to myself, so I left a note up front directing her to ring the buzzer.

At 12:10, she was at the front door, hair windblown and cheeks red from the cold. Wow, what a knockout she was. She was dressed in black, no hat, red scarf around her neck, and a warm gray wool coat, which she had already unbuttoned. Her smile sent my blood rushing.

Back in my office, she said, "So this is the lion's den. Where is the rest of the pride?"

"Probably out in the fields stalking little round white balls."

"Golf, in this kind of weather?"

"You know Seattle. Golf nuts play, rain, snow, sleet or hail. Sunshine is a treat."

"True."

"Come on, I'll show you the office, and then let's cut out for lunch. We can talk business there."

"Oh! You're not going to do business with me, right here among all this splendor?"

I smiled, wished I could, but said, "Now, this over here is our trading department." I led her across the hall. "Down this way is our accounting office." I showed her some of the other offices, Old Spit and Polish's with the hand-carved sailing vessels, Jiggs's office with the collector vases and expensive paintings on the wall. Those she noted carefully. She knew of the painters. Then I showed her Mr. Bylor's spacious office, sterile of personal effects.

As we passed Mr. Hackett's office, her nose turned up. "What a messy office."

"Not messy, he's just busier than hell, has lots of things going."

"How does he find anything?"

"Believe me, that's not a worry. He's an octopus. He has his hands into everything."

"No thanks. I'll settle for Broker Jim."

"Pays to watch him too."

There was that Mona Lisa smile again.

We walked back to my office. "Have a seat while I straighten things up."

I put things away that I didn't want to leave on top of my desk, and then said, "Let's go to lunch."

I helped her with her coat. My blood tingled when her hair brushed my arm. "We can walk," I said.

All during lunch, I tried to pick up nerve enough to ask her out. A "no" would have shattered me like a boot heel on a frozen pond. I didn't want to chase her away by being pushy. Sven had told me that she had been divorced for three years. When her husband left town, he took all the assets and left her all the bills. Would she risk another man? Would I have a chance? She might be so sour on men in general, that she would tell me to go jump.

"Now down to business," I said. "I've picked a couple of ideas that I think would be a good investment for you."

"Jim, like I said, put me into anything you think best. I'll trust you, with my money."

"Is that all?" I said, and gave her a playful grin. My time had faded. I had to act now, or I'd miss my chance.

She smiled in return.

As we got up to leave, I blurted out like a green school kid, "How about a date tonight? Let's take in a movie."

"Okay."

"I'll be by at six-thirty."

I could have stormed the Bastille, I was so elated. I had found my CBB. She had it all, character, brains and beauty. Now if I could just get her to accept an MRS degree, my life would be splendid. I hadn't told Sven Nordoff that my interest in her had grown to more than just a client relationship. I'd surprise him. When I got her to say yes, I'd ask him to be my best man.

My friendship with Sven had grown. It was more than just business. He had become a pal. I even enticed him to go for a sail with me on my yacht, the $200 plastic sailboard boat that required a bathing suit. When he hesitated, I gave his ego a thump. "I thought Vikings were not afraid of water."

It was a Saturday afternoon in late summer when we acted like true Vikings and set out to conquer Lake Washington on my plastic sailboard. A big cruiser came by on its way to Lake Union and probably headed for the Chittenden Locks and out to Puget Sound. The cruiser's huge wake flipped us over. While I righted the boat, my Viking friend scrambled to recover his cellophane-wrapped cigars floating all around him. We crawled aboard our little boat and made for shore. Both of us burst out laughing at ourselves—two grown men on a plastic board on a lake. On shore, we found a park-like spot and recouped our dignity with cigars and beer. There truly was a life after Lois, and a damn good one.

A few weeks passed, and Sonada's couch had become quite familiar, her kisses longer and harder. I didn't know how much longer I could hold off. One evening when I took her home, she invited me in. That night she had left David at the babysitter's home. She fixed the coffee and it smelled good. It wasn't cold, but I built a fire in the fireplace. We sat close and I held her hand. I turned out the light and kissed her and kissed her again. We lay on the couch close and tight with me almost on top of her.

The flickering of the firelight cast shadows on her face. I said, "Sonada, will you marry me?"

"Did you have to ask?"

"Sonada, you're the only woman I have ever really wanted."

"You have me. Isn't that enough?"

"I love you, and I want to marry you."

She raised up and sat on the couch, looking at the fire, not at me.

"Jim, don't spoil it. No way will I ever marry again."

"I want you to be my wife."

"Let's enjoy each other's company and leave it at that. The only permanent man I have room for in my life is David."

Backing off with a temporary defeat, I said, "Sonada, sounds like your first marriage ended up in hell, just like mine."

"You might say that, but let's drop the subject."

We retreated back to light love, until it was time for me to go.

Monday morning, when I went into the office, there was a note that Sven Nordoff had called. I returned his call just before the sales meeting. "Jim, there is some bad news you should know about."

"What is it, Sven?"

"Olga. She had a stroke, died almost instantly."

"No! Not Stidem's wife."

"Yes, she died Sunday night."

"Sven, Olga became one of my favorite people. Stidem okay?"

"He won't show it, but you know it hurts."

"He's got quite a surprise coming, Sven."

"What surprise?" he asked.

"Can't say right now, Sven, but you'll know, soon. Are you sure Stidem's all right?"

"I don't know. Always macho. But now he's like a shipwrecked sailor, lost. Olga always managed the house," he said.

"I'll give him a call."

"He'd appreciate that," he said.

"Thanks so much for letting me know, Sven."

I had grown to like Olga very much. I would miss her earthy country philosophy. I decided to wait until after the sales meeting before I called Stidem, and before I told him anything about his good fortune, I had some things to square away.

After the meeting I called Stidem and expressed my condolences. Later, at the funeral, for the first time I saw him in a suit. The pants were too short, and they made him look like Ichabod Crane. Of course, we didn't discuss any business there.

When I called Stidem a few days later, he sounded calm. I could almost see his stiff upper lip through the telephone line.

"Stidem, I think it would be wise for you to come in. I have some important business to discuss with you."

"The stock market don't interest me none," he said. "I don't pay any attention to it."

"I know, but Olga did. You need to find out what she did for you."

"I'll be right down."

Stidem stood in front of my desk not more than thirty minutes later. "What'd she do to me?"

"I don't think it will smart too much, Stidem." I could have poked the son of a bitch in the nose, right then.

"Well, what did she do?"

I pulled out his personal account sheet.

"That looks pretty good," he said. "I only gave her $3,000, and you show it's worth $5,000 now."

"Yes, it beats bank interest," I said.

"I'm happy with it. Guess I gave Olga a bad time. At first she'd tell me what she did, and then she quit saying anything about it. I figured she'd lost money and was afraid to say anything."

"Stidem, there's more."

"What do you mean?"

"Olga invested some of her own money that she had in a cookie jar."

"She never had any money. I always paid for everything, 'cept the groceries which she shopped for."

"She came up with $2,000 from somewhere, Stidem."

"So that's what she did. Knocked down on the grocery money."

I didn't respond to that.

"Fifty thousand. That's what she made it grow to."

"What!" You've seen fat men whose bellies bulged over their belts through unbuttoned shirts. Well, that's the way Stidem's eyes looked, when he said, "I'll be damned. When can I get it?"

"Right away, soon as a copy of the death certificate and instructions of the executor are made available to us."

"I can give that to you right away," he said, and reached into his coat pocket.

"We can draw up a check in a week after her account is liquidated. I presume you want to sell at market." I did not mention income tax. Let him sweat that out later. But to save his ego, I didn't tell him that I had already obtained the paperwork from his sister-in-law, releasing her interest in the account, as previously arranged by Olga.

"Good."

"Sure you don't want to put some of it to work for you?"

He smiled. "I'll take the cash, and by the way, Jim, go ahead and sell my other stocks."

"You mean the convertible bonds?"

"Whatever you and Olga bought," he said.

Stidem got up to leave. I shook his hand. I was out when he came by a week later to pick up his check. After that I never saw him again. Stidem wasn't too bashful to quit a winner.

TWENTY

My take-home commissions now averaged three grand a month, against the $360 that had been my last pay at Montcalm. I made almost as much money as the governor did, if you did not count his perks. I felt rich, but I stayed in my $65 a month third-floor walk-up. All my debts were paid and I had some investments on my own. I smugly felt that Lois had abandoned ship too soon. I heard that they were okay up there in Alaska. Her contractor husband's business prospered, but I wondered how many years he'd keep it up.

My stock choices seemed infallible. Everything I bought went up, but then again, most everyone won in 1968, just like almost everyone lost in 1929. I wondered when corporate blood would run again. Mae Belle felt so flush that she pulled $5,000 out of her account and hired a geologist to work on her dead Joe's mining claims. Sven Nordoff sent me more of his Boeing friends. Benjamin Ergstein, my Dow Theory plunger, left town when his wife divorced him, and I lost contact. His former father-in-law, Mr. Toola, as well as his bridge partner, Mrs. Tremble, sent more and more people in to me. I thought they had sent all of their friends in, but still more came.

There were no black Mondays. Big names joined Bing Resources board of directors. Support for their oil drilling limited partnerships shot up like gushers. Bing's private jet sucked more money out of the investment community than air through its jet engine vents. Stockbrokers from all over the country were given free rides to the headquarters of this fast-rising oil company to participate in their "educational" meetings.

Mr. Hackett had gotten pretty chummy with Bing by now. We all decided to take advantage of their educational program. Mr. Hackett, Daniel Lews, Jim Swenson, myself, and of course, the ever present Ralph Bailor, all flew down to San Francisco by commercial airliner. From there, Bing's private jet whisked us on to Denver for a three-day "educational" seminar.

I had never before seen so many drunks seeking an "education." We stayed up way past midnight and almost until dawn. We drank cocktails, wine, hard liquor, and visited with pretty girls, mostly airline hostesses on their spare time, all good clean fun. I never heard that any of them raised their skirts higher than they should have. Next morning, a breakfast of steak and eggs; then bleary-eyed, we torturously tried to stay awake during class sessions.

At lunch break, I said to Mr. Hackett, "You know, if they'd cut out these parties and let us get to bed at night, we might learn something the next day."

He just laughed and said, "Bradley, who in the hell is interested in learning anything? These guys are down here for a party. Relax and enjoy yourself. They'll give you lots of reading material that you can study when we get back."

I didn't learn much on that trip, met mainly other stockbrokers, most of whom said they thought Bing was a good investment. On the way back, still in Bing's plane, pretty girls bobbed wine bottles up and down like oil pumps filling us with booze. They served crackers with some kind of spread that you could hardly see in the dim light. Everyone made a big to-do about it. Personally, I didn't care for it, and said so in an undertone to Daniel Lews, "What the hell is this stuff?"

In a boozy, loud voice, he shouted, "You dumb-ass, don't you know what caviar is?"

"I've never really tasted the stuff before," I said.

Monday, after my return from Denver, Sven Nordoff sped into my office about midmorning like a whirlwind. He was downtown on an errand for Boeing, and was aglow like Northern Lights. "I might get married," he blurted.

"Who's the lucky girl? I thought you said, 'Never again.'"

"I won't say. Not 'til I get a final answer, but I'm close."

"That's just great, Sven. I'm happy for you."

"Would you be my best man?"

"Certainly, would love to, just say when."

With that emotional release gone, he left as fast as he came in.

Everything important seems to happen on Monday. That evening, after everyone else had gone home, Mr. Hackett came into my office. He sat down, which struck me as unusual. He always called me into his office, held his conferences in between phone calls, as he paced around his desk. He seemed pensive as he sat down. The tips of his fingers came together as though in meditation or prayer. He sat there quietly. I got the strangest feeling that something was on its way that would shatter my world.

"Jim," he said, "I want to give you something to think about. Whatever your decision, this meeting didn't take place."

"What's on your mind, Mr. Hackett?"

"Well, Broker Jim, my friend, I have made an irrevocable decision."

"What have I done now, Mr. Hackett?"

"I'm leaving Jones Bylor."

"You're leaving Jones Bylor!"

"Yes."

"The way you came in here, I thought I was leaving."

"Maybe you will."

"What do you mean?"

"Brodrick Bylor is satisfied to stay just as we are," Mr. Hackett said. "I don't want to piss away my life in a small firm forever. I want to grow."

"You leave, we won't be Jones Bylor anymore."

"Then how about Tiger Hackett & Company?"

"What's that?"

"A new firm I've organized."

"Who's Tiger?"

"Our symbol or logo. No pussycats allowed!"

"Sounds exciting. Am I invited?"

"Why do you think I'm here?"

Mr. Hackett stood up and paced around like his old self. "I want you, Lews and Swenson to join me. That gives us a start of five partners."

"Who's the fifth?"

"Malcomb Baskum, you know, that client of mine with megabucks."

"This is a surprise. I'd always assumed that you would take command of Jones Bylor when Mr. Bylor retired."

"I don't want to waste that much time."

"Frankly, Mr. Hackett, I'm shocked and a bit confused."

"Let's go over to Trader Vic's and talk. Don't want to be accused of proselytizing here," he said with a smile.

As we left the office, I said, "Brodrick? I've never heard Mr. Bylor called that name before."

"He didn't want you to. He's a junior who hated his father, so he goes by B. Bylor. Frankly, I think he'd rather be called Lord Bylor."

"So that's why the old heads call him BB. I thought it was because he's so short."

"Nope. That's his name, Brodrick."

As we took our seats in the richly furnished Trader Vic's, we ordered brandies and lit our cigars while our eyes adjusted to the subdued lights.

To lighten up, I said, "Guess this setting makes the old fellows feel safe when they're out playing footsie under the table with young secretaries."

"You, Lews and Swenson can each buy up to 5 percent," he said. "Baskum gets 25 percent interest. He's put up some big bucks and a substantial block of subordinated capital."

"Who gets the rest?"

"I do."

"How much is this 5 percent going to cost me?"

"Ten thousand. With Baskum's fifty cash and hundred subordinated, ten each from you guys, we'll make it. With mine, we'll have a base of two hundred fifty thousand.

"That's not a lot of capital."

"We'll make it grow."

"I don't have $10,000."

"Can you put together five?"

"Probably."

"Good, get busy and find five, and I'll get Baskum to loan you the other five."

"That's pretty generous."

"You'll earn it."

"When do you have to know?"

He looked a little hurt. "Pronto! When I tell Bylor tomorrow morning, that's the end of my Jones Bylor career."

"How do Jim and Dan feel about this?" I asked.

"Swenson's in. You talk to Lews. He's your buddy, isn't he?"

"We commiserate together."

"Good. Bring him in and you're each a vice-president."

"A?"

"Yes. I've saved "the" for some big game."

"I'll see what Dan thinks."

He then stubbed his cigar out in the ashtray. "Cigars first is a bit ass-backwards, but now let's have some dinner, soon as this smoke clears."

"It'll be a tornado tomorrow!" I said. "Mr. Bylor will be on the warpath."

"Worse than that. Wait 'til word hits the street."

"Mr. Hackett..."

"Don't call me that anymore. You're a partner. Just John."

"Well, Mr. Hack... uh' John, you backed me when I was on the way out. Mr. Bylor was ready to dump me. I appreciated that, deeply. I'm sure I'll go along, but I'd like a couple of nights to sleep on it, and talk with Dan."

"Sure, just give me a call." He scribbled a number on the back of one of his cards. "Here's my home number. Doubt seriously if I'll be around here after tomorrow."

"I'll touch base in a couple days," I said.

Mr. Bylor conducted the sales meeting on Tuesday morning. He discussed the potential of a local electronics company. I thought he would say something about Mr. Hackett, but he did not. I looked at Swenson, but he gave no sign. Dan Lews didn't either, but I had not talked with him yet. After a thirty-minute dissertation on the merits of the new underwriting, Mr. Bylor asked for indications of interest. Then he dismissed the meeting.

About noon pandemonium broke out. Clerk whispers started it "Have you heard? Mr. Hackett's leaving."

All stockbrokers immediately came under suspicion. Who's going? Who's staying? It didn't take long for me to learn that the old guard were all "stays." I was shocked at the animosity expressed towards Mr. Hackett, even after all that money he made for the firm with his different deals.

Spit and Polish said, "Who'd want to join that scalawag?"

"Hackett will be on the rocks in less than six months," was Jiggs's response.

"I'd hang the son of a bitch," said John Lucas.

Only one person had a kind word for Mr. Hackett, and that was Miss Shirley. She praised his past good works.

My old competitor, Jim Swenson, told management right off, "I'm leaving."

"You can clear your office in an hour," Mr. Bylor told him.

Management regarded Dan and me as young, naive and, unfortunately, subject to Hackett's bad influence. We must be protected from our own folly.

Jiggs said to me right after the meeting, "Let's go to lunch."

He took me to his country club and we rode in his Rolls Royce. This was the first time that he'd invited me to lunch. The club was a palatial place. They had uniformed waiters.

"Now see here, Jim, old friend, we mustn't have you making any hasty moves. Charming fellow, this Hackett. Nice one to know, but a risky one to tack your fate to. You've done well here, Jim, and you have a fine future with Jones Bylor. Stay with us, my friend, and I will recommend to the executive committee that you be made full partner, and soon. Your destiny lies here with Jones Bylor, not with this Hackett fellow."

I didn't interrupt Jiggs. He gave speeches and didn't like to be cut in on, just like he must have when he headed his own sizable firm. I let him finish, and when he was talked out, he touched his lips with his napkin. I figured then it was safe to have my say.

"Jiggs, I really appreciate your thoughts and especially your friendly advice. I've always valued your wise counsel."

"I told Miss Shirley from the very beginning that this fellow, Jim, had the makings of a successful broker. I really mean that," he said.

"I'm still cogitating, Jiggs, and here's my problem. I love this firm and I like all the people. Everyone's great, especially you, Mr. Tedmore and Mr. Lucas. This decision isn't easy for me."

"Wise decisions never are."

"I honestly feel a strong loyalty to Mr. Hackett. He stuck by me when Mr. Bylor and the executive committee were ready to sack me." I could see him wince at that. He was a member of the executive committee.

"Oh."

"Mr. Hackett argued them out of it. You see what I'm up against. I still want a few days to think."

"Take your time. I know you will come to the right decision and stay. You stay here, old friend, and I'll guarantee you'll get down the road a lot faster than you will with this Hackett fellow."

"I'm still thinking."

We drove back to the office, and on the way we stopped in front of a large chemical plant. Jiggs pointed, "That's where I spent twenty-five years. Started in that little shed over there, mixing and selling paints. My laboratory wasn't much bigger than this car."

"That's some plant. Was it all yours?"

"Yes, I sold out just five years ago. Comfortable now. Just play around with my own investments at Jones Bylor."

We drove on and Jiggs parked his car in the basement garage. As we got out, he said, "Now, Jim, when the time comes for you to buy in as a partner, you let me know if you need some money. I'll back you."

"Thanks, Jiggs. I appreciate that. I just might take you up on it."

He smiled at that.

There was a note on my desk from Miss Shirley when we got back at two o'clock. "Mr. Bylor wants to see you at two-thirty."

I wondered if he was going to fire me. Had the executive committee already decided to sack any of us who were the least bit friendly with Hackett? Mr. Bylor had never paid much attention to me, but now that his ego was at stake, it looks like he was coming alive.

I walked into his office. Mr. Bylor sat behind the fortress of his massive mahogany desk. Its top was as clean of current work as the desk of any major executive at Montcalm. I often wondered when executives did their work. He pointed to the side chair, close up to his desk, reserved for special friends. "Have a seat, Jim."

I was being honored, and he knew that I knew. He called me Jim, to let me know that I had arrived. The firm had always maintained a formal tone. We called each other Mr. This or Miss That. It helped to maintain cachet, and kept the clerks respectful. Prior to this time, I was cub-class, who the hired clerks called Mr. Bradley, because they had to.

I sat down. "Thanks, Mr. Bylor."

"Jim, we've been quite pleased with your progress. You've come quite a way."

"I've tried hard to not get dumped."

He ignored that. "We've developed a great deal of respect for you. You've done well." With his elbows on his desk, his thumbs under his chin, his hands pyramided in front, which hid his mouth, he looked straight ahead, not at me. "I want you to know, Jim, that the executive committee strongly favors offering you a partnership position as soon as this unpleasant situation clears."

"That would be a great honor."

"Are you going to be here to receive that honor?"

"I appreciate all that Jones Bylor has done for me. The only reason I hesitate is that I feel a certain obligation to Mr. Hackett. He stood up for me when I was down."

The corners of his mouth tensed. "Like I said..."

"Mr. Bylor, I will give you a decision Monday. I want the weekend to firm up my mind."

"Okay, that will be all right. Let's get together at nine o'clock Monday morning." He marked his calendar. "We shall put this unpleasant matter behind us." He stood up and extended his hand.

As I left his office, I decided there would be no Saturday stockbroker work. I would spend that day in deep thought. I would make a final decision on what I really wanted to do. If I stayed with Jones Bylor, I was headed right to the top. If I went with Mr. Hackett, there were risks. To the investment community we would be outsiders. Mr. Hackett was not a member of the Rainier Club, nor the Tennis Club, like Mr. Bylor.

The two people that I most dreaded to offend were John Lucas, my rancher friend, and Bill Tedmore, old Spit and Polish himself. Both had given me so much of their time. They helped me with ideas and encouraged me when I first started with the firm. They were always there when I had a problem. I also felt a strong friendship for Jiggs too, even if he was a bit of an old fuddy-duddy and way above my financial class. The thought that they would no longer be close friends and work comrades distressed me. What would be best for me? Mr. Hackett was always too busy putting deals together to give Dan and me much of his personal attention. I liked the people of Jones Bylor and would be perfectly satisfied to spend the rest of my work years with this firm. Yet, when all was bleak, Mr. Hackett was the one who stood by me, when everybody else would have cast me overboard. He had given me my first break and had come to my aid when I was desperate. Did that mean nothing when balanced against personal advantage?

Drained from this conflict of wishes, I looked forward to my evening with Sonada. I wondered what her reaction would be. As I left Mr. Bylor's office, I passed the door of John Lucas. Old Spit and Polish was with him. I suspected I had been the subject of their conversation, because they invited me in.

"Come, sit a piece, Pard," Mr. Lucas said in his best rancher's manner.

That's all I needed right now, another confrontation with these two. They motioned me to sit down. Right after Jiggs, I had received the luncheon treatment from each of them, individually.

"Hi, fellows. I'm still cogitating."

"That's dangerous. Too much of that ain't good for you," John Lucas said.

"Jim, I hope you haven't let Hackett scramble your thinking," Spit and Polish said.

"Ride the high country. It smells better," Lucas added.

"Look, you guys," I said as I got up. "My final decision will be made this weekend. I'll see you Monday." I left. I didn't want them to prejudice my thinking.

I went across the street and called the office. I disguised my voice and said, "I'd like to speak to Mr. Lews."

Miss Shirley said, "Certainly, Mr. Bradley. You got a cold?"

"I guess so," I said.

I stood there on the street with a pay phone in my hand for a good five minutes, and waited for Dan to get off the line.

"Dan, can we talk?"

"We need to," he said.

"Can we meet at the Sixth Avenue Bar & Grill?" I said.

"Good. I'll be right over."

"Won't that look suspicious?" I asked.

"Maybe, but we've got to talk. I'm going nuts."

"Let's make it at lunch. Then it won't look so funny," I said.

"Can't. I've got a lunch appointment with Mr. Bylor."

"Okay, let's do it now," I said.

I reached the Sixth Avenue Bar & Grill first and took a seat near the window overlooking a tiny swimming pool. I was in the restaurant part of the motel, near the bar, which was just around the corner. From where I sat, I could watch the pretty legs of the two barmaids as they moved about serving drinks. In the pool two young lovers frolicked, kissed and put on a show, like sex had been invented for them.

Dan came in, a harassed look on his face. He sat down across from me.

"What are you doing, Jim?"

"Danged if I know."

"Why did Hackett have to screw up a good thing, and start his own company?" Dan said. "Everything was going so smoothly."

"I know. I wish I could tell him to go jump, but I feel a strong loyalty to him. He stuck by me when nobody else would."

"Same here, but Jim, I'm just crawling out of being dirt poor. I think I'll stay."

"Mr. Hackett says he wants to grow, and Jones Bylor is going nowhere."

"Jones Bylor looks solid enough for me," Dan said, as he watched the swimmers kiss, then looked at his watch, and then back at me.

"Mr. Hackett also said for me to pass on to you, Dan, that you and I can each acquire 5 percent of the new company for $10,000, and be full partners."

"I don't have ten grand."

"Neither do I, but they will loan us five of it."

"I could raise $5,000," Dan said, and looked at his watch again.

"They also would make us a vice-president."

"That's what he said?"

"Yes. Tempting, isn't it? Owning a piece of the company could make us some real money if it goes."

"Jim, are you going to? I'd sure hate to be left alone with city slickers like Bailor."

"Dan, I just don't know. I want to, and I don't."

"You saw how they treated Swenson," he said.

"Yep. He was out in an hour."

"You think they would do that to us, Jim?"

"I know damn well they would, if we tell them we're going. I told them that I'd give them my decision Monday."

"They let you have that much time?"

"Yes," I said. "I told them I'd give them a firm answer Monday morning. Damn sure spoils my weekend, to have to wrestle with that problem."

Dan stood up. "They said they wanted an answer from me today."

"Well, what are you going to do, Dan?"

"I don't know. Why in the hell did this have to happen? Hackett gave me my first break."

"I know, Dan. I feel chained to two mule teams, each pulling in the opposite direction."

"Jim, I've got to get back. Someone is coming in half an hour. Then I've got lunch with the Old Man."

"Your turn for the good boy treatment, eh?"

"You're lucky, a whole weekend to think about it. I've just got this morning, and it's going fast."

"Let's hope we do the right thing," I said. "See you Monday."

He turned around as he reached the door. "Maybe," was his parting word.

Six-thirty, I freshened up and headed to Sonada's on Capitol Hill in my little green bug. It would be a special evening as I had made two reservations at the Space Needle. We'd have an hour to chat before we headed out to dinner. I thought I should get her involved, since I planned to make her the other side of me. She was one smart Aphrodite and she wasn't going to get away. I'd take her, legal or not. Her thoughts might influence my decision.

I couldn't understand how such a beauty could have a romantic interest in me. I wasn't handsome, still had some freckles left over from my youth. She could have anyone she wanted. I saw the glances that men gave her when we were out together. I could have killed the bastards for what I knew they were thinking. I didn't want her to slip away, like I had dropped all those German Club girls.

She finished touching up her make-up while I sat on the couch and waited. I must have been pensive.

She asked, "Is anything wrong?"

"No, Sonada, just thinking. I have a decision to make. I'd like your input."

"What's on your mind?"

"I've been offered a position as vice-president and a partnership interest in a new brokerage firm that's being organized."

"Congratulations!"

"Problem is, I love being where I am. I like the people."

"Then why move?"

"That's the problem. I like and feel a strong obligation to the guy who's starting the new company, and I'd like to join him."

"Deep down, what do you really want to do?"

"It's tough when you've got good friends on both sides. Either decision, you are going to lose some of them."

"Forget about your friends. What's good for you? That's the question."

"That sounds like good advice, but it doesn't make it feel any better."

"Just do what pleases you."

"I'm sure that I will, but deciding what pleases me is the problem."

"Don't worry about it. The answer will come."

"Tomorrow I'll give it some more serious thought."

She smiled and said, "I wish I could stick my problems in little boxes, and think about them only when I want to. I thought you had something earthshaking. God! All that turmoil in your face, just to decide where you're going to work."

"You do bring one back down to earth," I said.

"They might even offer you the presidency, just to keep you where you are," she jested.

I glanced at my watch. "We better be gone. We have reservations at the Space Needle."

"That's nice. I haven't been there since the Fair. Gee, you must be flush."

Atop the revolving Space Needle as the sunset neared, the whole western sky became a crimson red. Windows of the downtown office buildings were golden, and the snow-covered Mount Rainier loomed in the distance as the tall buildings cast their shadows towards night.

I looked at Sonada and smiled. Long amorous kisses in the car, at the door and on her couch, but we had gone no further. I wanted her, but also I wanted to save that moment until she was really mine. I had best get her to say yes soon. My morals wouldn't stand many more tests. Those pretty legs struggling to get out of my Volkswagen made it worth keeping the old clunker.

While we enjoyed the wine, the view and dinner, the golden scene turned into night, with a silvery hue of city lights. A lady's purse made its way towards us. Someone shouted, "There's somebody's purse." All of the women in earshot grabbed for theirs.

"It's mine," an embarrassed lady said as she ran to retrieve her purse, and then retreated back to her seat, feeling stupid. That happened often up here in the

187

Space Needle, especially during tourist season. The unwary placed their purses on the stationary outer ledge at their side and forgot that the inside restaurant section revolved, which gave a 360 degree view of the city. As the restaurant slowly revolved, the purse would slip away unnoticed.

Sonada's smile was like turning on the lights for me. It made me shudder at the thought that she might lose interest and drift away. I feared that she must have other dates, because I saw her only once or twice a week. I cut out all other females, once I met her. Occasionally, I felt guilty at the way I had treated those girls at the German Club, dated them once, then dumped them if they didn't meet my character, brains and beauty criteria. I didn't want to risk another Lois. I would like to have gotten to know Bette better, but I supposed that she must have gone back home. Like Sonada, I also feared to fall in love again. I remembered the misery, the unhappiness with Lois. Yet, the thought of Sonada drifting away was like waving goodbye to the one you loved, not knowing, but fearing, the ship might not come back.

The Space Needle's prime rib shamed a Montana steakhouse. When they poured our dinner wine, Sonada raised her glass in a toast, "To the big success in your new job, Mr. Vice-President."

"Thanks, but I haven't made that decision yet."

"You will."

"I'll think about that tomorrow. Let's get to something important."

"What's more important than a promotion to vice-president? I'm proud of you."

"I want you. Marry me, Sonada. That beats any vice-president's job."

Her smile fell away. Worry wrinkles lined her forehead. "Jim, I thought I had made that clear. I don't ever want to marry again. Marriage just spoils the zest and the fun of a friendship. Let's don't run that risk."

"Just think how much more time we would have together."

"That's the problem. After the new wears off, come the contentions and the infidelities."

"Never."

"That's what you say now. How will you feel when I'm a household drudge?"

"Ha! That will never be."

"Let's stay single, and you will love me longer."

"We could be so happy, Sonada."

"Weren't we happy before you brought that up? Don't spoil the evening."

I could see that she still meant business, and I knew the future. She would lose interest, or find another, or just drift away to avoid marriage. I tried hard not to show my disappointment.

I tipped her a final toast, "To more positive days."

She returned the pledge, and I helped her with her wrap. I felt a sadness. Neither of us said anything on the way home. Sonada, looking out the window, seemed in deep thought. I kept both hands on the steering wheel, and looked straight ahead. Was this the way it would end? I would simply lose her because I asked too much.

We stopped in front of her place. Streetlights were sparse. Moonlight gave a silvery tint to the old wooden two-story. Her place had once had been a mansion, but now was broken into four individual apartments. Under the moonlight, the street looked like a river that ran through a forest of elm, maple and birch. I got out, walked stiffly around, and opened her door. As her feet touched the ground, I pulled her up. We walked up the steps. I held her hand. I felt her hand squeeze mine. We stood in the shade of the porch overhang. It was sheltered and dark there. But for the tree shadows, the moonlight painted everything a silvery hue. I turned her towards me for a goodnight kiss, maybe a goodbye. My arms encircled her, and my hands pressed her hips tightly up against me. Her kiss was long and deep. It felt like a farewell. She clung to me and I kissed her again. In the shadowed moonlight I caught her eye. There was an innocent look upon her face. She laid her head against my shoulder.

I heard her whisper, "Won't you come in?"

"Sure."

She found the key in her purse. I took it and unlocked the door. She turned on the table lamp at the end of the couch near the door.

"I'll put the coffee on, and bring us some wine while it brews." She pointed to the couch, and quickly disappeared through the door into the kitchen.

I heard her movement in the kitchen, and then she disappeared into another room. Moonlight, through the window, cast a dim light on the pictures on the wall. They had been rearranged more than once since that first night when Sven brought me here. Lois moved furniture; Sonada moved paintings.

Sonada's taste in art was mostly originals by local Northwest artists. There was only one print among them, and that was Picasso's *Lady In Blue*. There were books everywhere; the shelves were full, and the overflow was neatly stacked in piles on the floor. Classic literature, books of poetry by Blake, Riley, Tennyson and many more. There were biography books, books on literary criticism and books on art. For a dental technician she seemed awfully well read, and from her conversations I suspected that she read them all.

Sonada came back, dressed in a loose blue robe that skimmed the floor as she walked. Two glasses of wine were in her hands.

"Quite a collection."

"Yes. Since I've been single, I've had lots of time to read and study art."

"I could," and almost said, 'change all of that,' but instead said, "enjoy reading all of those books."

She lit the fire in the already prepared fireplace, and sat down beside me. In a few moments the flames flickered and took away the need for the lamp, so I turned it off. We sat, held hands and gazed at the fire, with no need for words. She moved closer. I put my arm around her, pulled her over and kissed her. The fireplace flames cast a cozy light. The couch was wide. She stretched out and I lay beside her. I kissed her on the cheek, the forehead, the neck and then the lips. I felt her hips rise and press against me. I thought of my sweaty, hot work days in the Oregon sun, when I stacked lumber, anything to uncock my pistol. My hands cupped her pyramids, like God holding the Egyptians back. I had never gone that far with her before. They were firm and full, and she didn't resist. I caught a glimpse of her eyes in the firelight, and they said, "Now." I thought of the Indian princess who sped away when I spurned her wish for love. I kissed her lips, her neck and then the peaks, and went for the rest.

Afterwards, I continued to kiss and caress her. I felt like a thief who had stolen that sacred moment. Why couldn't I have waited? We continued to lie there mesmerized by the flames that licked the air, enraptured by just being together. I felt guilty, but after more kisses and hands that wandered, I was ready again. After a two-year drought, I couldn't get enough love. Who needed heaven with paradise like this?

"Can I see you tonight?"

"Sure." She snuggled closer and said, "Must you go?"

"Yes, it's a big decision today." I quickly dressed, bent down and kissed her hard, and said, "I'll see you this evening?"

"Make it about seven."

I kissed her again and left.

TWENTY-ONE

Outside, it was dawn. Decision day, to stay or not to stay at Jones Bylor. I thought I had better get some rest and make that decision with a clear head. Monday was reckoning day.

On the way home in my VW, I didn't drive. I glided through heaven. She did love me. She would say yes. Hell! I didn't fornicate. I made love to my future wife. Future, hell, she was already my wife. I didn't need some judge or preacher to tell me that.

I bounded up the three flights of stairs, pulled the bed down and crashed. It was ten o'clock before I woke up. I walked down to the Pike Place Market for breakfast. That place was always best for heavy thinking.

At the counter downstairs I ordered hash browns, eggs, toast, and bacon. I carried my coffee mug up the long steps to the top of the cafeteria. They would bring breakfast to me. This cafeteria had been the birthplace of the famous Manning's Cafeteria chain. Now it was Lowell's Cafeteria. The broad view, the harbor gave me a different perspective. I first discovered this place at one of my low points after Lois left. It amazed me how much more there was to the world when I was alone and took a broad look outward.

Before breakfast came, I savored my coffee, and thought about the one thing I would miss most if I left Jones Bylor. It was the cheery enthusiasm and support that I had received from Miss Shirley. She went far back, even to that first day in Seattle.

Big ships came and big ships went. Smaller fishing vessels and some pleasure boats passed. The larger vessels mainly plied the waters of Puget Sound, while the smaller boats utilized the little inlets and the waters of Lake Union and Lake Washington. Large ferryboats gorged on cars and people, after first expelling an earlier feast. Giant cranes nipped at the world's newly-mades, like dinosaurs feasting on treetops.

It was an immense world out there that didn't give a damn whether Jim Bradley stayed or didn't stay at Jones Bylor. Yet, I thought of the terrible difficulty that I had gone through, just to get that spot at Jones Bylor. It wasn't something to toss away like a candy-wrapper. Never again did I want to in be in such position that I would have to hock my watch for food. If Tiger Hackett failed, that could happen again.

The world of power and property and money that I viewed out there in the harbor came from risk-takers, not those who cringed in safe harbors. Those fat ferries, now operated by the state, got their start from some young fellow who may have hauled people around in a rowboat. He prospered, and then built up a fleet of larger ships. He could have played it safe, and stayed with his rowboat. Wealth came to those who took risks, who braved the storms, the setbacks, and went after bigger game. That's where wealth came from, own a piece of the action, set the policies, and enjoy the profits. Hackett was that kind of man. He was the type who should be my partner, not the stuffy, play-it-safe Bylor. Jones Bylor had been good to me, especially when I became successful. But it was Mr. Hackett who threw me the life belt, not Bylor and his executive committee.

That's where my loyalties belonged, with Mr. Hackett, regardless of the outcome. Why all this agony? Go with Hackett, that's what I really wanted to do. We'd make the Seattle investment community take notice. They'd wish they had worn steel-toed shoes, when Tiger Hackett & Company stomped onto the scene, especially those birds who had a chance to hire Broker Jim, and didn't.

I hadn't noticed when they brought the heaped-up hash browns, bacon and eggs. I tasted the hash browns. Cold, but what the hell. What were a few cold taters to a future millionaire?

I could hardly wait until that evening to tell Sonada my decision. No sense to go to the office today. Someone might drop in, even on Sunday, and I would have to bear the questioning looks. I had told them that I would let them know on Monday, so let them wait. These good friends would likely turn into vipers, once I told them my decision.

That evening when I picked up Sonada for our evening out, I said, "I've decided to join the Tiger Hackett outfit."

"I knew that's what you'd do all along," she said. "First thing you know, you'll be president of your own firm. You are that kind of guy."

"How can I lose with that kind of support?" I said, but my thoughts were really, "Somehow I've got to make this relationship a permanent alliance."

Monday, as I entered the offices of Jones Bylor, I could appreciate how Daniel must have felt in the lions' den. I could have used some of Sonada's confidence right then. I waited for the storm to break. I didn't see Daniel Lews anywhere, and Miss Shirley wasn't there. All during the sales meeting, I could see the question in their eyes. Are you with us, or are you a traitor?

As the meeting concluded, I stood up. "Gentlemen, there is something I must say, and afterwards, I hope we're still friends. I think you all know I feel a deep sense of obligation to Mr. Hackett. He stuck by me when my world crumbled.

That I cannot forget. Even though I have strong affection for all of you and this place, I have no choice. I must go."

I could see all eyes turn toward Mr. Bylor, and wait for his reaction, but he showed none. The seconds ticked away in silence. No one said anything.

Then I heard a throat clear, and it was John Lucas. "Jim, a man who does what he thinks he ought to do, can't be no polecat. I'd still be proud to consider you a friend."

"Same here," Old Spit and Polish said. I saw Jiggs nod his head in approval.

Then Mr. Bylor said, "Jim, we all hate to see you go, but if it doesn't work out, you're welcome back."

"Thank you. Thank you all so much." I felt a lump in my throat, and didn't want to show the depth of my feeling. I left and went to my office and cleaned it out. In less than half an hour I had my desk calendar, fountain pen set and all the personal things from my desk packed in a cardboard box. I quietly left, and caught a cab over to my new destiny.

I found the offices of Tiger Hackett & Company located on the seventh floor of a modest-priced office building. "Welcome aboard," Miss Shirley greeted me. She sat on the window ledge, making notes in her steno pad. I felt a glow of happiness from my nose to my feet and a renewed confidence that I had made the right decision. Here was Miss Shirley, still with us. I couldn't imagine what Jones Bylor would be without her and Mr. Hackett.

I didn't see Mr. Hackett. Jim Swenson and Dan Lews sat on the floor, and were calling their clients. They each waved. They worked out of cardboard boxes. There were no desks or chairs.

"What happened?" I asked.

"Phones are in," Miss Shirley said. "Furniture won't be here until tomorrow or the next day. Some mix-up in the shipping. Mr. Hackett has gone out to rustle us up some temporary chairs."

Swenson, off the phone, yelled, "Hey, Jim, they kick you out?"

"No. Surprisingly they were very nice to me."

"I'll be damned."

I said to Miss Shirley, "It's a wonderful surprise to find you here. What were their reactions when they found out that you were leaving?"

"Mr. Bylor was hurt. I could tell it in his voice. I called in this morning, early, and talked with him. I hated to not give him notice, but I couldn't work there after telling him that I was leaving."

Dan, off the phone, got up from the floor, came over and shook my hand. "Well, friend, we meet again."

Finally Mr. Hackett came in, puffing. He carried five fold-up chairs. "Hi, Jim. Sorry about the mess. This is only temporary. Soon as it's completed, we'll move into the newest, most prestigious office building in town."

"Got our license yet?" I asked.

"Not yet."

"Been two weeks, hasn't it?"

"Any day now," Mr. Hackett said. "Meantime, get on the phone, and make your clients aware of the change. Get them to send letters transferring their accounts over to us."

"Won't that hurt our clients if they can't do business?"

"Don't worry. We'll hold their letters until our license is effective."

"How long do you really think?"

"At most, I would say two more weeks," Mr. Hackett said.

Two weeks passed, and four more. What we forgot was that the bureaucracy has its own clock. I was embarrassed to call clients, and give more excuse for delays. I began to worry, and almost wished that I had stayed with Jones Bylor.

On the seventh week, we got the letter that our license was effective. You would have thought that we had won a revolution, not just a license to do brokerage business. The noise, the celebration, the dance of the jig. Mr. Hackett came up with two bottles of champagne and that expensive, awful stuff that you put on crackers.

A week later, all of Seattle who read the financial pages knew that Tiger Hackett & Company was a force to be reckoned with. A huge orange tiger with darker orange stripes was overprinted on the New York stock quotes. Also, printed in bold orange letters was TIGER HACKETT & COMPANY GREETS YOU. How John Hackett managed to get the newspaper to do such an overprint over the stock quotes, and how much it cost, was to remain a mystery. Our friends at Jones Bylor, who had gone after our clients like tigers, reacted in a sorehead fashion, "The audacity of that Hackett." The rest of the local financial community just chuckled.

All but three of my clients transferred their accounts over to Tiger Hackett & Company. I considered those who came to be saints to have stayed with me that long, and resist the efforts of the Jones Bylor brokers who pursued them.

Six months later, we were in our new headquarters. It was the penthouse on the seventeenth floor of Seattle's newest office building. I looked out my window to the north, towards Lake Union. Small dinghies, stinkpots, large cruisers and sailing yachts moved across the lake. Some of the larger ships were headed to the government locks and on out to Puget Sound. Others were on their way back home to their berths on Lake Washington. After dark, the lights of Queen Anne Hill danced like fairies with lanterns in the night. I hated to go home to my gloomy little apartment.

Immediately, Mr. Hackett put his deal-making genius to work. He put mergers together, and took bigger companies apart, and we watched the pieces grow. With our buying support, many of these stocks zoomed. This new market action did not go unnoticed by the street. Twelve more brokers, all experienced men, came from other houses and joined our firm. Nobody wanted to be left out. Many of those, who didn't join us, participated in our market action. Jones Bylor, smirkingly, waited for the fall.

In one of Mr. Hackett's deals, we put real estate into an inactive corporate shell. The stock moved from one dollar a share to fifteen. We raised money for an oil company, and it hit a gusher. The stock went up ten times. Many of our other deals also did well. There just seemed to be no losers.

That first year, our capital grew from $250,000 to over $1 million. That made my 5 percent worth fifty grand. My clientele doubled. Any stock that moved up brought in a flock of new clients like a shot at a covey of birds. Their friends and their friends' friends called you. Little accounts suddenly became big accounts, when they brought out their serious money. Sonada's $500 account had grown to $6,000, and she still said no to marriage.

Christmas, Tiger Hackett threw a party for our clients, prospects and the rest of the investment community to commemorate our first year. Sonada came with me. We filled our champagne glasses from streams that flowed out of a fountain. Hors d'oeuvre tables must have outclassed many robber baron splashes. A first-class band played music; some danced, but most people just ate and drank. From Mr. Hackett's penthouse office we could see city lights all around as we danced.

Many individual brokers from other firms came. The ever-present Ralph Bailor from Jones Bylor was bold enough to show up. Not quite out of earshot, I heard him say to another outside broker, "Leave it to Hackett to put on such a gaudy display."

Monday, comments were bantered about in brokerage offices all over the city, some good and some bad. Those who snubbed us wished they had come. Marilyn Whittman, our cashier, had made all the arrangements for the party. She had come over from Jones Bylor one month after we opened for business. Her decision to join us surprised everyone. She was a big plus, one of the best cashiers in town. She acted powerfully possessive of Mr. Hackett.

Sonada and I continued to date at least twice a week, and sometimes made heavy love. Every so often I would ask her again if she would marry me. She would get uneasy, and then nonchalantly say, "I'd rather not."

I had a date with her Saturday night, but it was only Friday. I felt an urge to see her that evening, so I called her about noon.

"Sonada, let's get together tonight. I can't wait until Saturday."

"Jim, I can't. I'll see you tomorrow."

"Okay. Sorry you can't make it."

I didn't understand. She'd never stalled me before. I stayed home and tried to read. I wondered, was she out with someone else?

Saturday night, when Sonada opened the door, I didn't see David. She had already taken him over to the baby-sitter. She was beautifully dressed in black. She wore a white blouse, black panty hose, and wore her hair like Veronica Lake, down past her shoulders. Stunning, when she didn't have it balled up in a granny bun, the usual way she wore her hair. She had an elegant Greek look. What a beautiful widow she would make, all in black, ran through my mind. She was so beautiful in black.

We went to Rosellini's 410 for dinner. No mention was made of her not being able to see me the previous night, but that still concerned me. Also, I was still puzzled about that time, when I first met her. Somehow, she had looked familiar. I couldn't place where I had seen her before.

After the wine server had left, I asked her, "Sonada, where have I known you before?"

She smiled and said, "You really haven't figured that out yet, have you?"

"No."

"Do you remember that time in Bellevue when you came looking for Lois?"

"No?! You're not Mitzie?"

"Could be."

"How?! Why?!"

"I needed extra money after my husband left town, leaving me all the debts to pay, and I didn't want my boss to know that I moonlighted, so I disguised myself."

"You did a good job of that."

"I let my hair down to flow over my shoulders, painted myself up and wore different clothes, so people wouldn't recognize me. At the dentist's office I used little makeup, wore my hair in a bun. No one recognized me, not even you."

"I think you're beautiful either way, Greek with bun, or flowing free."

"It took you long enough to recognize me," she said.

"Why'd you keep me in suspense so long?"

"I thought it would be better to let the past die, but you've been so insistent."

"Then you knew Lois."

"We were slight friends. I came to her rescue one time when she got into a squabble with another girl in the rest room."

"She told me something about that," I said, "but I never made the connection."

"Got a note from her a few weeks ago. They're quite happy up in Alaska."

"I'm glad she makes someone happy."

"When did you leave that job?"

"Not long after I first saw you," she said. "I found out that some of the local housewives had a side business there, so I left."

"At least there's one thing I found out tonight," I said.

"What's that?"

"Barmaids can be nice girls."

"Hostesses."

"I stand corrected. Say, do you think David would like to go for another ride on my yacht tomorrow morning?"

"If you mean that plastic board? He'd love it."

"I'll pick him up about ten in the morning."

"You know you've become quite a hero to him."

"I'd rather be his father."

She hesitated and then said, "I never mentioned this before, but after you had been here a time or two, David said to me, 'Mommy, let's marry him.'"

"Sounds like a future stockbroker to me, a man of fast decision, who gives good advice and yet, only six years old."

She smiled. "He'll be ready at ten."

Later, back at her place, as we lay on the couch before the fireplace light, I took her hand and braved it once more. I said, "Sonada, let's get married."

"Okay." She said it so nonchalantly, I almost missed it.

"You mean you will?" I couldn't believe it!

"Sure, let's do it. If you think you can stand to live with a ex-barmaid for the next fifty years."

"We can get married in one day over in Coeur d'Alene, Idaho," I said. I didn't want to give her a chance to change her mind.

"I think David will be willing to wait until next weekend for that sail on your yacht," she said.

The next morning, we were on an early flight to Spokane. We rented a car and drove on to Coeur d'Alene, not quite seventy miles away. We told no one except her brother, who would look after David.

Saturday morning by nine-thirty we were in Coeur d'Alene, Idaho. Marriage in Coeur d'Alene is a well-organized institution. After we purchased the license, we were directed to another department for a blood test. Next, we selected a preacher. Both of our previous marriages had been to Catholics. She was born to it and I, a convert to marry Lois. A Protestant preacher was our only choice if we wanted a religious ceremony. Catholic priests would not marry us, because our former partners were still alive. One preacher would be as good as another, we figured. Our first try, from the yellow pages, was a Baptist church. That line was busy, so we next tried a Presbyterian church.

That preacher said, "I'm not too well-dressed, been raking leaves. You come by in a couple of hours, and I'll be ready."

"Fine, we'll have lunch first," I said.

After lunch we walked to the preacher's house. He greeted us at the door with a big smile and a friendly welcome. With his gray hair and dumpy tweed suit, he was more like a jolly elf than a preacher. His home, a white-painted wooden frame with red roses in the front, was neatly furnished in fifties furniture.

"Please sit down," he said. "Let's chat for a moment. Are you Presbyterian?"

"No."

"You are of a religious denomination, are you not?"

"Yes, both of our previous marriages were to Catholics," I said.

"Do you have any children?"

"Sonada has a small son. I have none of my own."

"Do you presently attend church?"

"When somebody dies, or gets married," I said.

"Well, how do you plan to raise your children, the son and any future ones you might have?"

"Hadn't thought a great deal about it," I said. Sonada nodded agreement.

"Well, you can't raise them atheist."

"Why not?" interjected Sonada, "The way I see Christians treat each other, it might be an improvement."

"Look, sir!" I said. "We came over here to get married, not to be lectured."

"You won't do your children any favor if you raise them as atheists," he sputtered on. "You two should sit down very soon and discuss it. Give the matter some serious thought."

"We'll do that," I said.

That satisfied him, that he had done the Lord's business. His sermon had not been a total waste. The wedding ceremony proceeded with his wife as a paid witness. We got the distinct impression that marriage was crucial to the cash flow of that town.

After the ceremony, hand-in-hand, we thrashed and kicked our way through a carpet of colorful maple and birch leaves. Our world was at peace. The rapes, the kills, the burns, the war that took place in Vietnam, and all the rallies against it were on another planet. At that moment, our world was each other. As we walked through the park, there was a background smell of fireplace smoke. A breeze brought more gently falling leaves. We wanted this moment of happiness to endure forever.

Then, it dawned on us, we had made no arrangements for the night. We scurried off to find a motel. We were lucky. It was off-season, so we found a good spot right on Lake Coeur d'Alene.

Married at last to Sonada! I was happy. These moments made up for all of the struggles, the turmoil and the fights with Lois. I resolved to give Sonada's needs first choice and to avoid arguments under all circumstances. No more marital battles for me! Life created enough battles. You didn't have to marry them.

Evening came. From our window we could see the ink-black lake and tiny stars above. We wanted to make it last. When the moon came up, the lake was painted silver. We opened the bottle of champagne that Sonada's brother had given us for the celebration. We drank it and the moment was so great we wanted the anticipation of lovemaking as man and wife to last forever. When the supreme moment for love came, soused and exhausted, we both fell asleep.

Sunday afternoon, we flew back to Seattle. That evening my wife saw how a bachelor kept house, and I wondered if she might have had second thoughts. I arranged with the landlady to store Saul's trunk in the basement for later pickup. We then loaded my meager movables into the Volkswagen, and I moved in with her and David.

First thing, Monday morning, at the office, I called Sven Nordoff to give him the good news. He didn't say much, but invited us to join him that evening for more of his famous stew, and to celebrate his continued bachelorhood.

When I went to the trading window to turn in some tickets, Ellen Simpson, our girl trader, glanced down and saw the wedding band.

"Oh! You got married!"

"Over the weekend."

"Who?"

"You wouldn't know her. Just one of my rich clients," I joked.

Not more than fifteen minutes passed, and the whole place was ablaze with the news. "Broker Jim bit the dust, no longer is he open game." I never knew I was anyone's quarry, or whether any of the single girls in the office were interested in me. Our office had plenty of young pretties, but I had paid them no heed. My Uncle Jim's advice had been, "Keep your hands off the hired help. They're the most expensive thing you can touch." I often wondered what triggered that advice.

Not everyone at Tiger Hackett had been fortunate enough to have had a wise uncle's advice. Some of the brokers began to refer in undertones that the place was Hackett's harem. There was no proof, but suspicions grew that John Hackett sampled forbidden fruit.

We were due at Sven's that evening. I was sure Sonada would be glad to see him again. After all, he had introduced us. She still had her job, so I called her at the dental office.

"Sonada, Sven has invited us to dinner this evening. Is that all right?"

She hesitated and then said, "No, Jim. I'd rather not. You go ahead and have your delayed bachelor party with him. I'll see you when you get home."

"I won't be too long."

That evening, Sven greeted me with a weak handshake. He handed me a mug of beer and said, "Skoal." He said nothing for a few moments and then, "Congratulations," but there was not the usual smile that he always offered.

The table was set, the candles lit. From the kitchen, there came the smell of fresh homemade bread.

"Sit," he said. "Let's enjoy a beer while the stew brews. Your news surprised me. I thought you just helped her with investments."

"Nope, but it took me almost two years to get her to say yes."

Sven expressed interest in our trip. He wanted to know all the details, such as when we got married, where we went, and everything. He was friendly, but there was a soberness that I had not seen in him before. We talked about what a mess the world was in.

"J.C. sure has screwed things up down here," he said. "Hope he has done a better job up there, that is, if there is a heaven."

It seemed a long wait, and there were some silences, but finally he served the stew and the fresh-made bread, still hot enough to melt butter. After we had finished our second bowls, I complimented him on how magnificent the stew was.

"Did you notice a little different taste in the stew?" he asked.

"No, I thought it was great," I said.

"It could be poisoned."

"What? What do you mean?"

"Just that. The stew could have been poisoned."

"What're you talking about, Sven? Are you kidding?"

"No, it could have been." With his elbows on the table, he folded his hands, and placed his thumbs under his chin. "I thought about it," he said, and did not smile, like he had made a joke.

"What are you getting at, Sven? Your stocks are doing okay."

"That girl you married. She was mine. I asked her to marry me."

I know my jaw dropped, and I sat there and looked at him in shock. "Sven, I didn't know! Honestly, I would never, never have even dated her if I had known that you were interested. You told me that she was just a good family friend."

"Not very perceptive, are you?"

"I guess not. Does this end our friendship?"

He looked at me for a long time and said nothing, and then said, "No, I suppose not, if the poison doesn't kill you."

"Poison!" My mind raced. Maybe the stew did taste a little funny. But he ate the same stew that I had. But then again, I had not watched when he served the individual portions. He could have doctored mine.

"Sven, I am so sorry about this. I never realized." I still didn't know what to believe about the poison. I felt all right.

"You know, Bradley, I really did think about it."

"What?"

"Putting poison in your stew."

"You really didn't poison it, did you?"

"No. Guess I'll have to live with it. Just call me Miles Standish."

"What changed your mind?"

"Good brokers are too hard to find." He tried to smile, but I could see I had broken his heart.

"I am sorry this happened."

"That's all right. I'll take it. I guess J.C. is just getting back at me. Having his fun, sitting up there and laughing. I guess it's not really your fault."

The evening ended amicably. On the way home, I shuddered. Poison! I could be dead. Sonada would have been a widow already, and worn her black get-up for real. Was this truly the end of it? Had he just temporarily lost his nerve?

At first, I thought I would say nothing to Sonada about how the evening went. It would be just as well to let it rest. What went on between them, I would rather not know. She was mine now.

That sounded okay to me in the car, but when I got home, Sonada was watching TV and without a second thought, I blurted out, "Sonada, what was going on between you and Sven?"

"What do you mean?"

"Why didn't you tell me you guys were sweet on each other?"

"Did Sven say something?"

"Yes. He said that you were his girl. He also said he actually thought about putting poison in my stew tonight."

"He what?"

"That's what he said."

Her face turned a pale white and then red. She said, "This is embarrassing. You remember that Friday night that you wanted to get together and I couldn't make it?"

"Yes."

"He called me at the office that day and insisted that he had to talk with me that evening. He had something most important to discuss with me, so I said yes, and that was before you called."

"Well, what was so important?" I asked.

"He embarrassed me. He proposed. I always thought of him as some kind of an uncle, not that way. His sister and family sort of took me in like one of them, when I was stressed out over my marriage breakup."

"What happened?"

"I told him no, that I didn't love him that way. I always thought of him just as a friend."

"How did he take that?"

"He cried. I felt sorry for him, but what could I do? To me, he was like family. I never had that kind of interest in him, never led him on. I was shocked at the thought."

"Was that all?" I asked.

"He asked if there was someone else. I didn't want to hurt him anymore, the state he was in. So, I didn't say anything about us. He tried to poison you?"

"He said he thought about it, but I think he is okay now."

Maybe Sven wasn't going to do me in, but it wasn't long before I found out that in the business world there was another kind of poison.

TWENTY-TWO

Our Tiger Hackett roll continued well into 1969. Some brokerage firms were resentful of our success. They eagerly awaited our downfall. We had become the firm that smart young brokers joined. Those who remained with their old firms had to explain to their clients why their investment ideas did not move up like those at Tiger Hackett.

We were in our prime. The striped orange cat had showered its blessings on us all. Then one day, at a sales meeting, Mr. Hackett's announcement came like a thunder blast.

"Gentlemen, I have some good news for you. We've grown so much that I think we need some top class help. I want you to meet our new executive vice-president."

We all looked at the not yet introduced stranger who sat in our midst. He was a beefy young man with heavy jowls, dressed in a smart green suit.

"This is Mr. Gordon Palimeer. He comes to us from Merrill Lynch."

We had good people. "Why hadn't he promoted one of us?" we all wondered. We were a different breed from Merrill Lynch.

The next day Palimeer conducted the sales meeting. Mr. Hackett was not there.

"I have a mandate," he said, "to improve the quality of the securities you hold in your clients' accounts. I've made a study of your investment positions. Most of these local securities, that your clients' money is tied up in, are junk and a waste of investors' resources. Why buy junk when there are so many good New York Exchange companies you can invest in?"

I felt my face turn red and snorted like a bull. This was in direct conflict with my whole philosophy. This man thinks he can make a big company whore out of me!

Over the next few days, Palimeer made more pronouncements of what he thought was in our best interests. My encounters with him were not hostile, but cool and formal. We saw less and less of Mr. Hackett. He was often out of town, on deals, mergers and finance. More and more of the day-to-day contact with brokers was handled by Palimeer.

Two months passed, and then one morning after the sales meeting, I found a note on my desk from Miss Shirley. "Mr. Palimeer wants to see you in his office at nine-thirty."

As I entered his big corner office, Palimeer sat behind a large mahogany desk, that was 5 percent owned by me. I sometimes believed bankers and brokers, who deal in dreams, like to have something real solid in front of them. Big-boned and fleshy, Palimeer looked like a gargantuan toad with glasses on. I almost expected him to hop onto his desk and lash his long tongue out for a bug. He glowered at me and I felt like that bug.

"Bradley, I've reviewed your clients' positions. Crap! Shit! That's all you have." I had never heard him talk like this before. Before the whole group, he had always been so formal and proper.

"My clients' cash registers might argue with that."

"Junk! Speculative junk! That's all your clients have! Clean out that shit. Sell 'em. I want to see some blue chips in that mix."

I knew there's a time to gamble when you can make big money, and there's a time to not gamble. What infuriated me most was that he was absolutely right. I had already started to clean out my more speculative issues. In true speculative markets, blue chips don't move. To make money then, you play the game, but you have to be nimble. I realized the flowers were in full bloom, and that the blossoms would soon begin to fall. I was already in the process of turning my clients' stocks into cash and more conservative positions, except for a few good local companies that we wanted to hold. Now, this pompous ass told me to do exactly what I was already doing. He could think, and say, that he had forced me to change my ways.

"What's good for the Rockefellers and Mellons is good for the country, eh?" I said.

"I want to see some immediate improvement in the quality of your holdings! That's all. You can go."

After that day our contacts were rare, and when together, cool. Every local investment idea that I chose to work in met with severe criticism from Palimeer. Finally, he said, "The only way you can deal in those stocks is on an unsolicited basis."

Access to Hackett was limited. To see him, I had to have an appointment. Most of the time he was away on deals. When there, he always backed Palimeer. He had little time for his original partners.

In sales meetings, Palimeer made more general announcements of his support for more mature companies, and each time he glared at me. There were some local stock issues that I still worked in and planned to continue to do so. To me, they were the seedbeds of the future giants. They needed and deserved the support of local money. They would get my support, Palimeer or no Palimeer.

Many of my clients were still interested in local companies. When I advised them of my problem, most of them said, "I would like to buy some of those unsolicited stocks. What looks good to you?"

Later, I was called back to Palimeer's office. "What's all this unsolicited business?" he asked.

"I don't know. Guess they know what they want," I said.

"I'll look into this. You can go."

He then called up some of my clients and asked how they had heard about certain stocks. Had Bradley called these stocks to their attention?

The answers he got, they told me later, were, "I read about it in the paper," or "My cousin works there," or "My kid sold the president some Girl Scout cookies and I trust him."

These responses brought more croaks from Big Mahogany. Palimeer reminded me of Brewster at Montcalm, who had recently died. I attended his funeral, and shamefully didn't know for sure whether it was out of respect for the dead, or that I just had to make sure that he was really dead. Anyway, I went. Some of my former associates were there too. I thought I saw guilty looks on their faces too.

It was Palimeer's arrogant manner that mainly irritated me. Never would I be someone's breakfast again, not after Bull of the Woods Brewster. If things did not change soon, I would say to Hackett, "It's either Palimeer or me." I had a pretty good idea who would go.

Weeks passed with no terminal eruption. Finally, I believed he came to think that he had a lost cause on his hands. He left me alone, and merely nodded when we passed in the hall.

Another six months passed, and I was working in my office. About midmorning, I heard a ruckus coming from the trading area down the hall. There were screams and yells and curses.

A female voice shouted, "You goddamn bitch!"

"You fucking whore," was the reply.

I got up and walked back towards the trading area, and caught the full view of the fracas.

Two women stood facing each other. They slapped and scratched. They bit each other's neck and yanked handfuls of hair. Screams and vicious yanks and torn blouses made quite a sight. I saw Palimeer step between them. One slugged him with her fist; the other one brought her knee up to his crotch. Bending over in pain, he lost his balance, and the full weight of his obesity squashed to the floor. The women turned in opposite directions, bellowing sobs.

Palimeer sat up, with knees spread apart, and his belly resting between them, not unlike Mr. Adams, so long ago, when he tripped over my stick horse. I felt like my mother must have felt back then; I wanted to laugh, but dared not.

Tiger Hackett turmoil grew worse. The hair-pulling contest proved up the Hackett Harem Theory. The two known female members of the harem, who tangled, were the cashier and the head-trader. As was his good fortune, Mr. Hackett was out of town. Elegant Big Mahogany had the bloody nose and Hackett had the fun.

Before Hackett's return, Palimeer dismissed the trader. Traders were easier to replace than cashiers. Hackett was left with the cashier. (Hackett's own wife soon left him.)

Genius strategies that had moved Tiger Hackett up from a quarter of a million to a multi-million dollar company began to malfunction. Our flagship investment was in trouble. The price of Bing Resources's stock tumbled. Its descent took along the coattail companies. The president of Bing, our golden goose, tried to swallow a bigger company and choked. When Bing couldn't swing the financing needed to complete the deal, the market said he was a paper tiger and ran for cover. Our inventory, mostly tied up in this company and its coattail dependencies, collapsed. Our capital disappeared like snowflakes in the sea. The $70,000 annual rent on our fancy quarters became unbearable.

First to leave was Palimeer. Tiger Hackett went into receivership. The predictions of the old heads at Jones Bylor had come true. We just lasted longer than they thought. Like many men in desperate situations, Hackett took shortcuts to save the firm. He temporarily borrowed some funds from an account, and didn't get the owner's permission. This was the end of his securities career.

Mr. Hackett left town with Marilyn Whittman, his new wife, and the former cashier of Tiger Hackett. His last words to me were, "I'm tired of this dream world. I'm only interested in investments that I can either kick or piss on." He went into the real estate development business in another state, and did well.

Except for a handful of Spokane mining stocks that had not been liquid enough to sell, I was broke. I lost everything. I had been a plunger and put everything back into the market. I knew better. This always seemed to happen to the big plungers. They don't know when to let go of the tiger. I suppose you have to feel the scratches yourself to learn the lesson. Sonada continued to work. She fed her embarrassed financial genius.

What could I do to crawl out of this disaster? After my experiences with Brewster and Palimeer, I did not want to ever again work for somebody else. My own firm was the answer, but how? I was broke. I still felt that the securities market did not meet the needs of small companies.

TWENTY-THREE

I went to see my old friend, John Lucas. His company, Lucas and Associates, was located just across the street from the Jones Bylor office. As I walked in, I found his headquarters an almost cavelike place. It was a long and narrow room, more like a hallway. There was only one window, which was located at his back. There were two other brokers and a couple of clerks towards the front of the room, near the door.

"I don't believe in too many hands," John Lucas said as he offered me a seat. "They cost too much to feed."

"I saw Bill Tedmore on the street the other day," I said. "He told me you had started your own firm."

"I finally had enough of Fancy Dan Bylor, so I got my own diggings. Been doing damn well at it."

"Bill told me you plunged out of the market about as fast as you plunged in."

"I did damn well. Them damn fools just sat there, uneasy, while the market went crazy. I cleared out ahead of time. Now, I got a barn full of cash."

"Looks like you're okay," I said.

"I keep busy."

His desk was covered with files. It looked like when he ran out of room, he just started another layer.

He saw me look at his filing system and smiled.

"Never lose anything. Spend a bit lookin' sometimes."

"I can see that."

"Jim, I heard you guys had some tough luck."

"I'm darn near busted right now, but I want to start my own firm. You have any ideas?"

"Hell yes! I'll loan you twenty grand to get started."

"Thanks, John, but I didn't come here to borrow money. I wouldn't impose on your friendship. Besides, I'm the stupid dolt who got myself into this mess. You warned me that a market crash was on its way. I didn't act on it. Thought you might have some ideas on how I can get back in the business."

"On the slim, eh?"

"Yes. I don't have much choice."

He pounded the desk with his big fist. "Say! I do have an idea," he said. "There's a one-man shop with a high-toned class of customers that might still be around."

"How's that?"

"Old man Biddle. He died a couple of months ago."

"I knew him," I said. "Nice old guy."

"Pretty well hung out with himself, but his customer list is like a "Who's who." His business just might still be available for the plucking. His gal is winding things down."

"That does sound interesting."

"Did you know that old man dealt with some of Seattle's oldest money?"

"No. I just met him a time or two at the monthly brokers' meeting. He didn't come very often, but I sat next to him once. He dealt mainly in convertible bonds, I think."

"He had some city slickers with lots of money."

"Picking up his client list sounds like a good idea to me," I said.

"Let me know if I can help. That old man's company just might be a good piece of ground for a young fellow to work." He handed me the daughter's name scribbled on a piece of paper.

"Thanks."

"Don't stand there prancing like a pricked-up stud! Get on over there and make a deal before those fillies stray."

I headed on down, but I didn't have the slightest idea how I could finance an acquisition. Where would I get money to buy a company, when my wife was feeding us? Get the facts and maybe I could figure out something was what I thought. Biddle International Securities, better known as BIS, was only a five-minute walk away. The office was in a pioneer building in the older part of downtown. Miss Biddle, his daughter, a slightly-graying lady in her early fifties, was busy at her father's old large rolltop desk.

"John Lucas suggested I come and see you," I said.

"How is old John? Dad used to talk about him. Said he cussed worse than a sailor."

"Only when there's no women around. Looks like you've got your hands full."

She turned around and smiled at me.

"Certainly have. Dad was such an independent cuss. He never told me anything, especially about the business. Now I've got to clean it up."

"How old is this company?"

"Dad started out as a one-man shop in 1930."

That sounded like a good omen to me. That was the year I was born.

"He considered it a matter of prudence to keep the business small. 'Too many crafty lawyers who pounce on any accumulations of capital' he always said."

"Sounds like your father was one smart man."

"He never left more than the minimum required capital on the books. When he needed cash for inventory, he just made the company a temporary loan."

I could see she was a talkative lady, so I said, "Miss Biddle, I'm interested in starting my own brokerage firm. It might give me a head start if I could begin with an established company. John Lucas thought your dad's company might be available."

"Hadn't thought about that. Would be nice if someone could carry on Dad's work. He'd like that. I was concerned about where his customers could go. He never liked the Big Board outfits."

A wild idea came into my head, so I said, "Miss Biddle, what I'd like to do is for you to keep any assets after all the bills have been cleared up, and let me take the company name and your customer list."

"There aren't any bills. Dad always paid cash. What's it worth to you?"

"I'd like to pay you $3,000, and here is how I'd like to do it. I'll give you 15 percent payment on any business that I generate from your old customers until you have been paid $3,000. Would that be fair enough?"

"Make it $25,000, and you've got a deal."

"Looks like some of your dad's savvy rubbed off on you."

"Twenty-five sounds like a good figure to me," she said.

"I'd have to gross over $160,000 to pay you off. That's a bit steep. Let's make it ten."

"I'll go for fifteen," she said.

"How about twelve-fifty?"

"Dad left me in pretty good shape. Would you take good care of his customers?"

"Yes, I can give you some references if you'd like to check me out."

"No. I don't think that'll be necessary. You look like a fine young man to me. I think Dad would have liked this."

"Then it's done."

She smiled and said, "I don't need the money. I was just testing your mettle. I think Dad would've liked you. You can have it for three."

"Good enough."

She shook hands and said, "I'll have Dad's attorney send you a contract to sign."

"Thanks. I'll try not to disappoint your dad."

"Let me give you some background on the company," she said, and then she told me, "BIS stands for Biddle International Securities. Dad's early ambition was to build a large firm. Even with the Depression in the 1930s, he developed a substantial operation with several stockbrokers associated with him. He finally grew weary of the constant hassle of broker turnover. Everyday he saw more and more government regulation. When he started as a young broker, the robber barons were still in fashion. He once told me he witnessed the initial invasion of the securities business by the SEC in 1933 when they moved in on the New York Stock Exchange. It got worse every year. Finally, he told me, 'I've had enough of bureaucrats.' He settled down into a one-man shop with a bookkeeper to keep his records. After that, they left him alone. 'They had bigger game to skin,' he told me."

With no out-of-pocket costs for the corporate structure and client list, my main concern now was to find the minimum $5,000 liquid capital. I didn't want to borrow the money. This business was too risky with only a small base. I considered John Lucas too good a friend to clip for $5,000. I had no collateral to cover him. Dan Lews, I figured, was in about as bad a shape as me. I knew he also had been hurt pretty badly by the Tiger Hackett failure.

That evening I thought I would give him a try anyway, so I called him. "Dan, I have made a deal with the Biddle estate to acquire a securities corporation with some pretty powerful clients left by Mr. Biddle when he died."

"I read about his death in the paper."

"Dan, I want a partner to join me in this new operation. I wonder if you'd be interested?"

"I'm broke."

"So am I, but Dan, I'd love to have you as a partner. There are some big clients in that company that you could help me work."

"I don't know, Jim. I've toyed with the idea of a Big Board firm. I'm just tired of risks. I don't want anybody else, ever, to blow my money away again."

"Wouldn't happen here. You'd be a major partner."

"Jim, I don't have any money, but how much do you need?"

"We've got to put together a minimum of $5,000 and we really need more than that after the haircuts they give your capital."

"Let me think about it. I don't know where I could find that kind of money. Tiger Hackett ate me up, took my clients down with it," Dan said.

"We could get well quick with those new clients to work with."

"Let me think. I'll let you know. Jim, I think First Securities might have a spot for you also. Are you interested?"

"No. I want to build a company to raise money for small firms," I said.

"I'll let you know, Jim."

"Okay, Dan, but we could have a lot of fun and make some real money if you join me."

"I'll sleep on it, but don't count on me," he said. "That First Securities deal looks pretty good to me. You should join me there."

"No. I want to stay independent."

A week passed by and I hadn't found any money, nor had I heard from Daniel Lews. I wouldn't beg him to join me. Besides, maybe he just couldn't swing it. Next I called Jim Swenson and told him my deal.

"No thanks, it's Merrill Lynch for me this time. Good luck, Jim."

Two months had already gone by since Biddle's death. Those clients of BIS would be snuffed up by other firms pretty quick, if not already. I didn't have much time. Maybe I too should just join a big firm. The thought of more Palimeers made my stomach retch and to become a big company whore made me want to outright puke.

When I came home that evening, Sonada sensed my distress, and then said to me, "I know how much it means to you to get your own firm, Jim. Maybe I can borrow some money on my retirement fund. How much do you need?"

"Five thousand," I said. "But, Hon, I couldn't take your retirement money. It's too risky. Looks like your financial genius isn't so smart after all."

"You've had a terrible market," she said. "I've seen those drops in the Dow Jones averages. That's beyond your control. I know that much."

"I could've pulled out faster, like John Lucas did," I said.

"I'm sure I could get at least $5,000 for you," she insisted.

"No, that won't do."

That morning the contract from Biddle's attorney came. It looked okay, but I didn't like the short time requirement specified. I signed the document anyway and put it right back in the mail. That tied up the corporate shell and customer list, but for only sixty days. I had to have my license and be in business within that period, or the deal was off. Her attorney must have tried to show that he earned his money, and added that little rub. I didn't have time to waste. I remembered how long it took to get Tiger Hackett's license approved.

This was the time when a lot of people thought gold and silver was the smart place to put your money. In the den, I pulled out the file with those worthless Spokane securities. I made a list of them and called John Lucas to see if he knew whether there was any value there. They were not generally quoted.

"I'll call Spokane and get some quotes for you," he said.

In a couple of days John got back to me. He said, "Jim, they're putting out some pretty good quotes for some of that stuff. Don't count on it though. If you try to sell more than a thousand shares, the price will take a dive."

"That doesn't surprise me," I said. "I know how thin those markets are, but it pleases me that there is quoted value."

"Do you want me to sell them for you?"

"No. I'll hold them for now, but may sell them later," I said.

The higher quoted value meant a lot more to me now, than what little could be raised from selling them. These stocks must have really moved up since the last time I had checked their markets. Then, they were worthless and probably still were if you tried to move any size. I totaled up the quoted prices. It was $7,000. All of them, together, had cost me over $15,000, but that was back when I had money to throw around. If I haircut them 30 percent, they would still show $4,500 on paper, close to what I needed. If I sold them outright, I'd be lucky to get $2,000.

I felt exhilarated. Just maybe I could do it. Another $1,000 or so and I was in business. Maybe my luck had changed.

That evening Daniel Lews called me and said, "Jim, let's have lunch tomorrow. I want to talk to you about something."

"Have you seen the light?"

"Won't say, but let's talk."

"Okay, usual place."

We'd often had lunch at the Sixth Avenue Bar & Grill, just down the street from Tiger Hackett. I used to kid him about his tapeworm. His body was not very efficient in converting food. He'd eat two full-course meals and not gain a pound. I just hoped that maybe he'd come up with something.

Dan did the cat and mouse game with me. He wouldn't say his mind.

"How many clients did Biddle's firm have?" he asked. "Who were some of them?"

"At least a couple hundred active ones, some of them big. I'm not naming names until you become a partner."

"Would I have to come in before eight o'clock?" he asked.

"Depends on you. I'd call that a partner's prerogative as to how hard you wanted to work."

"How safe do you think our money would be, Jim?"

"Safer than Tiger Hackett, I'd say. We only need it for show capital. We won't take in any inventory, at least not for a while. I'd say it's pretty safe."

He stuck out his hand, "Then count me in, Jim. I'll put in five thousand cash for 30 percent interest."

I returned his handshake. "Done," I said.

"Jim," he said, "you know I work hard when I'm there, but I like to take off about three o'clock."

"I have no problem with that, but how did you come up with five grand?" I asked him.

"I got to thinking about it pretty hard. I decided I didn't want to be just another number in a big outfit. I've seen the money Hackett made before he started chasing skirts."

"I thought you were broke."

"I am, but I called Dad and Mom and told them what I wanted to do. Dad told me, 'The money's yours.' I suspect he mortgaged the farm because he said he needed interest and wanted a payback in two years."

"I think we can do that, but what made you ask for only 30 percent?"

"I figured if you put in five, plus you tied up all those clients for us, that's a fair deal."

"Dan, I think we'll be okay partners. We'll find ourselves a little office and get going."

"Done, partner," he said, and we shook hands again. "Jim, you find us an office and I'll get a letter out to those Biddle clients saying what we're doing."

"Fair enough."

We now needed to pass the state's principal's exam in order to qualify to run our own securities business. I called State Securities in Olympia. Some male clerk answered the phone. "Next scheduled tests are the fifteenth of next month over in Spokane."

"That's thirty days away. I can't wait that long."

"Why not? Everybody else does."

"I want to talk to your supervisor."

"Won't do you any good. Why waste her time?"

"I said I want to talk to your supervisor."

"All right, but it won't do you any good."

A more friendly voice came on the line. "This is Ruth. What can I do for you?"

"I need to take the state principal's exam. We've made a deal to buy a company whose owner died. It's critical that we get going quickly or we'll lose his clients."

"Who is the gentleman who died?"

"Mr. Biddle of Biddle International Securities."

"I thought that's who you might say," she said. "I knew Mr. Biddle. A nice old fellow. Never gave us any trouble."

She hesitated a moment, and then said, "I'll be working Saturday doing some catch-up work. Why don't you come on down Saturday morning, and I'll personally give you the tests and grade them while you wait?"

Had I heard her right? Had I actually found a bureaucrat with a heart that ran with real red blood?

"We'll be there Saturday morning for sure," I said.

Friday night, a blizzard came. When I woke up, there must have been two feet of snow. Even the gods were against us, I thought. We were supposed to be in Olympia for our tests at nine o'clock. Overnight the storm dumped more snow on the west side of the mountains than had happened in any of the past fifty winters. I didn't even have chains for the car. To drive down in a car would be hazardous. People went nuts around here when there was a snowstorm. They didn't know how to drive in such weather, it was so rare.

I called Olympia again at eight o'clock. Ruth was already in the office. "With this blizzard, I was wondering if we could reschedule it for next week."

"Can't," Ruth said. "I'd be delighted to give you the test later, but first of the week I'm going back East to spend the holidays with my family, and I'll be gone three weeks."

"Is there anyone else who could help us?"

"No, I'm it. There's just the commissioner and me that could do this. I'm bending the rules, you know."

"Will you be there long?"

"All day," she said.

"We'll be there by two o'clock. Is that okay?"

"That should work. I'm here all day."

"We're on our way. I'll get there if I have to walk."

"You better get moving. Sixty miles is quite a distance to cover in six hours on foot."

From the comfort of our Greyhound seats, we saw cars stalled all along the highway, a jumbled chain of chaos.

"I hope this storm doesn't foretell our future," Dan said. There was a look of concern on his face.

"Dan, don't think negative thoughts! We're going to build a business that even the governor will sit up and take notice."

We walked across the Capital grounds in single file. Tree branches were stacked so high with snow, a cough could create an avalanche. The crunch of snow under our boots sounded like the chug of an old coal-burner. Dan trailed behind me like the caboose. A billow of smoke from my cigar wafted skyward like that of an old pioneer train.

The State Securities Commission was located in the State Highway Licensing Building. The Securities Commission was small. The Commissioner and an assistant or two was the whole show. I had heard that when small companies wanted to raise money, they could go in and talk directly with the commissioner. He would give them his thoughts, ideas and guidance on how to write their own prospectus. This was before the whole industry became so lawyer-dominated that it took a legal opinion before you dared to go take a squat.

The State Securities test was reputed to have a lot of trick questions that could be logically answered several different ways. They didn't disappoint us. It was a puzzle. The correct answers, of course, were their answers. They were the only ones that counted. We had thought we knew the material, and that had given us confidence. We already had our NASD principal's licenses. We got them on an ego trip at Jones Bylor. Both Ralph Bailor and Jim Swenson had their NASD principal licenses. Those two yahoos were not going to best Daniel Lews and me.

We sat across the room from each other. We couldn't talk, but we looked at each other. Dan looked as exasperated as I felt. Two hours dragged on. Finally we turned the papers over to Ruth. She put her work aside and graded them one by one.

We sat there and waited and watched her facial expression. She'd make a good poker player. We wondered what we would say if we didn't make it. We simply couldn't fail, but what if we did? Neither of us had a good feeling about the tests. I could tell from the expression on Dan's face that he was concerned as I was.

Finally, Ruth looked up and smiled at us. "You passed the tests, and beat the minimum requirements, slightly."

"Thank you! Thank you so much! Can we buy you lunch?"

"Thanks, but I've got lots to do yet, reports to get ready for the Commissioner."

We were so elated we walked back to the bus station on soft cotton. Such a modest showing didn't alarm us. We knew the material, that's what counted. To heck with the score. We passed!

Back in Seattle, I filled out the broker-dealer forms, paid the required fees and shipped the application off to the State Securities Commission. We registered with the SEC and the NASD. We didn't get on our knees, but we each said our own little prayer that the bureaucrats didn't delay us they way they had at Tiger Hackett's.

We rented a three-room office downtown in a well-kept older building. Dan took the smaller office with a corner view. Mine, slightly larger, had no view, but was right behind operations. As president and chief administrative officer, I needed to be close to operations. Kathy was our operations and girl Friday. She was both cashier and receptionist. At Tiger Hackett we called her Don't-Look-Up-Girl. She was a no-nonsense, hardworking girl. Our first choice and offer had been made to Miss Shirley. This had been out of my sense of loyalty for her past support, but she hurt our feelings. She spurned our offer. She said our proposed salary did not meet her requirements. "That wouldn't be much more than unemployment," she had said. "Think I'm better off to take a year's paid vacation."

Five weeks later, just before our deadline expired with Mr. Biddle's daughter, BIS, Inc. was back in business. It seemed like a miracle, compared to the time it took Tiger Hackett to get their license approved. Mr. Biddle's good reputation must have helped us.

Now that we were in command of our own fate, we thought life would get easier. To our dismay, we, as bosses, faced a lot of perils. Never had we imagined that there would be such a deluge of regulations. Management at both Jones Bylor and Tiger Hackett had been our shield. Now we were naked before the enemy.

Nearly every mail brought another stack of regulations and rulings and bulletins that we must study and often act upon. These missiles came from the SEC, the Federal Reserve, the NASD (National Association of Securities Dealers), and the State Securities Commission. They were like bullets aimed at our business heart, fatal if we did not comply. Each piece of paper had to be read, interpreted, and a determination made to deep-six or act on it. Most of the administrative duties fell to me. I was almost afraid to throw anything away. The lowliest bureaucrat had a knife at our throats. We weren't really our own boss. We also found out that if you hired someone to work for you, there is another whole set of rules and regulations to follow. There was a whole country full of damn fools like us, eager to take all the risks and stay harnessed to the treadmill, like trained mules, while our government stood back and threw rocks at us. Corporate tits began to look pretty good.

No wonder most of the smaller broker-dealers had gone out of business. I talked to my clients only when they called me. I had no time to call them. Thank God, I still had Dan as a producer of business. What had we gotten ourselves into?

Dan was in my office and we discussed the latest missile from the SEC, and wondered whether it applied to us or not. Kathy had taken a coffee break. Outside the counter, which separated the operations department from the reception area, stood two men. I had not noticed them until I heard one of them cough.

Catching my eye, one of them said, "May we come in?"

"Sure," Dan and I both said at the same time.

They introduced themselves as Jerry Bell and Bob Blakely. Jerry, the short, dark-haired, nervous one was the first to say something after introductions. "We've got a real moneymaker. Are you interested?"

"Depends," said Dan.

"We'll make you rich," said Jerry.

I smiled at this favorite line of most con men.

They went on to describe their sophisticated home security system that raised an alarm when break-ins tampered with windows or doors. They demonstrated a prototype with all types of electronic gear that would tell the victim which window or door was being molested. At the same time, alarms would be quietly set off at a nearby security station.

Prestige Systems, which they called themselves, had financed the research and development of their product by a limited partnership. Their friends and relatives were the limited partners, and they were the general partners. Prestige Systems needed additional money from the public to finance the manufacture, assembly and distribution of their systems. The company had authorized 2 million shares, and Jerry and Bob had already issued themselves 1 million shares for their general partnership interest. They had issued half a million shares to their limited partners, so 1.5 million shares had been issued for the total investment cost of $100,000.

They would generously share 12 percent of their future good fortune with the public for an investment of $200,000 at a dollar a share. This put a $1.5 million value on shares owned by the previous investors.

"That deal sure makes you guys rich, but I don't know about us and our investors," Dan said.

"You're absolutely wrong," Jerry said. "It's a fair deal."

"It certainly is," Bob backed him up.

"My! Aren't we being generous?" I said. "The public pays $200,000 for 12 percent interest. You guys end up with almost 90 percent of the company, which cost you a total of $100,000."

"Gosh. That is a real fair deal," Dan mocked.

"Doesn't make any difference! The product is ready to go and we'll sell millions of units," Jerry said.

All four of us crowded around the small desk in my office. Kathy shut the door, after she came back and was out front. She held up the phone calls. It was an erratic battle, attack-retreat, attack-retreat, attack-retreat. It went on for three hours. It turned into a shouting session, with insults thrown back and forth, but a decision was made. I wasn't sure they were in total agreement or just wanted to get away from my cigar smoke. We finally convinced them to turn back enough shares, so that after the first underwriting, their group would own 1 million shares among themselves, and the public would hold half a million. We would place half a million shares at forty cents a share, which would net them $170,000 after our costs. Later, when they needed more capital, another half million shares could be sold. Then the share positions would be equal between the public investors and the insiders. For our efforts, we charged a 10 percent commission on what we raised, plus 5 percent more for expenses. In addition, we'd get a five-year option to buy 50,000 shares at seventy-five cents per share if we successfully raised them the $200,000. We wanted the underwriting, as we thought it would be a winner, but we wanted a fairer break for our clients.

We were gullible enough to believe we could pull it off and easily raise the money. We were convinced that their project would make a great deal of money for all of us. But when we got to selling, it wasn't so easy. Our clients were not as enthusiastic about the future of Prestige Security Systems as we were. Besides, President Nixon bombed Cambodia. The general market crashed. How could we excite people about some new home security system when the world was exploding? Bob and Jerry did what they could to help. They spoke to groups of potential investors who would come to see their prototype and hear their spiel. Most people, when they saw how the prototype worked, liked it and were impressed. Some not only bought stock, but also placed orders for the system to be installed in their homes. Still, it was a tough job to raise the funds, and we had to raise most of the funds ourselves. Four firms committed to help us. Two backed out and the other two firms committed for only 50,000 shares. Dan and I placed the remaining 450,000 shares. It took six months of agony to sell that issue. In better times either one of us could have moved the whole thing in three or four days. Even with the heavy price we paid, it was a victory. We had completed our first underwriting. Prestige Security Systems was funded and on its way, in spite of the stock market crumble.

We celebrated that success and our first year in the business. It wasn't a celebration that you could compare to Tiger Hackett's first year splash. We got a temp to catch the phones. Dan and I closed the office for a couple of hours on Friday afternoon. We took Kathy to lunch at the fancy French restaurant on the top of the highest building in town. We all needed a break. Kathy was swamped with paper work.

Our final glass of wine, we clinked to Kathy, and I said, "To the best damn Don't-Look-Up-Gal in town. I think we need to stretch out and get you some help."

"I'll drink to that," she said.

Little did we realize we faced far greater problems.

TWENTY-FOUR

We had just gotten back to the normal business of calling our clients and going over their portfolios with them, when it happened. A stern-faced, cotton-headed kid came to our office. "I'm Ted Baxter from the NASD," he said. "I'm here to audit your books."

"Fine, no problem," I said. "There are the files. Here are the books. Yell if we can help."

Over the next three days he yelled and he yelled a lot more. Constant interruptions. "What's this? What did you do here? Don't you know you aren't supposed to do that?" He stuck his snout into everything. We tolerated it, with our fists clenched in our pockets.

After three days of this regulatory water torture, Baxter stood and engulfed the entrance to my office door.

"Well, I'm finished," he said. "I have the results."

"Do we get to stay out of jail?" I asked.

"Mr. Bradley, you have three infractions," Cotton Head said with great satisfaction.

"What are they?" thin, wiry, and hyper Daniel Lews asked as he walked into my office. He stood at my side with his hands on his hips, ready to face God's judgment with me.

"In the first infraction of the rules, you allowed a client to pay for his stock one day late and the second infraction you allowed another client to pay three days late. You didn't seek our permission."

"If you think this is serious, we'll be more careful next time," I said.

"Serious? It's critical," Cotton Head stomped his foot and shouted, dumbfounded at my incredible stupidity.

Dan asked, "Do you think they'll cut our penises off?"

Cotton Head ignored this. "You should have canceled the transaction or called the NASD for permission not to cancel."

Dan scratched his head and asked, "If we had called you and asked permission, would you have given us permission to not cancel?"

"Certainly."

"Then why bother?" Dan asked.

Cotton Head's cheeks puffed up and his blue eyes glared. "It's the rules!"

"Oh, I see," I said. "What's the other crime we committed? I think you said there were three."

"That Prestige System underwriting you just completed."

"What about it? I thought Dan and I did a good job. We single-handedly raised them $200,000, with very little help from any of your other NASD brokers."

"Yeah, and two of them welshed on us," Dan said.

Cotton Head stood with his arms crossed at his chest. "You filed the registration papers on Prestige Systems with the SEC on September fifteenth. You did not file with the NASD until October fifteenth."

"So?" Dan said, still at my side.

"The rule states that members of the NASD must file registration papers simultaneously with both the SEC and the NASD."

"We are a small firm, and have no lawyers on retainer," I said. "The attorneys for Prestige Systems handled the filings and negotiated it through the regulators."

"You are the underwriters and members of the NASD, therefore, the responsibility rests with you."

"Prestige's attorneys told us not to sell any stock or make any solicitations until all filings had been completed and approved through both agencies, and we didn't," I said.

"Still an infraction and your problem."

"What difference did it make?" Dan asked. "We sold no stock until the offering was approved by both the SEC and the NASD."

"No harm was done," I added. "I thought you guys were on our side. After all we are an association of brokers and dealers and we pay you dues."

"Doesn't make any difference. It's an infraction of the rules. You will most likely get a citation from the District Director." With that said, he left with the smugness of a MacArthur who had just returned to the Philippines.

"Dan," I said, "I actually think the man had an orgasm from all the excitement of catching a couple of crooks like us."

"Son of a bitch. Big deal," Dan bristled. "No stock was sold. No damage was done. Pure bureaucratic tyranny. That's what it is."

"No time to fret. We got to get busy and do some business. Cotton Head cost us almost three days of business," I said.

"Yeah! I agree," he said. "I couldn't get a damn thing done either. How can you work up any enthusiasm with an asshole like that, right in earshot all of the time?"

"You don't sell much stock with a deadpan voice," I said.

A week later a certified letter came from the NASD District Director. "Dan! Come on in," I shouted. "Let's see what they've done to us."

They listed the three crimes spelled out by Cotton Head. "They've censured us, Dan, and fined us $100."

"The sons of bitches."

"This places a black mark on our record, Dan. I'm going over to see the Director right now," I said. "You coming?"

"No! They'd throw us both out of the business. I'd probably poke the son of a bitch in the nose," he said.

It was a three-block walk to the IBM building where the NASD had their regional offices. The sunshine and golden autumn leaves of the mimosa trees, planted for the 1962 World's Fair, certainly didn't reflect my frame of mind. I walked so fast I was puffing. When I got there, the receptionist sensed my anger and ushered me right into the Director's office. All in one breath, I blurted out, "I'm Jim Bradley of BIS, Inc. We just got a citation. No stock was sold and no sales solicitations were made until all the filings were done and approved. We don't think you're justified in hitting us with this censure thing, and the $100 fine is unfair!"

"Rules are made to be followed," came the voice of authority from behind the big mahogany desk.

I said, "As a matter of principle, we think this black mark you put on our record is wrong, unfair and should be rescinded, along with the fine."

"Sorry, nothing I can do. The committee's decision has been made. You can appeal it, but I don't think it'll do you any good."

I went back to my office in a stew. Arguments with bureaucrats are about as fruitful as spitting your anger at heaven. You're the one who gets wet. We paid the fine. We learned fast. You don't butt heads with bureaucrats. You lick their boots if you're small and want to stay in business.

Two days after we paid the fine, here comes two country boy types from the SEC. "You've been in business a year. 'Bout time for us to see how you screwed up," said the fat jolly one who looked like Jackie Gleason. The other one was thin. If he had been taller, I might have called them Mutt and Jeff.

They spent two days and went over the same stuff again. Everything the NASD did, they also did. They asked the same questions that Cotton Head had asked. They kidded us along a little, and made a few sensible suggestions, like in the future, we might do this and not do that. By the time they left, they had convinced us that maybe all bureaucrats weren't bad.

A day or so after the SEC boys left, I casually mentioned to our banker that we were drowning in confirmations and stock transfers. Our operations found it tough to keep up.

The banker said, "We want to expand our computer services. We're interested in expanding our services to include confirmations and accounting for the brokerage community. Would you be interested in our doing that for you?"

This sounded like the voice of God. "That would be great!" I said.

"If you're interested, we will experiment with you."

"With or on?" I asked.

"We'll make the cost modest. Handle all your confirmations to clients and do all the necessary paperwork. Are you interested?"

"I might be," I said. Fantastic lights exploded in my brain. An escape from paperwork and a buffer between us and the regulators. Unbelievable! I tried to hide my enthusiasm. Kathy was swamped, and I had a multitude of reports to fill out. Now they would save us from all this!

"It's a program I think you'll be happy with," my banker said.

"When could you start?" I asked.

"First of the month okay?"

"Yes, but how about the cost, how much?"

"I'll call you shortly and confirm it in writing."

The next day we received a letter that confirmed our arrangement with the bank. We started the first of the month. We hand-carried forms to the bank each day, with the names and addresses of our buyers and sellers, and the details on the actual transactions. The next day we received duplicate copies of the bank's confirmations to our clients. At the end of the week, they sent over a recap sheet, which listed all the transactions for the week and the transfers of funds into and out of our account. For all of this they charged us three bucks a ticket. Paradise! We could talk to clients again. No more paperwork!

"We don't even have to handle the money," I said to Dan.

"Now maybe you can get back to work. It's about time you sold something again," Dan replied.

"Who knows, maybe we can even find time to hire and train more brokers, and maybe even begin to make some money," I said.

Two months of this bliss, then paradise crumbled. Our reconciled figures did not match those of the bank. People paid late for their stocks, and we were not notified. Cotton Head from the NASD came back to our door with more infractions of the rules and another citation. He couldn't intimidate the bank, so he took it out on us. This time the fine was $200. The bank put our paperwork in worse shape than when they began. It took more time to reconcile our differences with the bank than it had to monitor Kathy's previous transactions.

At midpoint of the fifth month, the head of the bank's data processing division called me on the phone.

"We've decided that we're no longer interested in the securities bookkeeping business. We will terminate our involvement at the end of this month."

"You'll do what?! Our records are in a mess. The NASD bangs at our door like the police, and you walk away," I said.

"You knew this was an experiment. We discovered that your business is too unrelated to what we're doing. Sorry it didn't work out."

"What about the $5,000 reconciliation difference?"

"Send us a check."

"Our records are so messed up, we don't even know if we owe you that."

"Just sign a note for the $5,000, and we can adjust it if we find any errors in the balances."

"If I sign a note with you guys for $5,000, that's what you'll collect," I said.

"No," he said. "We can adjust any differences."

"Bankers are as tricky as lawyers," I said. "You'll find a loophole somewhere."

"What do you mean by that?"

"You'll just assign our account to someone else to collect, and he won't remember this conversation."

"Hogwash! We're a big bank; we don't operate that way."

"I'll make you a deal." I said.

"What kind of a deal?"

"We'll take our back paperwork mess, and you write off the $5,000 that you say we owe."

"I don't think so, but I'll take it up with the committee."

Another month passed, and we received a bill for $5,000 plus one month's interest.

I wrote back and said, "We won't pay."

Their attorney called and I told him the same thing.

Then a collection agency called, and said, "This account has been assigned to us. It is no longer the concern of the bank. We expect immediate payment in full, or an acceptable arrangement of monthly payments."

"I suggest that you go down to the base of Madison Street and take a swim. Go jump, Buster," I said, and hung up.

I called the bank president and said, "We're bringing suit against you for $50,000 in damages to our business. I've called a press conference to make the announcement this afternoon." Then I hung up.

Twenty-five minutes later, the bank attorney called me back. "We've decided to write off the $5,000 if you'll sign the settlement agreement."

It took me two more months to straighten out our messed-up books. Cotton Head from the NASD was no help. He was in every three or four days to nit-pick. I worked evenings until midnight and sometimes later. Finally we got our books back in shape. Once more there was peace with the NASD, and the Cotton Head kid stayed out of the patch. It was wonderful to have peace again.

That same evening, just at quitting time, Daniel Lews came into my office and sat down. He wasn't all tensed up and mad at the bureaucrats this time. His fight was gone.

"Jim, we can't lick the bastards. Let's join them."

"What's on your mind, Dan?"

"Let's bag it and go to work for a bigger outfit."

"Can't do that, Dan. I've told you I'd rather be a contractor with my own wheelbarrow and haul muck than go work for someone else."

"Well, Jim, I was afraid you'd say that. I'm sorry to leave, but I got to. I've had enough. I'll leave it with you."

"What do you mean, Dan?"

"I've been offered a job with a Big Board outfit."

"Dan, you can't do that now. We're almost there."

"I've already accepted their offer. There's room for you if you'll come along. They'll take us both."

"No, Dan, I'm afraid I'll have to tough it out here."

He stood up. "No sense to linger. I don't like goodbyes. I've already cleaned out my desk. You can settle up with me when you can, Jim. I don't want to cause you any hardship." He shook my hand and briskly walked away.

This was false bravado. There was sadness in his face, and turmoil. He was choked up, and I could see he had to get away. He must have fought off telling me until the last moment. At the door he turned around and waved a salute. There were tears in his eyes.

TWENTY-FIVE

Dan's departure hurt. I heard his footsteps go down the hall. We'd been friends a long time, partners and spiritual comrades. Now he was gone. I felt my grip on tomorrow's rope slip. The chasm below was deep. Gone were most of the smaller securities firms. We'd seen them go, pop off like a black bean in the Mexican Revolution. They quit in despair, or merged with larger firms, or went broke.

There *had* to be an answer. An independent broker-dealer was still the best hope for local companies and start-ups. Banks were not the answer. Venture capital companies were not interested in risk. They wanted something seasoned, and even then they took a big bite. Price movements in the stock market create excitement. Excitement makes people want to invest and even gamble. Any new venture is a gamble. Not everyone wanted a General Motors tit to suck. Yet you'd think there was a conspiracy to keep capital safe for banks and savings accounts and provide play money for the big guys. There simply had to be a way around all this regulation. Alone, I wouldn't last, unless I could come up with some way to outwit it. Complying with all the rules and requests for information, there was no time to serve my customers. The SEC, NASD, and the State Securities Commission's blizzard of regulations created an avalanche that could only crush or smother me. Maybe I should just bag the whole idea. Let the little guys go to hell. Close my business and join a Big Board outfit, just like Dan and the others.

The next day was pandemonium, my own calls and calls from Dan's clients. If he wasn't there, where was he? Were we going out of business? I gave them Dan's new phone number, and said I was sure he would call them shortly.

"No, we're in business to stay," I said. "We've got a new concept I'll call you about soon."

Now I had to find the concept.

After lunch, when the market closed, I said to Kathy, "I'm out for an hour or so. If anyone calls, tell them I'll get back to them in a couple of hours."

I wandered down to Lowell's Cafeteria at the Pike Place Market. I picked up a coffee and carried it up to the highest floor level overlooking the Sound. Then I lit a cigar. It didn't take long for thoughts to flow. Best thing to do when bad breath heads your way is to get out of its way.

What if I registered only with the state as a state broker-dealer? Maybe then, I could eliminate two bad breaths. Without the NASD and the Securities and Exchange Commission, I might survive the lesser halitosis of the State Securities Commission. The SEC was mainly concerned with interstate commerce. If I confined my business to the state, then they were not likely to bother with me. If I did not have to concern myself with the SEC and NASD regulations, I might be able to survive. I didn't know any firms that did that. They were all registered with the SEC and the NASD. I had heard of intrastate firms, but they were mainly organized to raise money for a single project. I could skip the NASD, but if I did, I wouldn't be able to deal with their members on a wholesale basis, which everyone said you had to do in order to survive.

I went back to the office and called Nathan Blattsworth. He was the president of an insurance company. We were the first market maker for his stock after he financed his company through an intrastate offering. We were still friends, even though he had outgrown our market-making activity, and was now supported in bigger markets by others.

"Nathan," I said. "I'm drowning in regulations. If I were just a state broker-dealer, do you think I could cut out some of the agencies that regulate me?"

"Jim, I don't know whether you could skip the SEC or not. Tell you what, though, I know Herman Hershel down at State Securities. Let's go down and talk with him. Maybe he has some ideas."

I had heard the name, Herman Hershel, before, but had never dealt with him.

"Sounds good to me. Monday okay with you?"

"Let's hit it early before they get busy," he said.

Monday morning at eight o'clock we were at the state capital. We waited in the Securities Commission's lobby for Mr. Hershel. "It'll be a few moments," the receptionist said.

The setup had changed since Dan and I had last been here. It was no longer a small office. Now there was a vast area of desks, separated by room dividers. There was the hum of voices and activity, but no longer the friendly, personal atmosphere of that earlier time. Now it was somber and all business. Finally, the receptionist pointed in the direction of Mr. Hershel's work area and we walked over.

"Herman, I want you to meet Jim Bradley, a good friend of mine. We want to explore something with you."

Mr. Hershel offered us two metal folding chairs, and we gathered around his desk in the cubicle office.

He looked to be of medium height, and most of his brown hair had taken leave, but there was one long tuft combed, optimistically, to cover a broad area. Most of his weight hung over his belt, and I secretly nicknamed him, "Big Belly." Then I recognized him. He was the flunky who had assisted the nice lady who had personally given Dan and me our principal's examinations ahead of time. She had since retired and was no longer there. The puppy dog innocence of youth had left Big Belly. He was friendly, but there was a glint of hardness in his look.

"Mr. Hershel," I said, "I want to start a new brokerage company to be registered only with State Securities. We plan to raise capital for local business and make markets in their stocks."

"Sounds like a good purpose, but why only register with the state?"

"If I can avoid the crush of SEC and NASD regulations, I might be able to survive as a small broker-dealer."

With a puzzled look, he said, "They are there only to protect investors. Why do you say that?"

"It's the paperwork and excessive rules and regulations that kill off most of the small broker-dealers."

He grimaced as he said, "Those other agencies, like ourselves, protect investors. We just do our duty. If you can't comply with the rules, you shouldn't be in the business."

"Just let them keep it up and there won't be any business to regulate, except maybe a couple of big outfits. Then where would you fellows be?"

He smiled. "That's not likely."

"Seriously, though," I said. "They make the cause hardly worth the effort."

"What's the cause?"

"My motive is to help small business and keep more investment dollars here at home."

"And make a few bucks for yourself," he added.

"Of course, but I think the little guy needs a break. My dad was a sharecropper, only because he had no way to get capital. Between the landlords and the banks, there wasn't much left."

Big Belly paused a moment, scratched his nose with a ruler, then said, "I like your purpose. It would be good for industry here."

"There's a real need in this area," my friend said.

I assumed that Big Belly was fairly new in this higher position, and had not yet acquired the rigid attitude so prevalent among those who had spent years in the same job.

He finally said, "I'd like to see somebody support local stocks. We need that."

"My question is," I said, "if we register only with you, and confine our business activities to the state, can we avoid all the paperwork and reports to those other agencies?"

"I don't know," Big Belly said, "but let's find out."

He picked up the phone, called the SEC division headquarters in Seattle and posed the question to them.

There were long pauses, while he listened to them, interspersed with, "Yes... No... I don't think so."

Big Belly finally hung up, turned to me, and said, "They say you're my problem. If all of your transactions stay within the confines of the state, you don't utilize vehicles of interstate commerce across state lines."

"Then we can be a broker-dealer without them?"

"I guess that's your answer. You file your state broker-dealer application, meet the capital requirements, and stay out of trouble, you won't have any problems from me."

Big Belly handed me a set of broker-dealer application forms. "Fill these out, get them back to me with the filing fee, and if your application looks okay, you're in business."

"Thank you so much, Mr. Hershel. I'll get it right back to you. I appreciate your help."

On the way back from Olympia, I said to Nathan, "I plan to publish a market letter covering local companies. There'll be write-ups on companies and listings of bids and offers on their stock."

"That's sounds great," he said.

"I'll print extra copies when there is a write-up on a company, which they can mail out to their shareholders. It'll help us both."

"Sounds good to me," he said. "We'll support you. Let me know how I can help."

Soon as we got back to Seattle, and I was in my office, I called Dan and told him I had something to talk over with him. "Come on over," he said. "I can show you my new office. You'd like it."

Sounded like he wanted to proselytize me. I walked down to his building. Dan's office was near the top floor of one of Seattle's newest skyscrapers. Maybe I could steal him back. He felt the same way as I did about small business. I was excited about this new concept of a state broker-dealer firm. With these new ramifications, he might still be interested.

Dan's new firm was First Securities Northwest. The layout was like most Big Board houses, with offices around the perimeter for executives and senior brokers, and a bullpen in the center for the up-and-comers and the on-the-way-downers. Dan seemed at home in his big Spartan bullpen. I told him my idea and suggested he might want to join me.

His reaction was swift and forthright. "Jim, you've got rocks in your head!"

"How's that?"

"Look, we can't keep up with all the crap coming out of Washington, DC."

"Dan! That's the whole thing. We don't have to mess around with the SEC and the NASD anymore. Not as a state broker-dealer. Come on back. We'll make some real money and be on our own."

"No, Jim, I'm through with the small businessman's fight. I'll stay where I am and fight for Dan."

"Come back. It'll be fifty-fifty," I said.

"No, Jim, not this time. That's my final answer." As a dismissal, he picked up the phone to return a call from the stack of messages on his desk.

I left. Without Dan as my partner, it would take the gusto out of the business. I'd miss his support and comradeship. Maybe he was the smart one, and I did have pebbles for brains. But still, I had to go on.

I liquidated BIS and settled up with Dan. I named my new company Local Securities of Washington, or LSW. I took a smaller office down the hall and found Kathy a job with another firm. I could no longer afford full-time staff. This was when Chrispina came to work with me. A young Filipina lady, she worked for a local produce firm and needed to earn extra money. Her mother and younger sister had just come from the old country. Chrispina spoke excellent English, had a sharp pencil and was good with figures. She worked each Saturday and kept my books.

Now I needed brokers. Good ones stayed with their old firms. When I advertised for some new men, I got the leavings. One old gentleman just sat there and looked at the phone all day. He waited for calls or the next Depression. I don't think he knew which. Another older guy, arrogant, specialized in estate liquidation. People did not die fast enough for us to make any money on his efforts. I brought new people into the business and trained them. They spooked easily, were skittish and had frail confidence in these smaller companies that I made markets in. First setback, they left me and scattered out to the larger brokerage firms, who were delighted to get the experienced men I had trained.

Without a partner, it was difficult to make any money. Other brokers around town told me, "Jim, you're nuts! You'll never make a living out of those little Northwest stocks." Sonada kept her job as a dental technician and that helped us to survive. One cloudy, overcast day, as my office filled with cigar smoke, I looked out the window and wondered if I did have pebbles for brains.

TWENTY-SIX

I opened the window to let the cigar smoke out. When I turned around, there were two men standing in the doorway. The tall, thin, gray-headed one stuck out his hand to shake, "Wayne Howard," he said, "and this is my associate, Rex Donovan." Rex was short, rotund, with red hair tinged with gray. An Irishman-like passion surged through his handshake.

Wayne, older, seemed to take the lead. He said, "Our company is Home Modules. We hold a patent on a new process in building construction. It has insulation factors that beats anything on the market."

"Tough as iron and fire-retardant," Rex added.

"Sounds intriguing. What can I do for you?"

"We want an underwriter," Wayne said.

I motioned for them to take a seat. "I'd be most interested, but I don't have a sales force. I'm it."

"We don't care. We can recruit a group. What we want is a public market," Rex said.

"Tell me more."

Wayne answered, "We can cast a complete room. We use an oil-based plastic foam mixture that is put inside a portable mold. Before we pump this material into the mold, we install steel-reinforced concrete studs. Then we pour in the plastic foam. This material has a high insulation factor, and can be put up quickly by relatively unskilled people. And it can withstand hurricane winds."

"That sounds like something you'd want to use in the third world countries," I said.

"Not only that, it's the best damn insulation against cold and heat that's been devised," Rex added.

Now they really caught my interest. This just might be the kind of issue I needed to put me on the map. "How does this stuff stand up in hot sun and winter's cold?" I asked.

"Wears better than a whore," Rex said. "It can take a rubber-melting sun. It'll ride out an earthquake rumble like a raft going down the rapids!"

Wayne, the quieter one, added, "We put the electric and plumbing lines inside the mold before the mixture is sprayed in. When we break the mold away, we have a finished room," he said, "ready and waiting to be combined with other rooms to make a complete structure, residential or commercial. How does that sound?"

"What about the cost factors?"

"Fifty percent of what it costs to build a conventional house with the same square footage."

This sounded fantastic to me, but I said, "To be honest, I love the sound of your project, but there is only me. About all I could do is reflect a market for your stock after an underwriting. My ability to raise money or support a market is limited. As I said, there's just me."

"We need an underwriter who'll make a market in the stock after the issue is done," Wayne said. "We can put a group of salesmen together. We can take care of that."

"You just back us up as a future market maker, and you'll make a piss-pot of money," said Rex.

"It's a whole lot easier to get salesmen if we have you as an underwriter," Wayne said. "Then they'll know that there will be an aftermarket for the stock."

"Sounds good to me," I said, hardly able to keep my enthusiasm in check. (Their idea was fantastic!)

"How'd you hear about me?"

"John Lucas said he thought you might be a good fit for us," Wayne said.

John Lucas referred them. That impressed me even more. "You got any background data I can study?"

"Tons of it," Rex said.

Wayne pulled a stack of material from his briefcase and handed it to me. "That'll keep you busy for a while."

"Let me look at this and I'll get back to you."

"Let us know by Monday," Rex said. "We have a couple other firms that have shown some interest."

I smiled at them, and Wayne returned the smile. We both knew that if they had someone else interested, they wouldn't be messing around with me.

Wayne and Rex came back Monday afternoon, after the market had closed. We put a deal together. In addition to a commission on anything I sold personally, I'd get an override on any sales their salesmen generated, plus a five-year option to buy stock at a price just slightly over the offering price. I'd make a fortune if it were a winner.

Home Modules moved fast. We had fifteen salesmen recruited, trained and selling stock within sixty days. We started the offering price at $2 per share, and within six months we raised $1 million. The company's exhibits at home shows created excitement and generated lots of interest both from people who bought stock and those who were interested in using the material in home construction.

I opened stock trades at $1.80 bid and $2.10 offered. Five of Home Modules's fifteen salespeople transferred their licenses and came to work for me, so I leased more space down the hall. Volume got so heavy that Chrispina was buried in paper work. We hired two more part-time bookkeepers. The price was up to $8 before I knew it. When it reached $10, five times its offering price, I started to sell stock short in order to maintain the market and keep the brokers working. At that price it should be easy to cover. Wayne and Rex had indicated that they would protect me. Every time I covered my shorts, the stock was a bit higher and I lost money. I was 10,000 shares short at $15 and no stock came in. Nobody wanted to sell.

It was Friday afternoon. I called up Home Modules and got Wayne Howard on the line.

"Wayne, you guys better find yourself another market maker. Monday, my company goes into liquidation. I went over the brink when I shorted all that stock to keep the market going. I need that stock you promised me."

"Jim, we've tried to find stock for you, but no soap."

"Then Monday, I notify State Securities Commission of my critical situation, and liquidate."

"God dammit, Bradley, you can't do that."

"Sorry, Wayne, but it can't be helped. I shorted to keep the market alive. It just didn't work."

"You can't do that. You can't walk out on us," he shouted into the phone.

"I thought I better warn you. Must go, lots to do." I hung up. I didn't have time to listen to his moans.

When I got home, Sonada asked, "Jim, is there something wrong?"

I brushed it off, "Got a few problems, but think I can solve them."

Monday, I was at the office early to start my stock liquidation. Usually I was the first one there, but not this time. Rex impatiently paced in the hall. "Well, my friend, what brings you down so early?" I said as I unlocked the door.

"We gotta talk."

"Talk time is over. I got to act."

"Jim, you got your tit in the ringer."

"You know damn well I have, and you do too. What do you think your stock will be worth when there's no market?"

"I guess you're right," he said.

"Who would've thought that no one would take profits," I said. "Stock up over seven times and not earning a dime, and still no stock comes in." I sat down at my desk and motioned Rex to a seat.

"Me!" Rex said. "We told you that it would go up and keep going."

"Yes, and it's only because you guys oversold the prospects of that stock. It'll be quite a while before you can generate any earnings, and you know it."

He smiled. "Guess it's a bit unhealthy for you, eh?"

"So you guys found no one who wants to take a profit?"

"What's it worth to you if we have?"

"What do you mean?"

"If you don't cover that short, you're dead, aren't you?"

"So?"

He twisted in his chair and looked out the window. "If I can save you, that would be worth at least 51 percent of your company, wouldn't it?"

"Rex! I tried to maintain an orderly market in your stock and it got me into this spot. Now you got the gall to take advantage of it."

"That's business, ain't it?"

"Rex, you and your damn stock can go straight to hell as far as I'm concerned. I've got work to do." I stood up for him to leave.

"Forty-nine percent of a going company is a hell of lot better than owning 100 percent of nothing," he said as he stood up.

"My partners stick with me. They don't pick my pockets when I'm down. See how much your stock is worth when there's no quoted market," I said. I was so mad I picked up the Big Cheese sign on my desk to chase him out with it.

"All right! All right! Jim, you can't blame me for trying. Let's forget about the partnership deal. Wayne and I've found four people who'll let you have 2,500 shares each at twelve bucks per share. That should allow you to come out okay."

"Was Wayne in on your proposed deal?" I was still boiling—him trying to take advantage of me.

"No. Just my own little private initiative."

"Don't try it again."

"Okay. Does this 10,000 shares take care of your shorts?"

"Just fine. Thanks."

"For God's sake, Jim, don't go short again! That stock could hit $25," he said.

"Without any income behind it?"

"You bet! Wayne and I had a hell of a time getting the four to part with that stock."

"Understood."

Rex got up to leave and at the door, he turned around and pointed his finger at me. "Next time it's your balls."

"There won't be a next time."

"I hope not. Look, Jim, you know the public don't have any damn sense. When they're hot for something, it's like throwing a chunk of meat into a pool of piranhas."

I grinned and said, "Seems there's piranhas on both sides of the net, but I don't think the public is so stupid. If they get the straight poop from the brokers, they know how to act."

He smiled and left with one more jab. "Just remember, it's your balls next time."

That was a close one. When things like this happened and everything looked hopeless, I wondered whether there was a power that looked after me. Or was it when you keep trying, maybe that's what triggers the help. Two weeks later, Home Modules's board of directors voted to split the stock three for one, and the stock price moved right back up to $10 a share. That made the original $2 stock now worth $30 a share with nothing earned. Nope. No more shorts for me!

A rivalry developed between two brokers. They tried to outgross each other on commissions, and that helped to develop underwriting clout, but I needed good people who would stay with me.

One week later, on Saturday morning, Chrispina said, "Mr. Bradley, there's a gentleman here to see you."

I looked up to see a distinguished older man with gray hair, a well-trimmed mustache, and dressed in a blue pinstripe banker's suit. He could have passed for Walter Cronkite, the newscaster, the way he looked.

"Major John Taylor," he said as he gripped my hand. "Saw your ad in the paper."

I motioned for him to sit down, and Chrispina went back to her books.

"Major, huh? Are you retired from the army?"

"Air Force. Been retired ten years. Banker last five."

"And now, you want to become a stockbroker?"

"Already am. We just raised $1 million for a little savings and loan outfit. Now we need to find a market maker."

"Maybe we can help you there," I said.

"Another fellow and I who worked directly for the company raised the bulk of the offering. We loaded these people up with all that stock. Now we'd like to see a market in it."

"We're small and limited, but maybe we can help."

He pulled out two cigars, handed me one. "Mind?"

"Hell, no. I smoke 'em by the dozen."

He lit his cigar in a weird way. He held the match about a half-inch away from the end of his cigar and sucked the flame up to it. "That's what I'm looking for," he said. "Don't like big outfits. Too much like the military, got to control everything."

"You do sound like my kind of man," I said.

"Thought so. Checked you out. You come up proud."

"What part of the country you from," I asked, knowing full well he was from my part of the country, with that accent.

"Texas."

"That's what I thought. I'm from Oklahoma. Sounds like we'd get on fine, jest fine," I said, sliding back to the sounds of my youth.

"I liked the action on that little underwriting you did."

"Home Modules?"

"Yeah, bought some. Already sold it though."

"That's smart. Getting a little pricey."

"I thought so."

"Tell me, Major, about that stock you underwrote. Maybe we can trade it."

"Hope so. I have a list of the shareholders. That should help. We're not a regular savings and loan outfit, but a general corporation that makes loans."

"I guess that keeps them away from all the bank regulations."

"Yes, more of a factoring outfit, but we make loans other than receivables too."

"Major Taylor," I said. (I'd already named him Major Gray in my mind, with that flourishing gray top.) "I'm curious about this other fellow, who helped you raise all that money. Do you think he might want to join us?"

"I've already talked to him. He's interested. I'll bring him in tomorrow. I came in to test the waters."

"Is he a good man?"

"He's different, but I'll let you make up your own mind."

I reached into my desk. "Okay, Major, here are the forms you need to fill out. One of them is an authorization for transfer from the other outfit. Two sets, one for you and one for the other fellow. Fill them out, get them back to me and we'll get going on the paperwork."

He picked up the papers to go. "I'll see you in the morning," he said.

The next day Major Gray was at my office door when I arrived. Beside him was a husky black man who stood six foot tall and looked like a warrior. "Jim," he said to me. "This is Sam Jackson, the man I told you about." He handed back the papers that I had given him yesterday.

If Warrior was good enough for Major Gray, he was good enough for me. I hired them both. If they didn't check out, I could always unhire them. They looked like doers to me.

I showed Major Gray his office and right away, he got busy moving in. That left Warrior and me to talk. Warrior started right off and said, "I'll make you more bucks than you ever saw before."

"I hope you'll do a lot better than that, or it'll be pretty skimpy," I said.

"You'll see. By the way, Mr. Bradley, I need forty bucks for expenses. Can you loan it to me?"

I handed him a $50 bill, "'til payday."

Within two weeks all their papers were in order. And in another week, both Major Gray and Warrior had moved big blocks of stock. At the end of the third week on Friday morning, Warrior called me from Oak Harbor, up in the San Juan Islands.

"Come on up," he said. "I've got an investor seminar all set. I want you to see how I operate."

"Okay. When is it?"

"Tonight at seven at the Sounder Restaurant."

"I'll be there."

When I arrived at the place, it was already crowded. The restaurant had given Warrior a small private banquet room. His advertisement had pulled in fifty curious people. People milled about, chatted, and nibbled the refreshments. We waited and waited. No Warrior in sight! It looked like I would have to take charge and come up with some kind of speech for them. Right then, I didn't have the best thoughts about Warrior. Twenty minutes passed.

About another fifteen or twenty minutes, in walked Warrior, making a grand entrance. Without a word, he walked to the front of the room. In the ashtray on the table in front of him, he put a cigarette, and to one side a bottle of Blue Brass Beer, and on a separate dish, a donut. Still, he said nothing. He ate the donut, chug-a-lugged the beer, then lit the cigarette.

"There, now I'm finished. And what do I have left?"

He had everyone's attention.

"Nothing," someone from the back of the room said.

Others nodded in agreement. I suspected that "Nothing" was a plant.

"You spend that much money everyday on trifles, and it's gone. Forever! Invest that in a local stock and you got something left for your kids. That's all you need. Anyone can afford that. You already spent it! So you see, anybody can afford to invest in local securities. For the cost of a cigarette, a bottle of beer, or a donut, you can buy a piece of local industry and build a future."

He told stories about different local companies, things I'd never heard. He finished with, "Buy stock in local companies, and it's like planting a seed. You can watch it grow."

"What'd you do if your garden gets sick?" someone from the audience asked.

"Chop 'em down and plant another crop," he said.

He ignored the chuckles. "Look! You don't miss the price of these luxuries. Buy five different stocks instead of this stuff. One of them is bound to take root, grow and fill your basket. That's your profit," he said.

All evening there were more of these homilies. People filled out cards so they could be on his mailing list. Some people made commitments right then. "I'll invest $2,000 with you," and then someone else said, "I might go $5,000," and from another person, "Call me." This went on the rest of the evening.

The program was more like a camp gathering than an investor seminar. He baptized them to a new awakening to local securities. Warrior's sincerity came through. He certainly delivered. The dollars rolled in.

That first $50 touch and the others that followed were among my better investments. I say investments because he didn't pay back his touches. I wised up. Never asked repayment, just held it out of his next paycheck. That strategy worked for both of us.

Major Gray brought in several large accounts and more brokers. Soon, I appointed him executive vice-president and sales manager. One of the first new brokers Major Gray brought in was a man wearing a turban. To me, he looked like some kind of rajah. He wore a business suit, but had this turban on.

"This is Raja Singh," said the Major. "He wants to join us. He's from India, just got his masters at the U" (University of Washington).

"What was your major?" I asked.

"Finance."

"How'd you happen to come to us?"

"There's this black guy. I heard him give a speech. People just threw money at his feet. I saw how he worked. I can do better than that."

"Do you have work papers?"

"Better than that. I've got an American girl as my wife."

We hired him. After he left, Major Gray said, "I checked him out and from the contacts the man has, I think he'll make us a good man, but he's a bit arrogant."

"You'd think he was some kind of prince, not just named Raja," I said.

"I suspect that's just his adopted American name," Major Gray said.

I kept in touch with my old partner, Daniel Lews, over an occasional cup of coffee. At first we tried to recruit each other, but after a while we both gave up. He'd say, "Jim, You've got rocks in your head to screw around with those small companies. The big bucks are over here." But it was a draw, so we just settled down to being good friends.

Everybody else in the business waded knee-deep in oil limited partnerships, but we stayed out of them. Money flowed into our company like golden grains falling into a bin. We got a reputation for never failing on an underwriting. We never stopped midway. We always plugged away until we finished each one, even the tough ones.

By this time we averaged three or four underwritings a year. We'd put together a quarter to half a million each, and made markets in all our previous issues. Our brokers did well. I split trading profits fifty-fifty with them. Warrior earned more than ten grand a month and Raja averaged almost twenty. More brokers came and they stayed with us. There was so much enthusiasm for our stocks that it was tough for me to hold the prices down to a reasonable level. It was scary. I knew what went up too fast, always came down faster. Maybe I became a bit smug because mistakes cropped up. Others lay buried deeper, like a hidden bomb.

TWENTY-SEVEN

Six months after I hired Frank Brocknor, he was our top producer. He even topped Raja. Through him, five new brokers came on staff, his college buddies. Six months more, he came into my office and said, "Let's go to Mignonne's for a cup of coffee." This was a Japanese-run French pastry shop, my favorite place away from the office when I wanted to negotiate.

Once there, I asked him, "What's on your mind?"

"I want to be a branch manager," he said.

"We don't have any branches."

"Let's start one," he said. There was a grim look of determination on his face.

"You got something in mind?"

"I'd like to start a branch up in Everett."

"Why Everett?" I said.

"It's a sleepy town, but we'll wake it up."

"Frank, from what I've seen you do this past year, I believe you might make it work."

"Can I take my five guys with me?"

"Sure, why not? You brought 'em in. They'd give you a good starting base, better than I had."

We rented space and outfitted an office in Everett, thirty miles north of Seattle. Frank recruited ten more brokers, and it wasn't long before their gross equaled ours. After six months Frank was back in to see me again.

"Let's start a third branch."

"Where do you have in mind?"

"I think Federal Way is ripe. It's an affluent area, and there aren't any brokerage firms down there," he said.

"Who'd run it?"

"Let me start it," he said. "I'll let Dave Connors operate Everett under my direction until I get Federal Way launched. This will give him some experience; then we'll put him in charge of Federal Way. Then I'll go back to Everett, but I'll also keep an eye on Federal Way for you."

"What do you want for all of this work?"

"Just give me a 5 percent override on any future profits on those locations."

Dave Connors had been the first of Frank Brocknor's college buddies to join us. He was ambitious and had made good progress. A little fast on the mouth, but basically a good man.

After the Federal Way office was underway, we switched Frank back to Everett and Dave Connors went down to Federal Way as planned. Dave Connors proved to be super at winning new business. It wasn't long before he added ten more brokers.

Now with three offices and forty-two brokers, we became a powerhouse in local securities. A hot national new issues market added fuel to our business. How could you fail with this kind of action going on all around you? Yet, I got an edgy feeling. I remembered Tiger Hackett's fast track dealings, and the crash at the end. This kind of success came too easy. Besides, I was feeling more broke. The bigger we got, the more money we needed.

Local newspapers and business magazines wrote us up with articles on our underwriting successes, our firm and on our more successful brokers. This gave us more credibility and brought in more business. Our clients saw their stocks go up 25 percent or 50 percent, and even double in six months. Other firms began to take an interest in our stocks. Our volume surpassed Tiger Hackett's at its peak.

All of this success didn't please everyone. A savings and loan company some sixty miles away complained to the State Securities Commission. "Too many of our customers have pulled money out of savings and transferred the funds down to some outfit in Seattle," they reported to State Securities. "We never heard of the outfit, LS something or other. What's going on?" They asked State Securities Commission to investigate. The branch of a Big Board house also asked the Commission to look into us. Our answer was, "Maybe our stocks go up."

Eleven o'clock, Tuesday morning, my old rancher friend from Jones Bylor, John L. Lucas, called. I hadn't seen him for six months. "God dammit, Jim," he shouted into his telephone, "let's have lunch."

"Sure, I've been meaning to call you."

Thirty minutes later, we sat down to lunch at the sumptuous private club of which he was a member. It had to be his money that got him in. He was an anomaly in this place with its fine furniture and hushed elegance. I noticed that the host seated us off in a corner, where John's burly form and lusty voice would not disturb the Brooks Brother suits.

"God dammit, Jim! You got too many goddamn wild horses!"

"What do you mean?"

"It's those goddamn pups you hired."

"You mean my brokers?"

"You're goddamn right! It's those damn stray pups you got in that damn Federal Way kennel that's going to kill you!" he shouted.

"What are you saying?"

He pounded on the table. I noticed people turning around to look at us.

"Fire the whole goddamn bunch if you want to survive!"

"What's brought this on? I haven't seen you this excited since President Kennedy tried to control steel prices."

"That goddamn den of wolf-pups you got down at Federal Way! I'd hang 'em all up by the balls if they were my men."

"They're the most productive crew I have."

"It's no goddamn wonder. They tell everybody your goddamned stocks always double; that you got lots of money to push them up. They won't lose any money on your stocks. You'll back 'em up."

"No, I haven't heard that story. You had any experience in hanging?"

"No, but I sure know how my old man would've handled horse thieves. That's what they are. They're stealing your business."

"Thanks, John. I'll get right on it. How'd you find out?"

"It's reliable. Let's just say some of my clients got pitched by your pups."

"Thanks, I appreciate your telling me about this."

"Expect you'd do the same for me."

Quickly, we finished our lunch. I had to move. This was a crisis. I had to put a stop this immediately.

Back at the office, I called Dave Connors. "Dave, I want you to tell your brokers to take the rest of the day off. Let the secretary take the calls. They can call their clients back tomorrow."

"But we've got a contest going!"

"Tell them to leave the office right now! I don't want to see them there until seven in the morning, period. Tell them now. Then get your ass up here, right now."

"Wha-what do you mean? Is something wrong?"

"Get a move on, right now." I hung up.

An hour later Dave Connors came into my office with an innocent, puzzled and greatly offended look on his face. "What's this all about, Mr. Bradley?" He took a seat before me.

"Dave, are you aware of what your brokers tell their clients?"

"Certainly. Is there a problem?"

"You bet there is! Your guys have told clients that our stocks always double in price. That they can't lose any money. Jim Bradley will take care of any losses personally!" I could see his defense antennae go up.

"That's a damn lie!" He jumped up from his seat and stood with his fists doubled while he glared at me.

"My source is reliable."

"He's a liar, whoever he is. My men don't say things like that!"

"We could all lose our licenses over this."

"We could?"

"Yes. Not only that, it makes us a laughingstock out on the street."

"It's a damn lie," he said as he slumped back into his seat.

"I don't think so. We will talk about it in the morning. Call your men up tonight and have them prepare a list of the people they have told this bullshit to."

"I'll find out who is doing it and put a stop to it," he said.

"I'll be there in the morning and we will get it squared up."

"What do you mean, squared up?"

"That's it." I stood up. "I called you up here to emphasize the importance of having your men there in the morning with those lists already prepared. Do you understand?"

"Yes."

"You can go now."

I dictated a letter we would send out to the clients. We would offer to buy back their stock immediately, at what it cost them, or at the current market, whichever was higher. The sales pitch that guaranteed them against loss was not appropriate and not permitted. I concluded the letter with, "We now offer you a chance to get out if you wish. If you choose to hold securities purchased under that premise after one week from this date, then the risk is yours, not this firm's." All letters would be sent certified.

Next morning at Federal Way, faces were grim. I made my short speech to twelve long faces. I asked for their help. They all feared I was there to fire them. You could see the relief on their faces when I asked for their help. They had their customer lists ready. Dave had warned them that I was on the warpath. Next, I read the proposed letter to clients. Relief rippled over their faces. There was even a smile or two.

Then I said, "I want a few minutes conference with each of you. Bring your customer list in, and we'll discuss what you've said to each one of them."

Dave Connors's face said, "What's the big deal?"

"Dave, I want to talk to you last." He gave me a "go fuck yourself" look.

I commandeered Connors's office for the private conferences. One by one, each broker said he had been coached to promise Bradley's backup support as the best way to move lots of stock.

I went back to Seattle and had the letters sent out that day. Then I waited. If everyone wanted out, I was in trouble.

At the end of the following week, Connors was back in my office. He wore a heavy black turtleneck sweater, like he must have worn in college. He slumped on the office couch. "Well, looks we like solved the problem this time," he said.

"Dave, there's no next time for you."

"What do you mean? It wasn't my fault. Nobody got hurt. I won't let it happen again."

"No, you won't let it happen again. I am going to do you a favor, and let you go. I hope you've learned a lesson."

"What do you mean?"

"Dave, I can tolerate mistakes. They can be corrected. A liar doesn't change. He can never be trusted."

A hard look came into his eyes, and he yelled, "I don't lie."

"They all said you coached them, 'Our stocks always double. Bradley only picks winners that double. You can't lose. He'll back up his judgment personally.'"

"They're liars. They're rats. You can't believe them."

"You picked them," I said.

"They lied just to save their own asses."

"I'm sorry, Dave. Better luck next time. Best to be absolutely honest with your next boss. With him, you can have a fresh start. With me, the scar is too deep."

"You can go fuck yourself," he said as he got up.

"Take this as a learning experience, and next time you're caught with your pants down, pull 'em up, buckle up and be honest. Don't lie."

Lines of anger crinkled across his forehead. "Your branch is dead. These guys will follow me. You won't have a branch."

I smiled back and said, "I'll take that gamble. Good luck to you, Dave, in your new ventures." I offered my hand in farewell. He ignored it and left.

He stuck his head back in the door and shouted, "You bastard! I'll get you!"

That didn't make me feel especially comfortable. I didn't need enemies. My friends were hazardous enough.

I sent Warrior down to take charge of the Federal Way office. He was good with young brokers and eager for power. He had felt snubbed because Brocknor and Connors had been made managers ahead of him. That was my fault. I had not asked him if he wanted to be a manager. He was such a great producer of business, I was reluctant to disturb a good thing.

The letter solved my problem.

I called John Lucas up to thank him.

"Did you get rid of them?"

"I got rid of the virus that was infecting them."

"I heard about that. Understand he wasn't too happy. Watch that fellow, Jim."

"I will. We were lucky. I offered to buy everyone's stock back, but had almost no takers."

"That's good. I'd watch 'em close."

"I will. Many thanks again."

When a Big Board house called for references on Dave Connors, I tried not to hurt him. I figured they were big enough to take care of themselves so I said, "He's young, ambitious. He needs time to grow, but he's restless. With the proper harness, he should make you a good man." I was honest, but I was glad they had him, and I didn't.

Warrior quickly got Federal Way back in step. None of the brokers switched their licenses over to the Big Board house when Dave tried to beckon them away.

Being on top was no fun. Money was tight. Every month we showed more profit, yet I felt poorer. The more business we did, the more money we needed. The more growth we had, the more help we needed. The more help we had, the more risks we had for screw-ups. Funds got credited to the wrong accounts, delayed stock transfers and improperly recorded information hit me everyday. When Chrispina and her part-time bookkeepers were my only staff, our operations were excellent.

Computers were new for small firms, so I hired a software company to set us up with a computer to handle the increased volume of business. They contracted to provide us with a full system and have it in place within sixty days. First one and then a second programmer was assigned to us. Each programmer came and went and the software firm stalled for time again and again. Our business grew. The computer firm went broke.

TWENTY-EIGHT

That night in Dallas, as I looked out at the city lights, my brandy and half the Cuban cigars Geologist had given me were gone. Thoughts of the old days were like dreams, rather than memories—of growing up, the failed first marriage, the struggles, the highs, the lows, the losses, and, yes, the successes. Now the uncertainty of reality hit me in the gut. I had always enjoyed my previous trips to Dallas and doing business with the oilmen. Now, with the SEC and State Securities ensconced in my office, I could only think how important it was to get back home.

The next morning Waterflood picked me up at the Dallas Towers. We headed out to the oil fields. In the old days, my little oil lease had produced thousands of barrels of oil per day. That was back when oilmen put down holes as fast as they could to outdraw your neighbor. There were twenty oil pumps on this sixty-acre tract, but only four still produced, and each one averaged only three or four barrels of oil per day.

Waterflood and I looked out over the field. The nearest pump rocked up and down with its own rhythm. In a slow Texas drawl, Waterflood said, "I figure that if we waterflood this, we'll clear close to a million and half on this little oil patch. That's after we cover all our costs."

"Our geologist friend tells me 3 million."

"Jim, when you've been in the oil patch as long as I have, you'll learn to take these geologists with a grain of sand. They're natural born optimists. How else can they catch pigeons?"

"Thanks a lot."

"I didn't mean you, Jim. A triple on your money is not anything to peck crumbs about."

"A million and a half and our costs back, I'll be his pigeon," I said.

Waterflood smiled and started the car. The pumps were the old-fashioned kind I had grown up with in Oklahoma. We farm boys, with nothing better to do, would climb up on the pumps and ride them like bucking broncos until the oil pumper, making his rounds, bucked us off with a few foul words, or a kick in the butt if he could catch us.

As we drove through the oil field on that flat Texas plain, we could see a few scrubby blackjack oak trees. If we weren't in an air-conditioned car, we'd bake like beans, it was so hot. Outside, the oil smelled pungent, but to me it was perfume.

"Think you can put the rest of the money together, Jim?"

"I think so," I said, partially lying. I had to show confidence, but my mind was on those snoops back in Seattle pawing my files.

I didn't want to think about them now. To be out on the Texas plain with oil pumps, scrub oak trees and sun-scorched brown grass sure beat Ulcer Gulch. This place was a kind of release for me.

Midafternoon, back in town, Waterflood and I picked up Geologist and South Africa. The four of us headed to Conan's banker. A cranky, faded Southern belle ushered us into his office. Conan, the little toad of thick girth, was already there, slumped in a captain's chair across from the banker, who sat behind a large mahogany desk studying his nails.

"How do things look?" the thin, somber banker asked.

"So-so," I said.

"Just took Bradley on a tour of the field," Waterflood put in.

"Interesting trip," I said. "Our only problem seems to be your friend." I looked at Conan.

Conan sat up, started to say something, but changed his mind.

"How's that?" the banker asked, looking at Conan with disdain.

"We made a deal for fifty down and the balance from our public offering. Now he presses us for more money up front. I thought Texans were men of their word."

"What do you mean by that?"

"Make a deal and then welsh on it?"

"This Texan doesn't," the banker said and looked at Conan.

Conan squirmed in his chair.

"I'm aware that Mr. Conan owes you a great deal of money," I said, "and you need some payment. Is that supposed to come from us?"

"Mr. Conan tells me your public offering is to be the main source of his funds," the banker said. "We can recover our money by other means." He looked at Conan with an expression that said his patience was near an end. "How long do you think before your funds will be available to him?"

"We must clear it through the regulators. I would estimate six months, maybe eight."

"I can live with that if you can assure the funds."

"We haven't failed on an offering yet," I truthfully said.

"Okay, I'll go along for now, but we can't wait much longer."

Conan stood up with his rimless glasses in his hand. He was a barrel-chested man, who looked like he suffered from emphysema. "Come on, fellows. I'll buy you lunch."

"Sorry. Can't make it," the banker said with a pained look, like maybe it was his money Conan planned to spend.

"Okay. We'll take you up on that," South Africa said.

At a greasy spoon cafe across the street, we each ordered a light lunch, except Conan. He ordered the largest steak on the menu, heaped with French fries. "You know you horse thieves stole this field from me. You'll take $5 million from my ground when you waterflood it."

"Horseshit!" Waterflood said. "We'll be lucky to clear $1 million, and that's after we gamble another $300,000 above what you conned out of us."

"That's not what the experts tell me," Conan said. His set jaw and fat jowls gave him a bulldog look. "I got other people interested. I want $100,000 more up front."

I stood up. "A deal is a deal. You can cram this oil field up your well-padded Texas ass." I headed towards the door. "Furthermore," I said, as I looked back, "I want my fifty grand back now, before sundown!" I figured Texans understood that kind of language.

"Now! Now! Let's calm down," Geologist said. He saw his fees go down with the setting sun.

Waterflood said, "Your oil patch isn't worth a goddamn' if we don't waterflood it. You would have flooded it already if you could have."

South Africa looked out the window like it didn't matter much, one way or the other.

I was almost out the door.

"All right, all right," I heard Conan sputter. "I was just joking. The deal stays the same."

I turned around and came back. "Okay, but I don't want to hear any more croaks from you. It'll take at least six months and maybe eight before finance comes through. Is that clear? I don't want to hear anything further about it."

"Done," he said.

I smiled, shook his extended hand. My bluff worked. I needed this deal a hell of lot more than he knew.

"I hear you're in the movie business," Conan said as he motioned for me to sit back down.

"I've financed a couple."

"After this deal is done, I'm moving to San Diego. Think you can get me a part?"

"What? You interested in movies?"

"I took high school acting. Made a good heavy."

"That fits," I said. "When you get settled out there, give me a call. Maybe I can give you a couple of names."

"You get me a movie part and we've got a deal."

I raised an eyebrow.

"Okay, okay! No problem," he said.

He pushed the tab towards me. "Yours, and the deal is done."

"I hear Texans are gamblers." I took out a half-dollar and flipped it. "Heads or tails?"

"Heads," he said.

I looked at the coin and pushed the tab back towards him.

He took the bill and paid it.

Monday morning, I was back in Seattle. I called Major Gray from home at five o'clock, "Let's meet for coffee before the market opens and we get busy," I said.

Sleepily, he replied, "I'll see you there," and hung up.

I looked at my watch. Didn't realize it was only five o'clock. I sometimes forgot not everyone got up as early as I did.

By six-thirty I was at our favorite coffee shop in the basement of the Rainier Tower. Major Gray was already there, and halfway through the day's first cigar.

"Jim, these guys think we're a bunch of crooks," he said as I sat down with a fresh cup of coffee. There was an agitated scowl instead of his usual smile. "The way these guys act, you'd think we were bookmakers instead of stockbrokers."

"How's that?"

"They've gone through every single file in our offices. I don't know what they want. They won't say."

"Typical bureaucrats. Intimidate you. Keep you on the defensive and guessing. Then hit you all at once with a truckload of piddling stuff that don't amount to a damn. That's been my experience with them," I said.

"Don't know about that. Their arrogant attitude, I think it's more serious than that."

"What makes you think so?"

"It's just the way they act, so self-satisfied."

"Sorry, John, to have left that mess in your hands. The problems down in Dallas wouldn't wait. What else happened while I was gone?"

"They pulled copies of all of our bank checks."

"I remember they had me sign a form giving them permission to do that. I really didn't have much choice. If I didn't sign it, they would just get a court order and make it that much tougher on us." Then another thought hit me. "Oh hell! Then our banker knows they are here," I said.

"Afraid so. They shook up all the brokers, too. They interrogated every single one."

"God!"

"Then they worked over the office help. Got Chrispina so rattled she talked Tagalog to them."

"That must have set them back."

"Not as much as it might have if they'd known what she said."

"How'd you know what she said?"

"I learned a little Tagalog when I was stationed in the Philippines."

"Well, what'd she say?"

He handed me one of his favorite cigars and lit one for himself. He said, "I learned some new words I didn't know. I thought a soldier could cuss, but she beats them. She even told them they could go suck a chicken's butt."

"I wish I could've seen their faces."

"The state man got so angry he almost shouted, 'Speak English!' She said to him, 'I hope you have chicken for dinner, and get stuck with the gizzard.' Then she smiled sweetly at him."

"Are they still here?" I asked, as I handed him a couple of "good" Cuban cigars Geologist had given me. He looked at me askance, then glanced each way to see if any Feds were about. Feeling safe, he smiled, and then put the contraband in his pocket.

"No, they left Thursday afternoon."

He retrieved one of the Cubans, savored the aroma, laid his old cigar down, lit the Cuban, and then let out a puff of pure heaven. "Didn't show up at all Friday."

"Any idea what they're up to?"

"No, sir, those gentlemen wouldn't tell me a thing. They just packed up their briefcases like a bunch of carpetbaggers and left without a word. How did things go in Dallas?"

"Conan pressed for more money up front."

"Did he get it?"

"Nope. I told him to cram it. The deal was off."

"Are we out of the oil business?"

"No, he got real nice, even apologized that he brought it up, and said our original deal was just fine."

"Out-pokered him, eh?"

"Could be, but sometime you have to just throw it to the wind and don't give a damn, unless you want to get pushed around."

"That's not always the best for the pocketbook."

"I guess not, but dammit, John, I wish I knew what those bastards are up to. They've loused me up for the bank loan. I've got to find some cash."

"I got ten grand if that'll help."

"Thanks, John, but I don't want to risk your retirement money. Picture is not that clear yet."

"If we give him an extra quarter, Raja can probably move 50,000 shares inventory and the rest of the guys maybe another 30,000."

"That would help, but still not quite enough. God! If only those bastards had stayed away a couple weeks more, I'd been in good shape. I'm sure the bank would have approved our loan."

"Do you think there's still a chance?"

"How can he loan me money with the cloud they brought? Until it's cleared, they've tied his hands. His board would hang him if he risked a single penny more on us. I can't even approach him until I know what our position is with these regulators."

"That's too bad, Jim. You're welcome to what cash I have."

"Thanks, John, but I wouldn't want to take your money, at least not until I see a clearing of this bureaucratic fog."

By that time we'd finished our Castro cigars. I said, "Let's get back to the office and see what we can do to clean up this mess."

We walked back through the tunnel under Rainier Square past walls covered with old photos of historic Seattle. Back at the office, to our surprise, our three bureaucratic friends were waiting. With only two chairs, Big Belly's man stood and the two Feds sat.

Stern-faced, the short Fed with heavy brown-rimmed glasses said, "Mr. Bradley, we'll see you in your office."

Major Gray left and went back to his office. I motioned the three of them to follow me to my office. I sat down and pointed to the chairs in front of my desk. They didn't sit. All three remained standing in front of me. They fired paper instead of rifles.

Big Belly's man said, "Mr. Bradley, we've suspended your license."

"Why? We don't have any problems that can't be solved. You suspend us, you've killed us. A lot of innocent investors, small companies and employees who depend on us will get hurt."

"You should have thought of that before," Big Belly's man said. "Here's a copy of an injunction that prohibits any further operations, and a statement of why this action has been taken. You will conduct no new business with the public. You will issue no more checks. No more stock certificates will go out, unless personally cleared through me or Mr. Hershel. Your salesmen will make no calls. You will transact no further business with the public."

"This puts us out of business."

"No, this does not mean that you are dead. It just means that your problems must be solved before you can actively engage in the securities business with the public."

After that, they left. I started to read their so-called Statement of Charges. It was far too complicated to read and to digest with them standing over me. There were no fraud or embezzlement charges. They didn't find a crook, and that's what they had come looking for. They said I had a net capital deficiency (not enough money in the bank). They said I was conducting an inter-state securities operation without a license from the SEC (some folks lived in another state). As a state broker-dealer, I had no need to register with the SEC.

Then I looked at the recap of the financial statements. They gave us no credit for our inventories (our equity in assets exceeded $1.5 million). They charged all liabilities against us (all payments due to customers and other broker-dealers, bank loans, accounts payable), yet no credit for our assets. It was unbelievable!

They said our markets were not valid (not unless we had two outside broker-dealers who made a market in the stock). We had created an independent market value for small companies (largely ignored by the big firms), and we did it with the blessing of Big Belly. He had been there, knew our plan of operations, and had given his okay. Now these guys treated us as though we were under the SEC and NASD. Maybe Big Belly was out for revenge because he now looked like an ass. Big Belly was the State Securities Commission. We were a state broker-dealer, and he was supposed to keep an eye on us. A hearing was scheduled before the SEC, and only two weeks away.

It was one-thirty, Friday, and a torrid August day. The room, however, was cold from the air conditioner, and the atmosphere, even more frigid. I sat there in that room in the Federal Office Building with everything on the line. Samuel Isaacs, my attorney, sat beside me, and next to him was his correspondent, a former government official who had a lot of experience in securities. Both were costing me plenty. I had decided not to use Blackhard & Funkelstein, the legal firm that did most of our prospectus work. They had an ongoing need to stay in the good graces of the bureaucrats.

At the head of the table sat a dapperly-dressed man, and down the opposite side from me, sat five SEC bureaucrats. To me, they looked like five fat toads with their long tongues ready to lap up this little fly. (Toads kept showing up in my life ever since I ran over one with my bicycle when I was a kid delivering papers.)

No bureaucrats from the state. Maybe they wanted to maintain the illusion that they were independent of the Feds. I knew in my heart that Big Belly would have loved to have been there for the kill.

Coffee was served in paper cups. Cream and sugar was on the table. No small talk. Just silence. The silence must have made the bureaucrats uncomfortable. Two of them fidgeted and coughed.

Except for the dapper one at the head of the table, all the bureaucrats were fat. At the precise moment the hearing was supposed to begin, the lean one stood up. His tweed sport coat, white shirt, off-shade green tie, and carefully cropped gray mustache gave him the appearance of a mild-mannered English country gentlemen, but his demeanor was more like that of a royalist who had one of Cromwell's men with his head on the block.

"This hearing is called to order. We will pass out copies of the charges and injunction." A young assistant came in the door and placed a stack of papers before each of us.

"If you will read these charges, I think you will see the business we have at hand," the lean one said. Then he looked right at me. I looked into his green eyes and wondered whether there were fangs under that thin mustache.

With the formality of a magistrate, Lean and Mean said, "Raise your right hand. Do you swear to tell the truth, the whole truth and nothing but the truth?"

"Yes," I said.

From a file he pulled copies of checks, and plunked one down in front of me. His knuckle hit the table. "Do you recognize this name as a client of your firm?"

"Yes."

"For the benefit of the court recorder," he said, "let exhibit number one reflect that check number 2504, dated August 1, 1983, signed by you and endorsed by John R. Williams is drawn on the Florida National Bank of Orlando, Florida, and was deposited in the account of Local Securities on August 5, 1983."

He turned to me again and said, "Do you know which of your brokers handled Mr. Williams's account?"

"Offhand, no."

"Let the record show that the broker on this account is Raja Singh"

Raja was at it again. Another nail in my corporate coffin.

"Mr. Bradley, when this check came through, didn't you notice that it was on an out-of-state bank?"

"Hundreds of checks come through our firm. No, I did not see it."

"You should have. A transaction across state lines makes it interstate commerce."

So that's why the SEC was involved. Looks like Raja really did me in this time. We were set up to deal only with people in the state, and not have to come under the SEC. Now they had me.

Lean and Mean pulled a copy of another check from his briefcase. "Do you recognize Balenda Brown as a client of your firm?"

"The name is familiar."

"Do you know who the broker is for this client?"

"No."

"Let the record show that Exhibit Number Two is a check signed by Balenda Brown drawn on the San Francisco branch of Bank of America, and was deposited to the account of Local Securities of Washington on August 8, 1983."

He pushed copies of both confirmations before me. "Do you notice that both John R. Williams and Balenda Brown live at the same address?"

"I'll be damned. They do."

"An odd coincidence, wouldn't you say, Mr. Bradley?" He smiled with satisfaction. "Were you aware of this?"

"I don't poke into the personal lives of our clients."

"It would appear that you do not know what is going on in your business either."

And so it went with another fourteen transactions. Ten were from Raja and four from Connors. It looked like my ambitious young manager in Federal Way had bit me, as well.

Lean and Mean wasn't through. Coming to number fifteen, he straightened up, stood tall, looked down at me, and smiled. He then faced his audience. A grin flickered across his face. Then he turned to me with a cold stare as he laid a copy of number fifteen before me.

"Is this Robert L. Bagley your personal client?"

"Yes."

He then placed before me a copy of our check made out to Bagley and signed by me. He turned it over. "Does this endorsement not show that Bagley deposited this check in an Idaho bank?"

"I believe it does."

"That is interesting, isn't it?" He smiled. "Can you explain why a resident of Idaho does business with you?"

"Yes, I can."

"It seems that the cat plays the same game as the mice." He looked at me, smirked, and then turned to his associates on their side of the table. They wore their stern expressions well.

"Mr. Bagley is a government employee with the National Park Service," I said. "He's been a client for many years."

"So?"

"He came to me one day and said he had been transferred and needed to sell his Independent Building stock for a tax loss. I had the only market, and he needed to sell it before he left town the first of the week. 'Sure,' I told him, 'but we can't mail your check out of state.' He said that was no problem. Just mail it to his old address, and his mother would handle it."

Lean and Mean looked bored.

"That's how I handled it. I didn't mail it across state lines. He must have cashed his check over in Idaho. I have no control over that."

"Your check was cashed out of state and that puts you in violation. You operated across state lines without a license registered with the SEC. That, my friend, is a criminal offense."

Lean and Mean gave me a condescending smile, and then fired his third volley. He stuck a financial statement in my face. There it was again, my file the SEC guy had picked up from the corner of my desk that first day.

Then Lean and Mean said, "Let the record show that Bradley furnished the State Securities Commission false and misleading financial statements."

He held the papers high above his head for all to see. Then he turned to me and said, "What do you have to say about that?"

"I am a little shamefaced," I said.

"You should be."

"It was really quite innocent, the way it happened," I said.

"Criminal activity is never innocent," he reminded me.

I continued, "I was in the middle of negotiations with my banker to increase our line of credit. My banker indicated that it would go through, that everything looked good. A couple of bank overdrafts were outstanding against the float, and I had charged them back to accounts payable. That's what they really were, as they had not been paid. If you guys hadn't come along, it would have been squared away the next day."

"You're also an accountant, eh?" Lean and Mean said.

I ignored his comment. "The state asked for copies of my financial statements, and since those statements were already prepared, without thinking, I hastily dropped them a copy in the mail."

"Fraud and deception, I'd say," Lean and Mean said.

"A matter of convenience and quick reply, I'd say."

Lean and Mean ignored my reply and stuffed his papers into his briefcase. "We will take these findings under advisement and you will hear from us. This meeting is adjourned."

As we came down the elevator, Samuel Isaacs and his associate tried to reassure me. Samuel said, "We'll meet with them the first of the week and negotiate some kind of settlement and get you back up and going."

His associate nodded his approval and said, "Yes, I think we'll be able to work something out with them. I don't think they're going to bring any criminal charges."

"How could they?" I asked. "I haven't done anything criminal."

"That doesn't keep them from filing charges," Samuel said.

Just then, I didn't feel like going directly back to the office. I walked down to Pioneer Square and had a coffee at one of those sidewalk cafes. Across the street was an old building named for Doc Maynard, the maverick pioneer and promoter in this part of town. He didn't get along too well with the downtown boys either. He'd been a friend of Chief Seattle and his Indian relatives, and unfortunately, when the doc died, his family didn't fair much better than his Indian friends. At that moment I felt a kinship with the old doc. The country was full of damn fools like us, taking risks and harnessing ourselves to the treadmill, while the big guys and their government toadies threw rocks at us. They said they looked after our interests, but took their perks and ended up with the goodies.

On the way back to the office, I walked past the new Federal Building. I gave a loud raspberry to that den of bureaucrats and their brothers. I hadn't noticed, but there was a street person just in front of me. He whirled around and struck at me. He would have landed his punch in my face if I had not been quick to duck.

"What's that for?" I asked.

"Nobody does that to me and stands up," he said.

"That wasn't for you. That was for the SEC and the gang of bureaucrats who hang out in that building."

"Oh! That's different, not a bad idea." He turned around and gave them a raspberry too.

I walked on down the street. At the corner I looked back. There he stood, facing the Federal Building, throwing raspberries. Not only that, but with his thumbs in his ears, he waved his fingers as he threw the raspberries. Then I saw a guy in a business suit approach him and say something. They looked my way, but I kept going. In the future I'd best release my spleen from the safety of my own car as I drove by.

It had been three weeks since my encounter with the bureaucrats. My attorneys still negotiated with the regulators. My business, maybe even my personal freedom, was at stake. The days passed and the legal fees grew. Then in the fifth week Samuel Isaacs called. "Jim, I've got some good news."

"I could use some."

"Come on down to my office. Let's talk. I think I can get you back in business."

"I'll be right down."

I left a note on the door that I'd be back within the hour. My hired staff had been reduced down to Chrispina, and she only worked on Saturday. The rest of the staff and brokers were on unpaid leave and lived on the hope that we would get things squared away and be back in business soon.

Samuel Isaacs had his office in a second story walk-up in an older building in the Pioneer Square section of town. I needed some good news and was excited to hear it.

The receptionist gave me a nod to go on in. "What's the news?" I asked.

"They are going to let us reopen," Samuel said. His eyes beamed.

"What kind of deal were you able to make?"

"I think we can live with it," he said. "First we put all your stock in a voting trust, independent of yourself."

"What do you mean?"

"I have a CPA friend we can trust to take responsibility as trustee to temporarily vote your stock," he said.

"You mean I can't run my own company?"

"That's the only way they'll let you reopen. We hire a new principal to run the firm, independent of you. He has full responsibility, monitored by the trustee. Also, you rejoin the NASD."

"Don't kid me. I take all the risk, but I have no say."

"You keep your broker's license and act as a registered rep (broker) under the principal's supervision."

"Rah! Rah! Do I need his permission to go to take a leak? How long does this crap go on?"

"Five years, they say."

"That's a deal? The cost will kill me."

"No, Jim, I think we'll be okay. Let's just do whatever they ask, and get you up and going again. Then, we'll re-negotiate and get the time cut down."

"They just want to kill us off but make it look like they're on our side," I said.

"No, but if we do it in stages, you'll be back on your feet."

"How's that?"

"First, do what they say. Hire the principal. Let him get us going, then we'll re-negotiate, saying he costs too much. I think they'll buy it, but let's get opened first."

The whole idea was repugnant to me, but I said, "Any ideas of a principal they would find acceptable?"

"Yes. My CPA friend suggests Malcomb Bailey. Good credentials. He's a graduate of Harvard Business School and has a master's. He's had several years experience with a reputable consulting firm that specializes in troubled companies."

"What would he cost?"

"I've talked with him. He'll go for $5,000 a month, if you'll throw in some options."

I blanched. "That's twice the salary I pull out of the company, and he wants a piece of the action too?"

"A man with his experience doesn't come cheap. Jim, if he gets you up and going again, he'll be worth it." Samuel said.

"Yes, but unless I get back in command fast, we won't last."

"That's why we better take their deal," Samuel said.

I was heartsick. My company had been stolen.

"I guess we'll have to try it for a while," I said.

My first meeting with Malcomb Bailey came off okay. He was in his early forties, a tall, string bean-type with dark hair. He was stiff and formal, just what the bureaucrats loved. I accepted Samuel's CPA friend as the new czar to vote my shares. Samuel, besides being my personal attorney, was also my corporate secretary. We jumped through the hoops. I resigned as president and chairman of the board, and the board elected Malcomb to replace me. I was a flunky in my own company.

Malcomb called a meeting with our brokers to give them encouragement. He had them study for their NASD licenses. He organized training classes with himself as an instructor. I was impressed with his sincerity. I sat in on all the meetings. I was treated with respect, but I said nothing, was nothing.

"Jim," Malcomb said, "if you'll get busy and raise more capital, I'll see what I can do about the liabilities."

I still had contacts and friends who remained loyal, so I said, "I'll see what I can do."

Malcomb put together a business plan in a fancy folder that impressed. It wasn't my style. Next, he organized a dummy corporation, negotiated with the creditors, which included legal fees, to accept notes from the new company and forgive LSW what was owed them. The securities company would treat these forgiven obligations as a subordinate debt to the new company, to be repaid as funds permitted. That way the old debts would not be charged against LSW. A shrewd move, I thought.

We filed for NASD membership. Did all the right things. Then they would say, "Now do this." We did, and then there was another, "Do this." So it went. Ninety days passed. We were still not in business. Costs continued to mount.

The place was like a tomb, it was so quiet, then early one morning, Frank Brocknor came by. Frank was hesitant. He had something to say, but did not seem to want to say it. Finally he said, "Jim, I don't think the regulators are going to let you get up and going."

"What do you mean? We've done everything they've asked."

"Yes, but have you noticed they always ask for more?"

"Yeah, it seems that way."

"Well, John Blackhard told me Hershel said as much." Blackhard headed up Blackhard & Funkelstein, the firm that had handled most of our legal work.

"How's that?" I asked.

"Blackhard says that Hershel hinted to him that you won't be back in business, no matter what."

"How is that possible? I've spent a fortune just to comply with their demands."

Frank twisted in his seat and looked out the window. "Blackhard says his firm will do the paperwork to set us up as a new firm. He feels confident that he can get it through the regulators without delay."

"How stiff are his fees for doing all this work for you?"

"Not much," he said. "He'll take a piece of the action."

"Oh? And who will run this great new firm?"

"I will," said Frank. "The brokers will come up with some capital themselves, especially Raja. I think some of their clients will back them."

"Sounds Jim-dandy! You, Blackhard, Raja and some of the others end up with my company, my staff. And you get it all for free and with Hershel's blessing!"

"Blackhard says he recognizes the value of what you've got here. He'll ask Hershel for permission to let you have a 20 percent subordinated, carried interest, but no control."

"That would make it hurt less," I said.

Frank left with a promise to get right back to me. Without the brokers, it would take months to rebuild. Perhaps a piece of a new firm was a way to salvage something.

Within two weeks, Blackhard & Funkelstein organized the new firm and had it approved through State Securities. NASD approval came shortly afterwards. The brokers were all excited. They now owned a piece of the action. They called themselves Bountiful Securities. Blackhard & Funkelstein convinced the brokers their services were vital. "Look what happened to Jim Bradley," they said.

Blackhard, Funkelstein and Frank Brocknor, along with Raja, had enough shares to control the new firm.

I called Brocknor. "What's the status on the 20 percent?"

"Oh, didn't Blackhard call you?"

"No."

"Jim, I'm sorry. He told me that Hershel said, 'I don't want Bradley to own any shares in the new company.'"

I didn't say anything. I just hung up. Bountiful Securities now had my staff of thirty-five brokers, organized and NASD-trained at my expense, for free. If I got back into the business, this firm, created, trained and paid for by me, would be my main competition.

I had no choice. I had to press on. Major Gray and Warrior decided to stay with me.

Major Gray said, "I'll just take a little vacation for a while, until you get it set up."

Warrior found a temporary job away from the securities business.

TWENTY-NINE

I was determined. Both Samuel Isaacs and Malcomb Bailey said the regulators had to give us our license if we fulfilled all the requirements. We got the SEC license, and Big Belly would have little choice but to grant us our state license, once we were registered with the NASD. We expected our NASD membership approval to come through any day. It was the last hurdle before we got back in business. Then we would hire new brokers. I sweated out each day as the costs mounted up. Payroll, rent, or any other cost felt like a jab in my gut.

One question bugged me. Why was I doing this? Wouldn't it be smart to just get out of the business? I had other abilities, but this business wasn't just a job; it was a passion, my life.

Bountiful Securities hustled our clients. They sent letters to them and said we were out of business, and that they were the old firm. (They had my brokers.) We then counteracted with another letter saying we would be back in business shortly. Blackhard's offer to me of a percentage in the new firm was a ruse he used while he stole my brokers.

Three more months passed. My costs continued to mount. Some clients stuck with us regardless of our problems. Sven Nordoff, now happily married to a lady of his own generation, had outgrown his urge to bump me off. He offered financial help. Mae Belle insisted on giving me a substantial personal loan under the terms of "pay me back when you can." She had sold one of her mining claims for over a million dollars.

John L. Lucas came by and said, "Let's have a cup of coffee."

Once we settled in at Mignonne's, John asked, "How're things going?"

"Not so good. Don't know how much longer I can hold out if we keep getting these delays."

John L. came alive. "You outgrew most of those little farts who said you couldn't make it. They can't tolerate a guy who succeeds too fast."

"Well, I guess that's the way the tape runs," I said. "I have little left to fight on with, but I think we might make it this time."

John L. then said, "Jim I can swing a few kopecks to help a friend. I'll buy $25,000 worth of your stock."

"John, you'd throw your money away. I've already run up tremendous legal bills. I even hired someone Isaacs knows, a high-up ex-bureaucrat to help me. Seems all I did was finance some expensive old boy bull sessions."

"Let's fight 'em some more. I can afford the loss."

"Thanks, John. I wouldn't let you do that, except I'm damn near broke."

"Done."

He handed me a check already made out. Without a look, I stuck it in my shirt pocket. He gave my hand a hard squeeze as he left, and said, "Jim, you'll make it. I don't take unjustified risks. You know that."

After he left, I pulled out my new lifeline to look at it. I couldn't believe it. The check was made out for $50,000.

The next morning I called John Lucas to thank him again. His office told me that in the night Mr. Lucas had suffered a massive stroke. He died instantly. That giant, that uncouth saint, was dead. My world suddenly grew narrower and empty.

Each Monday brought another disappointment. There was always another requirement, another week's delay. Then the IRS sent me a greeting card attached to a penalty notice. They wanted our annual report submitted on a computer disk. (We had submitted a manual report.) Now this was something new. We were not even on a computer, not yet anyway. Then began the dialogue between their computers and me. They'd bill, I'd write back; then they would send another bill, like they had not heard from me.

One time I wrote, "Dear Mr. Computer, when they invented typewriters, they didn't outlaw pencils."

Their reply, "Delinquent $11,000. Remit."

Then I wrote back, "Mr. Computer, I don't think it's constitutional for you to outlaw manual bookkeeping."

This went on for weeks. After ignoring my responses for so long, Mr. Computer got nasty and threatened to confiscate my assets. Now I was upset. I wrote again, "Dear Mr. Computer, if you sons of bitches haven't read the Constitution of the New Nighted States, I suggest you do so." Strangely, I never heard from them again.

We finally got word from the local branch of the NASD that everything was in order, and that their recommendation for approval had been forwarded to Washington, D.C. for final okay. It was just a matter of routine. Another two weeks went by. Then on the special day, Malcomb Bailey assembled us all around the large conference table for a special letter-opening ceremony. His vice-president and financial guru, Ralph Striggler, was there, and Major Gray and myself. Even Samuel Isaacs, with his meter turned off, came over to join us for the great moment. At last we'd be back in business. Malcomb had brought champagne for the celebration.

With a flourish, Malcomb opened the letter with the Japanese hara-kiri knife he had brought home from his tour of duty in Japan. He started to read, first to himself. Then his smile dropped to a frown. It was the first time I heard Malcomb use profanity.

He slumped in his seat, and under his breath, muttered, "Goddamn."

He then slowly began to read, "The documentation on the transfer of your liabilities to Skywalk Corporation from Local Securities, Inc. is not properly made. It is necessary that you obtain corporate resolutions from those firms which have granted release of debt to LSW, Inc." (In other words, the signature on the contract by the responsible local officer or branch manager was not acceptable to them.)

"To get corporate resolutions from companies, like AT&T and national leasing companies, even if possible, could take weeks," I said. "We'll be broke by then!"

I had already gone through most of John's $50,000. The NASD would not have liked to hear what was said that day. I was busted. My financial sources had dried up. Even your best friends lose faith, when so much time passes with no results. John Lucas must have sensed this. Why else had he come forward? "Let's meet in the morning," I said.

That night with brandy and a multitude of cigars, I ruminated. Sonada wondered why I was so quiet, but she did not question me. She knew what I'd been through. Bless her. It was she who fed us, while I blew thousands of dollars to breathe new life into a dead company. She acted in blind faith that I would bring it through, or out of loyalty. How could I fail her now?

Should I borrow more money? Should I hock the house? I still had friends who might help, if I asked. But how long would it all take? And what else would they ask, when we got to that point? I began to think they were surprised we were still alive. I couldn't prove it, but I wondered if there was a conspiracy here. There was that hint dropped to a fellow bureaucrat; there was the takeover of my business under the pretext that I was not a responsible administrator. Then there was the string of roadblocks, one after another. Regardless of how many roadblocks we overcame, there was always another one.

Yes, we had a problem with a heavy volume of business and too lean a staff. Big Belly, incompetent, had not done any monitoring, had never asked for an annual report. To him, we were now an embarrassment and safer dead. That evening, I made a decision. It was not what I wanted to do, but circumstances dictated no other course of action.

The next morning after Malcomb Bailey reassembled us around the conference table, I stated my position. "Folks, I'm afraid this is the end. Like Chief Joseph said, 'I will fight no more forever.' It's been a whole year they have stalled, delayed, and now they've starved me out. I'm leaving the business."

Protests erupted. Malcomb said, "We should sue them," and looked at Samuel Isaacs. Before Samuel could answer, I said, "No, it costs too much."

We made a plan to phase out the business and then adjourned the meeting. I felt sick but did not let on. I had never been a quitter, but I was defeated. What next? I did not know. I had spent most of my adult life, my whole career, as a stockbroker and investment banker. I had lived, eaten and slept with that mistress. She had given me a zest for life. Why did I not foresee earlier what was happening? In some ways I was more bitter at myself, than with the bureaucrats. The losses created a huge burden of guilt. How would I face Sonada?

Life went on. Major Gray stayed retired and took his ease. Warrior already had his new career in mortgage finance. Malcomb Bailey, now a registered principal, went to work for a Big Board firm.

I had a mountain of debts to pay. Business debts I had guaranteed personally, unpaid legal fees (for services that produced only more fees). I was such an independent cuss, who would hire me? I always said, "I would rather be my own man with a wheelbarrow and a contract to move muck or dirt, than be somebody else's coolie." Downtown one day, I saw Malcomb Bailey coming up the street, on his way to lunch probably. I called to him, but he pretended not to hear and ducked into a building. Maybe he thought I was going to tap him for a loan.

I wandered down to the Market to think. I picked up a mug of coffee at the lower level of Lowell's Cafeteria and climbed up the steps to the upper level. There, with a good cigar and coffee, I watched the ships moving in and out of the harbor. It's a big world out there, and most of them paid little heed to the stock market. They dealt in real things.

I thought of the good things that still worked for me. I had good health. I still had Sonada. David was doing well in school. Even if Daniel thought I had rocks in my head, I still had some smarts and was capable of a comeback. Back in high school, I had wanted to be a writer. Even had a few small successes (I got paid money for writing fillers.) Why not combine the writing with the market? I knew something about both of them. Might even rebuild my fortune, and get in a few licks at the bureaucrats. Bad publicity, they feared most. Independents got pushed around, and their pockets legally picked by the politicians and lawyers. I might be able to help small business.

That was it! I'd get into publishing. Put out a publication for independents, raise some hell. Get small business organized, give them some clout. When they got picked on, give them publicity for their side. That would certainly have helped if someone had clamored for me, pushed for my side, instead of running for cover.

To have a goal again, it was exhilarating. I'd hit 'em with writing and publishing. I remembered a session I once attended at the state capital. It was a Business Meet Government thing, and an old politico told me, "If you want to accomplish anything down here in Olympia, get an organization behind you. That way we'll listen to you." That's what I'd do—I'd create an organization they'd have to listen to.

My high school journalism teacher always said, "The written word was more powerful than the sword, and probably caused more blood to flow." What a way to get back. They abhorred bad publicity. Publicity, they'd get! We'd put it out in public, then they couldn't hide it in some committee and let it die. We wouldn't let them forget it. We'd hit them, and give the other side fair exposure, not just a list of charges like what most newspapers published. We'd use freedom of the press to bring about corrective remedies. We'd get the legislature's attention. The big guys may have the money, but we had the votes. Every independent had friends, customers, suppliers, and some even had employees. All the independents needed were a direction and purpose.

Washington Independents, that's what I'd call it. I sketched on a napkin a rough design for a masthead. Two columns, with the subtitle above it, Twin Pillars of Liberty. One pillar would be labeled Free Press, and the other, Free Enterprise.

On the way back to the office, I stopped in to see Daniel Lews. He crossed checks with me for $1,000. Now that I had a project, I needed some capital.

I called Major Gray. "How would you like to sell advertising?"

"What do you mean?" he asked.

"I've started a newspaper, " *Washington Independents*," something to support small business. Want to join me?"

"Why not? I'm bored here at home. When do we start?"

"Right now. I'll write and do interviews. You sell the ads."

"Be down tomorrow."

We were in business. We didn't need much capital. We had brains and energy. Sure enough, Major Gray sold ads right off. There were other independents who liked what we were doing. With the ads, we could finance the first issue. I raised hell, put some humor in it. I interviewed individuals about their experiences and struggles and how they succeeded. Many people I interviewed gave me good ideas for editorials, things that needed support. I had ideas of my own, and over the years I wrote them down. I had a wealth of accumulated material.

I mailed copies of *Washington Independents* to some of my former investors, stockbrokers, members of the Chamber of Commerce, the state legislature, and even distributed them by hand to local businesses.

Some small business people were skeptical; so at first my new publication was not grandly received. Some thought the twin pillars, which stood for freedom and liberty in my mind, were a political slogan for the Far Right. The president's secretary of one company wrote and asked that I please remove her boss's name from my mailing list. Another lady, who received a free copy in the mail, demanded that her name be removed from our mailing list immediately.

The corker came when I left a copy with a restaurant in Renton. I thought it might be a good place for lunch; so I continued my rounds of distributing free sample copies. Time for a lunch break, I came back. There in the wastebasket sat my copy of *Washington Independents.* When the owner came up front to seat me, I walked over and rescued my copy of *Washington Independents* from his wastebasket. I smiled at him and said, "I think I know someone who would like to read this," and left. I found a more pleasant place to eat.

Down came the pillars on my next issue. I just printed *Washington Independents* across the top with a new subtitle, "For and About Small Business." This set better. I began to receive Letters to the Editor from people and small business owners, who said they liked my magazine and that they found it a good help in their business.

One morning a man called up and said, "Who wrote that editorial about unseen bureaucrats?"

"I did."

"I liked it. I want to buy your lunch."

"Suits me. When?"

"How about today?"

"Whom am I speaking with?"

"I'm Carl Baxter, Tacoma Collections."

I hesitated. Now why would a collection agency call me? Was he representing one of my unsettled trade debts left over from the securities business? Was he using subterfuge to gather information on my current activities in order to press for collection, before I could afford to pay? I accepted his invitation, and agreed to meet him at a fancy restaurant in Old Town down on the Tacoma waterfront.

At the restaurant, Carl Baxter was waiting for me. Short Napoleonic-like man, but a quick smile and a firm handshake. I was cautious. I knew the game. I had used subterfuge to get information on some of my earlier insurance inspections, and used the same kind of friendly greeting.

"Tell me, Carl, what made you call me?"

"I just wanted to meet the guy who wrote that editorial," he said. "Someone who had the guts to tell it like it is."

"You in the collection business, Carl?"

"Yes, for now, but I don't want to stay in the business forever. Too many of them kill themselves."

"Really?"

"Yeah, it finally gets to you."

"Tell me, Carl, was it really my editorial why you called me?"

"Yes. I think things are in a mess. Weak-bellied politicians have turned the country over to the bureaucrats. Now, they don't have the balls to take it back."

"You could have written that editorial," I said. "You sound like a soul mate."

"Jim, quite frankly, I think you're too late. You're just a voice in the wilderness."

"So was John the Baptist."

"You know what happened to him?" he said.

"Yeah."

When I realized Carl was not trying to trick me, I said, "Carl, I've been through some tough times. I thought you might be playing cat and mouse with me."

He laughed. "No, Jim, but I think the good you do, is that you make people stop and think about where we're going."

"Thanks, but it gets a little lonely. Sometimes you think you are speaking to an empty hall."

"Jim, I want to support you. Here's my check. I want to subscribe and take out an ad."

"Thanks, Carl, your support means more to me than you think."

His reaction was a moral boost. He later introduced me to other business friends in several local organizations. Often, when things didn't go so well, I remembered that lunch. Like when one of our former clients sued Raja and included me in his lawsuit, since I had been head of the firm. I'd had enough of the SEC, so I got a lady attorney who specialized in securities law to represent me. She appeared before their hearing in my place. Nothing came of the proceedings as Raja agreed to settle privately with the client.

But what my attorney said to me, privately after the hearing, disturbed me.

She said, "They didn't say there's anything wrong, but they wanted me to let you know that they're watching you."

"Haven't they heard of freedom of the press?" I said.

"They said, 'That disclaimer in the credit section of your magazine that members of your staff may from time to time own shares of stock mentioned in your publication will not protect you in the event you trade in any of those stocks, and take unfair advantage of the public.'"

"They don't want to let go, do they? Once a broker, always a broker," I said.

I'd never taken unfair advantage of the public in the past. Why would I do so now? Their insinuation grated me. They wanted to let me know they were still boss, but I just put them out of mind. I made some more bold strokes, and said exactly what I felt about things. People liked the magazine. Subscriptions and advertisements continued to grow. If I didn't wear out or die, I'd succeed.

Major Gray and I went through the same steps to build the publication that we had gone through in the brokerage business. We courted potential subscribers and advertisers, gave them lots of attention. We went back regardless of how many times they said, "No." Then, all of a sudden, it started to work. Business rolled in. The free copies of *Washington Independents* we sent to members of the state legislature and to the stock brokerage community gave us admission to centers of influence.

Members of the legislature began to pay attention. We got letters from senators and representatives who commented favorably on our editorials and articles. One state representative even asked for copies of our back issues. He thought there might be material that could be incorporated into legislation. I wrote back and expressed appreciation for his interest, but suggested that he go easy on new laws. The wise course I thought best was to wipe out, or rescind some of the laws and regulations we already had. He must not have agreed because I never heard from him again. Our crusades brought in more subscribers. Then we began to get exposure in the outside press, some agreed and some disagreed. All this was good; it got us known.

One morning an official-looking letter came in the mail. It was from the governor's office. It set a date, the first Monday of November at 9 A.M. Would I please come down for a conference? If the date and time were inconvenient, please advise and they would try to reschedule.

I wondered. Was this a prologue to another indictment or injunction? What had I done wrong this time? With my battle scars, I was apprehensive. The letter was signed "Ben." Who was Ben? I didn't know any one in government named Ben.

THIRTY

On the appointed day I went to the governor's office in Olympia. A lady receptionist guided me to a small cubbyhole of an office. Books were on the floor, all around the walls. Behind a tiny wooden desk sat a small man who looked vaguely familiar.

He jumped up, grabbed my hand, and shook it with enthusiasm, "How good to see you again, Mr. Bradley."

He saw my confusion. "Don't you remember me? I'm Benjamin Ergstein. You were once my stockbroker."

"Of course! My Dow Theory friend. I wondered what happened to you."

"I went back east and went to law school, when my wife and I broke up."

"Ben, what the hell have I done this time?"

"Mr. Bradley, I always believed you got a bad rap. You'd been a real godsend for small business."

"How did you hear about me?"

"I've followed your career for years. That magazine you publish has some real good ideas."

"Thanks."

"I'm the governor's assistant. I've set you up for an appointment with him. We think you can do some good down here."

"What do you have in mind?"

"We'll save that for the governor to say."

Ben escorted me over to the governor's office, and turned me over to an attractive older lady. He picked up a batch of material on her desk from a bin marked with his name and said, "I'll see you later."

The lady took me in to see the chief executive of the state. Now he had the awesome power of life or death, if you awaited execution. The large desk engulfed the little man. His demeanor was solemn, contemplative, like he was deep in thought about something. Then, after we had his attention, he smiled, stood up, and his eyes sparkled with friendship. This chief of the bureaucrats stood taller than he looked, sitting behind his mammoth desk. He came around, shook my hand, and motioned me to a couch on which we both sat.

"Mr. Bradley, Ben speaks very highly of you. We think you've bayed at the moon long enough."

"What do you mean, sir?"

"I think we might give you some claws and teeth as well as a voice."

"What do you have in mind, Governor?"

"I have a position open at one of the bureaus, and I think you'd be the right man to fill it," he said.

"You mean, make me a bureaucrat!?" I said.

He smiled. "You might say so."

"Which agency are we talking about?"

"Ben thinks you would make an excellent Deputy Securities Commissioner," the governor said.

"Those people have not been my best friends," I said.

"From your editorials I have gathered that you don't greatly favor bureaucrats," the governor said, "but you just try to run a government without them."

"Yes! I do sometimes have such dreams."

"Down at the implementation level," the governor continued, "quite seriously, government would be in chaos in less than three months, without bureaucrats. No! Bureaucrats are vital when your civilization outgrows tribal status."

"I don't hate bureaucrats. I just don't like their arbitrary ways. I know there have been some good ones. Some have died."

Except for a brief smile, he ignored my sarcasm. "Once you get involved, you'll find that rules are essential. They're the only way you can develop continuity and stability in government."

"Isn't it really a love affair between their rules and regulations, and you know who gets it?" I said as I thought of Cotton Head and my experiences with the NASD.

"I haven't heard it put quite that way before," he said.

"I think they abhor change," I said.

"That's why we don't get many innovations from below," he said, "which brings me to the point of my request for this meeting."

"About the appointment?"

"Yes. Mr. Bradley, I've always liked mavericks. I'm too shy myself. Not bold enough to be one," the governor said.

"I've been called worse than that," I said.

"Mavericks often bring a fresh approach and take a different look at established procedures."

"That's true, but the establishment would rather treat them like cabbage heads in a polo field."

"Mr. Bradley, I don't play polo, but if you are interested, I'll give you a chance to do something about those things you've complained about."

"I'll take you up on that, Governor, but I don't think I could work under Big Bel..., I mean Mr. Hershel."

"I didn't say you'd work under anyone. You'll probably run things. The Commissioner is not in the best of health, but we'd like to keep him on a while. He's nearing retirement."

"With the same staff?"

"Pretty well. You know, these days with civil service, it's hard to change things unless someone dies or retires."

"That's what I've always heard."

"Mr. Bradley, as Deputy Commissioner, your suggestions will be taken seriously, not only by the staff, but by the legislature."

"Sounds like a good project for me," I said, but I thought of my next encounter with Big Belly.

"Do you have any questions?"

"Governor, do you think I have the technical background to handle this job? I'm not a lawyer."

"Thank God! This town is infested with them."

Soul mate. I toasted him with my upraised fist.

"From your editorials, I believe you have a grasp of the situation. Our follow-up indicates that regardless of your previous run-in with the department, you have integrity, ability and stamina for the job, so go to it."

"If you think I would be useful, I'd love the challenge, but when do I start?"

"Sixty days will give me time to prepare the staff for the shock, make announcements and go through the other procedures," he said.

"I think it will be fun," I said.

"I know there will be fireworks, Mr. Bradley. Just don't burn the house down. I might get scorched."

"Fair enough."

"Use the influence of your position to get some of your ideas across to the legislature. I like the sound of them. I come from a big company background, so I know what the little fellows face."

"I'll do my best."

"Act fast! I'm here only two more years."

"That, I'll do."

"By the way," he said as I left, "If you're only half as smart as Benjamin says you are, it will be like a breath of fresh air over there."

"Thanks."

I departed with my ego inflated, but still puzzled by the fickleness of this wheel of fortune. Me, a bureaucrat?

The next sixty days, there was much criticism of my appointment, mostly because of my past problems with the securities people. The main critic was the Securities

Commission, but the governor would not back down. He prevailed, and when my appointment became effective, Sonada and I moved to Olympia. Major Gray took over the publication until I could sell it.

During my first week on the new job, I didn't see Big Belly anywhere. An old-timer helped me get familiar with the internal procedures, and I had him schedule a general staff meeting. There would be questions that concerned the new policies I wanted to implement. I prepared well, yet I knew some would watch for a slip. Hershel was still listed on the staff roster, but his big belly was nowhere in sight. Perhaps he was on vacation or out of town on business. I didn't want to call attention to our previous encounters, so I said nothing.

After I returned from lunch, on Monday of the second week, I found a note on my desk from Herman Hershel. He asked for an appointment. So at last, the great moment had arrived. Would I make Big Belly eat crow, or would my earlier Baptist background spoil the fun? Make me forgive and forget? Life had taught me that being good did not always help you to prevail in this world. I gave the note to my old-timer sidekick and suggested that he set up the appointment for Wednesday, two days away. Might as well let Big Belly sweat it a while longer. How I hated that pompous, fat-bellied bureaucrat. All the miseries and years of struggle he had brought me, and all the while he luxuriated in a secure state job that was financed by my tax payments. I found it hard to forgive his vindictiveness. I remembered well his reported statement to John Blackhard that "Bradley will never be in the securities business again." Five years had passed since I had been so humbled by Big Belly. My family had been deprived of its livelihood, and we had lost our home. Now, I was his boss.

My first general staff meeting had been scheduled for Friday afternoon. That's when the fireworks would begin. I looked forward to it. I wanted them to have the weekend to think about my recommended policies, not gossip between the desks. I hoped to bring a change in attitude on corporate finance for small business. It's about time that they discovered a crook didn't hide under every securities prospectus. Their time might be better spent if they looked at some of the offerings by the Big Guys, who used smart lawyers with paintbrushes to cover up the muck.

Wednesday, just before Big Belly's appointed hour, a gaunt, gray-haired, little man whom I had seen around, but did not know, stood before my desk.

"Mr. Bradley, I presume you will want my resignation."

"Sir, why would I want your resignation?" I smiled to put him at ease.

"I'm Herman Hershel."

I made no response, but I was shocked. This was not the fat, arrogant bureaucrat.

When I did not show any signs of recognition, he said, "Perhaps you don't remember me."

A closer look, then I recognized him. Gone was his trademark, the big belly, and the arrogant hostile attitude. "What kind of sweatbox have you been in? You don't look like the Herman Hershel I once knew."

"I've not been well, sir."

Big Belly saying *sir*, to me! Now here's this poor, withered shell of a man standing before me. The joy of conquest collapsed like a stepped-on puffball. "I'm sorry to hear that," I said. "What would you like to do?"

"I have only three more years to retirement. I would like to continue my work here."

I actually felt compassion for this little raisin who had been the scourge of my existence.

"Mr. Hershel," I said, "I owe you a great deal. Without your help, I would not be in this position today."

"Wha—What do you mean, sir?"

"You forced me out of the securities business. Otherwise, I would still just be peddling stocks."

A look of relief on his face, and he started to say," I didn't mean to be..."

"No. I don't want your job," I said. "I would like your cooperation. I need your help to institute some new policies. Can we work together?"

"I'll give you all the help I can," he said.

"Okay. Then it's settled."

As he left, I said under my breath, "Ah shucks, some revenge."

Little Belly made as good an ally as Big Belly an enemy. At the staff meeting, the little fellow came alive. He defended and argued my position. From the attitude of the others, you could see he still had some clout. Whatever it was that plagued his health, he overcame it. He took on a robust look, and developed a missionary's zeal for small enterprises. He still kept a sharp eye for scams. Crooks come in big and small sizes and never go away. Where there's money involved, they are like ants after sugar. When young companies came in and asked his advice, Little Belly tried to assist them as much as the law allowed. He even helped to take the scare out of government. It was no longer, "No, you can't do that." His response became, "What can we do to help you?" or "Maybe this might be a better way." This once bitter enemy had become a good friend and mainstay. He exerted great influence with his fellow bureaucrats and that helped to change the attitude of the whole staff. From the snippets of conversation I overheard, I knew he took some ribbing about his change in attitude towards me. I felt a little ashamed of myself for the animosity I once held towards this man. He had honestly tried to do his job, protect the public against crooks, which he sincerely, but falsely, believed that I was.

Two years with the Commission, we changed the posture of the organization. Its attitude became "What can we do?" and "Let's help." Yet, we kept up the guard to protect the public investor against frauds. We pursued and eliminated some of the real crooks. But even after two years, I still didn't wear the stripes of a bureaucrat that well. With the governor's term up, I resigned my position.

I decided to not go back into publishing. Yet, at almost retirement age, I felt too young to retire. I had no more empires to build or to run. What I really yearned was to get on the phone with an investor. Sell him an idea. Convince him to put his money in the right places. Then, I could feel the satisfaction that comes to a good stockbroker who helps people make money to buy their dreams. I wanted to work with the heads of local firms and get them to pay attention to the interests of their investors and their employees who are the ones who make things happen, not just their own selfish interests. I had seen enough of that in this age of greed.

Money-wise, I was comfortable. When I joined the Securities Commission, I sold off my publishing business for $50,000. This, I turned over to my old friend, Dan Lews, to operate as a blind trust. Dan made a chunk for me, even with his conservative ways. He had stayed away from investments that might have created a conflict of interest.

Sonada had shared my bad times. I had plunged everything into the business. There had always been another deal, another claim on the money. This time it was going to be different. When we took our leave of Olympia and returned to Seattle, I put all my assets into an investment trust for Sonada, out of my control and ability to tap, except for $50,000. This I was going to use to start over again and build a small broker-dealer firm. Sonada had reacted quickly, "God! Are you never going to learn?!"

After arranging everything with my attorney, I started walking toward the Pike Place Market. It was spring again. At Lowell's I grabbed a cup of coffee and climbed to the top level of the cafeteria. I savored my coffee while watching the ships come and go. I always liked the broad look outward. I chuckled to myself when I recalled what Daniel Lews had said way back then, "You have rocks in your head messing around with those little companies." And when I asked Major Gray if he would like to join me in my latest venture, he just laughed and said, "No thanks, Jim. I'll stay retired this time, but I'll say this, you damn sure got balls."

My answer to them was that stockbrokers may be smart or dumb, or even greedy bastards, but I had no more empires to build or run. What I really yearned to do was to get on the phone with an investor. Sell him an idea. Tell him, "Hey, Charlie, I got a good idea for you. I think it will make you some money."

Any damn fool can be successful if he has money, and sense enough to hire others who have brains, integrity and ambition. The real genius is the guy who can build something from nothing. That's the challenge and the fun.

ABOUT THE AUTHOR

Lubic & Lubic Photography, Defiance MO

J. Glenn Evans

J. Glenn Evans can spin a good story from his more than twenty years as stockbroker-investment banker, with ten of those years as president of his own firm. He also operated a mining company in Idaho (a second novel?) and co-produced a cowboy Christmas film featuring Slim Pickens.

Originally from Wewoka, Oklahoma, a graduate of East Central University in Ada, Oklahoma, with a major in business. He also attended Oklahoma State University, Stillwater, Oklahoma and Santa Rosa Junior College in Santa Rosa, California. While in college, he worked in a Prineville, Oregon lumber mill.

Evans has lived in Seattle since 1960. A Seattle Chamber of Commerce brochure sold him on the idea that Seattle was a great place to live. He is a member of Seattle Free Lances, Washington Poets Association, Academy of American Poets, Seattle Writers Association, PEN, the Association of King County Historical Organizations, and Pacific Northwest Historians Guild. He has written two books of poetry, several local histories, two biographies, and a book on old Sweden. He is poetry editor and publisher of *PoetsWest*. A poet activist, he received the Washington Poets Association's 1999 Faith Beamer Cooke Award in recognition of service to the poetry community of Washington State. *Broker Jim* is his first novel.

Printed in the United States
48548LVS00003BA/7-30